Francisco Solano López and the Ruination of Paraguay

Francisco Solano López and the Ruination of Paraguay

Honor and Egocentrism

James Schofield Saeger

ROWMAN & LITTLEFIELD PUBLISHERS, INC.
Lanham • Boulder • New York • Toronto • Plymouth, UK

ROWMAN & LITTLEFIELD PUBLISHERS, INC.

Published in the United States of America
by Rowman & Littlefield Publishers, Inc.
A wholly owned subsidary of The Rowman & Littlefield Publishing Group, Inc.
4501 Forbes Boulevard, Suite 200, Lanham, Maryland 20706
www.rowmanlittlefield.com

Estover Road, Plymouth PL6 7PY, United Kingdom

Copyright © 2007 by Rowman & Littlefield Publishers, Inc.

British Library Cataloguing in Publication Information Available

Library of Congress Cataloging-in-Publication Data
Saeger, James Schofield.
 Francisco Solano López and the ruination of Paraguay : honor and egocentrism
/ James Schofield Saeger.
    p. cm. — (Latin American silhouettes)
 Includes bibliographical references and index.
 ISBN-13: 978-0-7425-3754-5 (cloth : alk. paper)
 ISBN-10: 0-7425-3754-4 (cloth : alk. paper)
 ISBN-13: 978-0-7425-3755-2 (pbk. : alk. paper)
 ISBN-10: 0-7425-3755-2 (pbk. : alk. paper)
 1. López, Francisco Solano, 1827-1870. 2. Paraguay—History—1811-1870. 3.
Presidents—Paraguay—Biography. I. Title.
 F2686.L82S24 2007
 989.2′05092—dc22
 [B]

                                                                2007000925

Printed in the United States of America

∞™ The paper used in this publication meets the minimum requirements of
American National Standard for Information Sciences—Permanence of Paper
for Printed Library Materials, ANSI/NISO Z39.48-1992.

For Jack

and the memory of Sue

Contents

Preface and Acknowledgments

To carry out a project such as this book one needs the assistance of many people and institutions. My dear friends gave me valuable insights: Sylvia Sherman Hoffman kept my spirits up and connected to the real world; Psychologist Roger B. Rattan gave me the benefit of his insights into the issues of personality; Janet Walters helped in ways too numerous to mention. My sons Jamey and Ted provided me perspective and support.

Two chairs of my department, Jean Soderlund and Mike Baylor, gave me constant encouragement. Financially, I am indebted to the College of Arts and Sciences at Lehigh University and especially former Dean Bobb Carson. His and the college's generosity allowed me to spend the better part of a semester at the Gran Hotel del Paraguay in Asunción in 2002. The personnel there made me feel a part of the family of a family-run place. The staffs of the Archivo Nacional de Asunción and the Biblioteca Nacional were unfailingly courteous and helpful, as were those at the Museo Mitre in Buenos Aires. Roberto Quevedo was kind enough to host a gathering for me at the Academia Paraguaya de la Historia, and the men and women who attended my talk and joined me in the wine that followed gave me the benefit of friendship, advice, and insights into Paraguayan history and culture.

Two great Paraguayan intellectuals who are no longer with us include my *patrón* and landlord, the wise historian Julio César Chaves, in whose house my family and I lived, and his friend the archivist, historian, and *pensador*, Hipólito Sánchez Quell. They shared with me their wisdom and helped me in numerous practical ways. Another former director of the

Paraguayan archive, Luis G. Benítez, welcomed me to dinner in his home. In his study, where we talked about his work and about the history of his nation, my ideas about the middle years of the nineteenth century began to coalesce, although my findings are far from what that historian sees in his nation's past. On a later visit, he made me a gift of his recent books, and he drove me around the city on both occasions. I am grateful to the Paraguayans, from a variety of occupations, who talked with me about what they knew and what they had learned in school about Francisco Solano López in 2005.

Bill Beezley, Barbara Ganson, and Al Millett read drafts of this book and gave me helpful criticisms. Three exceptional graduate students, Andrew Stahlhut, Adam Bentz, and Sarah Pomerantz, have been brave enough to read an early draft of the manuscript and to tell their professor where they think that he has fallen short. Andrew arranged my courses so efficiently and has himself done such excellent work as to give me time to finish the book. Friends have helped me to see more clearly. Mark Burkholder has continued to teach me about how we should study history. His advice has guided me since we took our meals together at the Hostal Toledo while working at the Archivo de Indias, when I first investigated Paraguayan political behavior. The late John Hoyt Williams gave me regular lessons on the political history of nineteenth-century Paraguay, the father and son López, and the nation's demography as we worked across the table from each other at the national archive in Asunción. Susan Socolow has helped in innumerable ways over a very long time, and she has set a high standard for all of us. Susan Deeds is a symbol of how one should approach our craft and has been a dear friend in good times and bad. John TePaske remains a source of inspiration. Bill Beezely encouraged me to write this book, and Judy Ewell gave the manuscript a close and penetrating reading.

No historian works alone. We all stand on the shoulders of those who have gone before. Francisco Solano López, Eliza Lynch, and the War of the Triple Alliance continue to fascinate. In 2002–2003, three histories of the Great War appeared. Those by Chris Leuchars and Robert L. Scheina accord with my view of events of that conflict, and I have used them with great profit. Although I disagree with many of Thomas L. Whigham's interpretations and conclusions—especially about López's character, his motivations, and military matters—his extensive research and vast knowledge of the history of nineteenth-century Paraguay have been invaluable. Two biographies of Eliza Lynch have recently appeared. That by Nigel Cawthorne is fun to read; Siân Rees's book breaks new ground. Several Paraguayan scholars—whom I will not name for reasons that the last chapter of the book will make clear—have given me pushes in the right direction. They have my eternal thanks.

Some forty years ago, John Gunther said that some outsiders in Paraguay resembled those in Balkan republics before World War II. He meant that their affection for an unusual place and one very unlike their homes was intense. In my feelings for Paraguay, I am one of those people. My affection for that country, however, does not mean that I am uncritical of its cultural icons when it is my job to do so. This biography of López measures the man and the creators of his legend in the twentieth century. The creators will undoubtedly be unhappy with what I have to say about their hero.

To all the many Paraguayans who have been kind to me over the years, you have my heartfelt thanks. I wish you well in your quest for a better country.

Finally, I must say the inevitable: that all mistakes of fact and interpretation are my own.

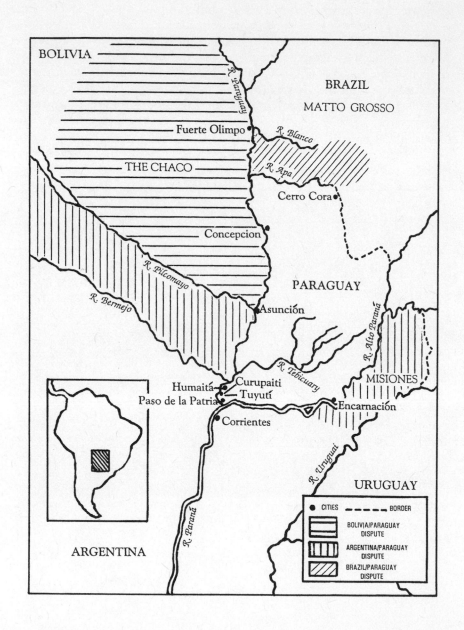

1

Introduction

IN THE PANTHEON

In the Paraguayan capital of Asunción, tourists can visit a four-block group of well-maintained squares in the heart of the city, one of which is the Plaza of Heroes. The plaza sits adjacent to the major business street, Calle Palma, and is a well-tended, grass-covered plot. A simple plaque in the center explains that this site was once the home of former Paraguayan president Francisco Solano López, born in 1827. The date listed is incorrect. López was actually born in 1826 and the wrong year is no accident. It is a purposeful revision of the historical record. Twentieth-century government functionaries and Paraguayan public historians, like López himself, knew 1827 to be incorrect.[1] He was born so soon after his parents' marriage that the true date shamed him, so he altered the year of his birth on record. As president of the republic, he reinforced 1827 as his birth year, both in his newspapers and reports. The alleged shame transcended the mere early arrival of the firstborn, as rumors abounded that his father was not his biological father. After he died, other Paraguayan leaders found the mendacious revision useful, because the fictitious date left their hero's name unblemished.

Also in the plaza, beside the López plot, once stood the home of the Supreme Dictator of Paraguay José Gaspar Rodríguez de Francia, the country's first dictator. His death in 1840 provided Francisco López's father, Carlos Antonio López, an opportunity to become the nation's second dictator. Unlike Francia, Carlos Antonio rejected the title of dictator, although his control of the country in the 1840s and 1850s was absolute. He

The Top of the Pantheon of Heroes

insisted that others refer to him as President López, like most other Latin American dictators. In 1862–1863, the first year of Francisco López's rule—and the nation's third tyranny—the new dictator acquired Francia's house, demolished it, and built the Oratory to the Virgin of Asunción, funded by the state. The dictator hired Italian architect Alexander Ravizza to model the building on Napoleon's tomb in Paris, Les Invalides.

Now called the Pantheon of Heroes, a two-man honor guard attends the Oratory building. These uniformed Paraguayan soldiers are attired formally in their white dress blouses, even in January and February, when the thermometer tops 100°F. Entering the building, one approaches a circular balustrade to peer into a gloomy basement. Three coffins draped with Paraguayan flags repose in the center of the room, surrounded by other honored dead. The middle casket honors an unknown soldier, commemorating the sacrifices of the men (and women) who died in the nation's service during the terrible wars in the nineteenth and twentieth centuries, to be discussed in detail later.

Flanking the nameless soldier are the coffins of Dr. Eusebio Ayala, president during the Chaco War with Bolivia (1932–1935), and Bernardino Caballero, a veteran general of the War of the Triple Alliance and president (1880–1886). Surrounding the coffins in circular fashion are urns containing the remains of Carlos Antonio López (consul and president, 1841–1862), Captain Antonio E. Yegros (hero of the independence era),

Plaque reading "Here was the house of Mcal. Francisco S. López, 1827–1870." The sign at the bottom reads "Please do not step on the grass."

and the Boy Martyrs of Acosta Ñu, children who fought and died in a late battle of the Triple Alliance war. A rectangular platform without an urn reads "Doctor Gaspar R. de Francia." It supports no urn because the remains of the supreme dictator (1814–1840) mysteriously disappeared shortly after his death. Hidden from initial view and beneath the visitor's feet as he enters the building is a bronze urn containing the purported remains of Francisco S. López. His resting place is tucked away, as if he had become an embarrassment, although few Paraguayans would admit this.

The first floor mezzanine displays several statues of official heroes. Upon entering the pantheon, on the immediate left, sits a bronze statue of an adult Carlos Antonio López. The sculptor charitably made him slightly overweight; in fact, he was obese. Moving clockwise, the next bronze statue is a representation of José Félix Estigarribia (1888–1940), hero of the Chaco War. Unlike Francisco S. López, he was a successful general who made good decisions and led his nation to victory. Further on, appropriately rendered in clay, stands the Blessed Roque González de Santa Cruz (1576–1628), a Jesuit founder of the famous Guarani reductions (missions) of Paraguay. At the rear of the room is a marble altar and the image of the Virgin Mary. She patriotically wears a sash of the Paraguayan colors, red, white, and blue. One then passes another clay statue, that of Mons. Juan

Sinforiano Bogarín, Bishop of Paraguay from 1894 to 1930 and Archbishop of Asunción from 1930 to 1949. He fits the right-wing political profile of the scene but is out of place here because he lacks historical significance.

Farther around the room, at three o'clock, one reaches the bronze statue of Francisco S. López. He is bearded, as he was in life, unlike his father or Francia. The sculptor renders him as a regular-featured man of average girth, unlike his increasingly debauched and expanding presidential self. Beneath his feet appears the legend "Vanquished Penuries and Fatigue." Another tribute, donated by retired military officers, reads:

> To the Marshal President Don Francisco Solano Lopez
>   Died at Cerro Corá, 1st of March of 1870
>   With his Sword in His Hand and the Country on His Lips, in Front of His Last Soldiers and on His Last Battlefield.

That he died at his last battlefield is true, but that he set a brave example for his soldiers is false.

On the wall at either side of the second López are bronze plaques. Paraguayan officials and public historians placed them there to honor him. Paraguayan organizations donated most tributes, and armed forces of nations such as Israel, Peru, Chile, and Ecuador also gave a few. Curiously, two memorials were contributed by López's archenemies in life, the armed forces of Argentina and Brazil. Only a few of these foreign homages specifically mention López; instead, they name merely heroes and soldiers. Of the twenty-four plaques clustered behind the statue, only four, including one directly beneath the López statue, refer to López by name. Another praises his best-known mistress and mother of six of his children, Elisa Alicia Lynch, an honored figure since 1961 when President Alfredo Stroessner officially rehabilitated her; according to Juan E. O'Leary, she was "the greatest heroine of America."[2] She played a memorable role in the life of López and Paraguay. Her reputation rose after fifty years of opprobrium and another thirty in limbo to her current place of honor.[3]

The statue of López faces that of Estigarribia. They occupy equal places of honor and similar wall space. The plaques to the two war leaders far outnumber the few surrounding Carlos Antonio López, a true builder of the nation, or the two priests, who have none. Above the statue of López, an almost out-of-sight plaque is from the Paraguayan Academy of History. So high that it is hard to read, its placement suggests that the official keepers of the historical myths of Paraguay feel embarrassed by López— or possibly by their own unwillingness to conduct a meaningful dialogue about him. In fact, many professional Paraguayan historians, too, are embarrassed by López's place of honor in the nation's pantheon. Better than other Paraguayans they know how the facts of his life contradict the carefully crafted public memory. In official and semi-official histories, including textbooks used in Paraguayan primary and secondary schools, López is eulogized as the nation's principal hero. One hard-working professional Paraguayan historian privately and quietly told the author in February 2002 that no Paraguayan scholar yet dared write truthfully about López. An objective presentation of his life, his presidency, or his war leadership was taboo for him and his colleagues. Even after Paraguay's experience with its own brand of democracy after the 1989 departure of Alfredo Stroessner—the last of the twentieth-century dictators who glorified López—impartial scholarly work on the man was not yet safe to conduct. Indeed, serious historical writing about the second López, the most important figure of the most important period in Paraguayan history, is meager, and the works produced by Paraguayans in the past half century are few in number.

LÓPEZ IN PROFILE: CONTROLLING THE NATION

Francisco Solano López's most important qualification for his presidency was a fortunate birth, having a father who was president of Paraguay before him. Beyond this, however, he possessed personal gifts that enabled him to run his father's government efficiently, to seize power for himself on his father's death, to retain it for eight years, and to persuade the people of Paraguay to make endless sacrifices in pursuit of his policies.

He was a fairly intelligent man and a "cunning" one.[4] Contemporary accounts all credit him with having a will of iron and a "fixity of purpose."[5] Although possessed of only a modest formal education, he read voraciously throughout his life. He was adept at languages and mastered of course his own two original tongues, Guarani[6] in the home and Spanish for official purposes. He also learned basic Latin and in his twenties became fluent in French, which he spoke almost daily from 1854 to 1870. Before his presidency, he explored the wider world and traveled extensively. He was a quick study and had an excellent memory.

In Europe, he acquired polish—he learned how to dress stylishly and to employ an ostentatious lifestyle that enhanced his image back in Paraguay. Industrious and energetic throughout most of his life, he was most likely the hardest-working man in the country. Before becoming president, he had mastered the intricacies of every important government department and of every military unit, ensuring that all functionaries were loyal to him personally.

He was persuasive. In personal relationships, he could be charming when he chose to be. At crucial meetings, López was a smooth talker with diplomats, one of his officers noted; he could make "them believe any-thing he wishes,"[7] an overstatement but not too far off the mark. In his daily habits, he was "careful of his appearance" and "fond of military fin-ery."[8] Attention to such details—and he often excelled at details—in-creased his stature in the eyes of his people. With an entire country for his audience, he was as persuasive on a grand scale as he was in private. He discovered how to induce men to give their lives for him. He kept his gi-gantic ego, which impelled him to aspire to the presidency, in check dur-ing his father's lifetime.

Until he was thirty-six, López was a hard-working, effective bureaucrat, loyal to his father but constantly preparing his own path to the presidency while mastering the politics of power. In the 1850s, his father delegated to him de facto control of the nation's army and navy, which he never relin-quished. He appointed and promoted only the men who were loyal to him. He respected his father, and he demanded that Paraguayans demonstrate their respect for him. His knowledge of the sources of power and his ab-solute control of the armed forces meant that on his father's death no chal-lenge to his claim to office had a chance of success. Francisco had acquired a monopoly over all military forces in the nation. In the armed forces, he se-lected commissioned and even noncommissioned officers for their loyalty to him and their submission to him, not their military aptitude. He employed few creative thinkers. Eventually he found a few men of intelligence willing to use their gifts to extol his virtues and promote his policies. He intuited that the Paraguayan people were unusually "respectful and obedient."[9]

For army and navy policy, López made all of the crucial decisions him-self. He enforced discipline and passed verdicts on infractions personally. He brooked no opposition to his orders and tolerated not a hint of disre-spect. When making decisions of consequence, therefore, he knew that men loyal to him alone would enforce them. He usually understood when to use the carrot and when to use the stick as motivators. He also learned that small gestures could please the people.[10]

Before 1868, López efficiently used nepotism to tighten his control of the nation, following his father's example. He appointed both brothers-in-law to cabinet posts, treasury and war ministry, but denied them real au-thority. In this way, he ensured that loyalists occupied crucial offices and blocked the way for other ambitious claimants.

López was an enthusiastic modernizer. He encouraged his father to adopt new technologies to develop the country and augment the family's domination of it. Hiring foreign technical experts from Europe, he strengthened the nation's defenses to deter Argentina and Brazil from at-tacking the small nation. He used the new telegraph to monitor develop-ments in the army when he was in the capital and in civil society when he was at forts and camps. He used the railroad for military mobilization, although a side benefit was economic growth. Unwilling to heed advice from Paraguayans on tactical or strategic matters owing to his boundless ego, he nevertheless bowed to the expertise of European engineers, architects, masons, and armorers on technical matters.

López's greatest talent was in controlling the nation. He mastered existing institutions. Through his choice of personnel, he achieved absolute control over the Catholic Church. He then used religion to enhance his own prestige and increase his power. On his orders, priests in the capital and in the field said daily masses for his welfare. He made them report to him information from the confessional. The bishop, Manuel Antonio Palacios, was his puppet. He instructed the priests to tell their flocks that López ruled Paraguay by divine right. To disobey him became a crime and a sin. His clerics told parishioners that those who died in the service of the nation would go immediately to heaven. When López justified his war on Brazil as a "holy cause,"[11] most Paraguayan clerics agreed. Those who disagreed ended up in jail.

Monitoring his own people, Francisco López was a good spymaster, as seen in his confessional policy. Throughout the country, he quickly heard of the gossip and grumbling that was important to him. He could thus silence potential opponents before they could speak out. In the army, he had his soldiers and officers spy on everyone else and report to him, not their immediate superiors. At the household level, servants reported to Francisco on the men and the women who paid their wages. Thus López "learned of the private affairs of the principal people in the country."[12] His spy system was both unofficial and official; Gumesindo Benítez headed his spy service until 1868.[13]

Francisco López had perfect pitch when assessing his people. He knew that Paraguayans distrusted each other, and he used their suspicions to increase his own ascendancy. In addition to his intelligence network, he effectively employed force, terror, and cruelty to enforce absolute control. Even his vice president was "desperately afraid of offending"[14] him.

In person, Francisco could be charming. When it suited his purpose, he was "very smooth and gentlemanly."[15] Because of his expensive clothing and his formal bearing, to most Paraguayans he *looked* like a president and later a field marshal. Appearances were important, and he knew it.

Francisco used his newspapers as tools of persuasion, "to bolster public morale,"[16] and as advertisements for himself. He employed them effectively, convincing the people that his cause and their cause, that his honor and theirs, were identical. His person and his policies inculcated in Paraguayans an absolute obedience to him. He convinced them that he *was* the government and that he embodied the nation.

With the enlisted men of the army he had a common touch. He spoke only Guarani with them, a motivational tool that promoted esprit de corps, signifying that they were all members of the same fraternity of Paraguayan men, not outsiders. His publicity efforts produced troops who had "confidence in himself and themselves, and with contempt for the enemy."[17] While maintaining a strong connection to the lower classes, he nevertheless presented himself as one far above them, emphasizing that he was a man of dignity. He required that even his brothers address him by his formal title, thought unusual in Paraguay even in the 1860s. He had friendly feelings for no one and distrusted everyone, which allowed him to make important decisions without being swayed by emotion or sentiment. López lacked a conscience, which also facilitated life and death decisions.

López was a master motivator of Paraguayan males, especially of the popular classes.[18] He used persuasion and terror effectively, as the occasion demanded. His use of the Guarani language continued the propaganda to his own people that he was superlative. He put a positive spin on setbacks and defeats, brazenly labeling them victories. He told men what they liked to hear, that he and they were the good guys; he effectively demonized foreigners, especially Brazilians, as the bad guys. Charging Brazilians with such crimes as cannibalism and biological warfare, he gave the nation's men an explanation of their condition. They accepted his claims, he knew, partly because they despised Brazilians, reflecting his own antipathy for persons of African descent. (Though a Portuguese colony with European ties, a large sector of Brazil's population was of African slave descent, which factored into his severe dislike of Brazilians in general.) López was talented at providing what a later generation would call disinformation, especially about Brazilian and Argentine motives. He also was proficient at stigmatizing enemies, including political opponents who fled into exile and failed and foolish commanders, deflecting blame from himself. He convinced Paraguayans, mostly illiterate and untraveled, that their small country was a great and potentially powerful one.

In wartime, he issued medals liberally, strengthening the bonds between himself and Paraguayan men, most of whom became soldiers after 1865. As in his choice of officeholders, he personally selected the recipients of these awards. He knew the value of good press relations and thus founded, supported, and controlled the content of several newspapers, in which he and the country were "civilized and enlightened,"[19] a claim most people accepted, believing also that their enemies were barbarous and unenlightened. That most Paraguayans were illiterate was not an impediment López's press offensives, because he had local officials spread his words to the unlettered. His functionaries got the word from the press, which they then read to the people. When he praised his own virtues, like his supposed self-sacrifice, bravery, and honor, his claims resonated with the core of the nation. To them, he was a man of great ability who was concerned about the welfare of the nation. After inconsequential battles and defeats, he convinced his men that they had covered his personage and themselves with glory and honor, which they were anxious to believe, and so he decorated them. Medal winners and their families believed in their leader, a common practice during wartime.

When he spoke to large crowds, he played on Paraguayan patriotism. He was an effective speaker, sometimes even inspiring, despite the handicap of poor articulation, resulting from the absence of several of his front teeth. He knew how suspicious his people were of outsiders and used their hostility to his advantage.

FLAWED PERSONALITY

He had qualities that hindered his ability to be a wise leader. Some of his traits caused him and his nation great difficulties. One was his ego, which was so great that it distorted his judgment of foreign adversaries. It is surprising to note that, for a man who led his people into a war and presided over the nation for four and a half years, López was a personal coward. This is clear from contemporary accounts. Although his faintheartedness seems to have made little difference to his people,[20] it would detract from his generalship.

A British officer in the Paraguayan army who rose to the rank of colonel noted a cowardly set of habits. After López moved his headquarters near the front in 1865, instead of setting an example to his followers, as commanders ought, he ate, slept, and worked in a heavily protected casemate, or bunker, which his engineers and soldiers went to elaborate lengths to construct for him. Staying in the casemate was seen as especially unheroic by foreign observers. Throughout the war, at the firing of the first shot he would rush to safety unceremoniously. He had his horse saddled every morning so that he could flee if the enemy drew near. More than once he was seen by his entire army fearfully galloping to the rear, leaving his mistress behind to face artillery barrages. None of this seemed to do him much damage in the eyes of his men, but his refusal to get close to the action hampered his communications with his subordinates and left him unable to respond rapidly to changing circumstances.

To be afraid in battle is natural. Soldiers surmount fear only after intense training and the monotonous drill, which promotes steadying habits. But López was never trained as a soldier, although he imagined himself one. He never took an order, except from his own father. To give good orders, an officer must first learn to take them, and his training here was deficient. Instead of setting an example as most able commanders did, he conspicuously avoided danger. Historically, good officers ask their men to do only what they themselves would, and he violated this tradition outright. Until the end of his war, he avoided doing anything demonstrably brave, but his propaganda said that he did. His indoctrination techniques and public relations were superlative within Paraguay. They were essential to his explanations of combat. Because López was a superlative disciplinarian and spymaster, his soldiers knew that gossiping about his want of courage would be fatal. Like defeatist talk, truth telling on this subject was punishable by death. Such conversations would be reported to López immediately.

After becoming prisoners of the Brazilian army, some of his soldiers finally admitted to witnessing acts of his cowardice—but only then. Customarily when a shell burst even a half mile away, López ran "like a scared sheep."[21] The precautions that he took to protect himself were at the time seen as demonstrating unusual timidity. During one terrible battle in 1866, he never "left the shelter of his works,"[22] meaning that he could revise no orders. López's "personal cowardice" "was so apparent, he scarcely took pains to conceal it." "His utter lack of courage was known to the whole army."[23] Even before he took his nation to war, it was clear that he lacked bravery. When boarding or disembarking from a ship, he ordered an officer to attend him on either side as he walked the gangplank, because he was afraid of falling in. To solemnize the onset of the Great War, he convened an Extraordinary Congress. As a North American historian recently noted, "He made a particular show of annoyance when members insisted that he refrain from exposing himself to enemy fire," a show of López's crocodile tears, because "the government officials had clearly coached the congressmen."[24] The charade was arranged so as to appear that *they* be seen as the ones who took the step of counseling him to avoid danger. But López's hand-picked representatives uttered no phrase, no word that had not been previously scripted by him. They followed "word for word the president's proclamations. . . ."[25] It was he who had ordered them to publicly beg him to avoid danger.

Another personal failing was López's total lack of empathy, a serious disability. Today some mental health professionals would consider this a clue to, or an associated feature of, an antisocial personality disorder, often referred to as psychopathy or sociopathy. Such a pathology would also explain the deceit and manipulation that was essential to the López character. Other psychologists might see his lack of empathy as an indication of narcissistic personality disorder.[26] He could have had a combination of the two; it is also possible that neither of these pathologies adequately explains his nature. Subjecting a man to psychological analysis more than a century after his death is at best risky. But the absence of any feelings of empathy in his personality remains a serious character flaw. It ultimately led to manifold troubles for the López presidency and for Paraguay. López enjoyed total control of the nation from 1862 to 1868. In the latter year, when he found that his domination of his environment was slipping away, he deteriorated psychologically. His invocation of excessive violence brought him back to his former stance of self-assurance.

As a military leader, López has much to answer for. He lacked formal military training and had only a brief military experience in a non-war situation, although his egocentrism caused him to think himself a military genius. He did significantly expand and modernize the military. He achieved total control over the army, the navy, and the police; lacking humility and self-awareness, however, his ego brought him to the belief that he was a great commander. Consequently, he made surprisingly inept military decisions, despite his wide reading in the literature of war, especially in French. The author of the best-researched study of the early years of Lopez's war asserts that in early 1865, "the marshal's plan was . . . not insane."[27] This modest assessment will find no disagreement here. The man was not insane, although he did lose his balance in 1868. But his war plan was a calamity for Paraguay. It was rooted as deeply in López's character as in the geopolitics of the Río de la Plata region. A determined leader, López "often used that determination more against his own people than against the allies."[28]

Another of Francisco's problems was the outsized importance he paid to honor (see the Honor Complex section below). Unlike the ability held by pragmatic men, he was unable to temper his pursuit of honor with practicality. He hungered for public acknowledgment of his honored status. When combined with his other personality flaws—his insistence on literalism in the honor code and his sense of honor magnified by his ego—this sense of impracticality helped bring tragedy to Paraguay. Rumors of his tainted birth were a threat to the family's reputation. He insisted that people go to excessive lengths to honor him, which goaded him into excessive behavior. He were so sensitive to the gossip about his mother's pregnancy by another man that he altered the year of his birth, changing the official date from 1826 to 1827. Even people who followed him to the very end whispered about the scandal. He could not control their beliefs, but all persons knew that he would punish them severely for gossiping about the matter.

HISTORICAL PERSPECTIVE

To explain the rise to power of Francisco Solano López, one must recall the history of the Río de la Plata and how Paraguay fits into it. To understand the López career, one must also look at the other two major players in the Plata region, Argentina and Brazil. From the sixteenth century, their affairs intertwined with Paraguay's. Indeed, parts of all three entities had once been attached to each of the others and the three disputed each other's boundaries.

After its founding in the 1530s, Paraguay built on the Guarani, Spanish, and syncretic traditions of the colonial centuries. When Spanish invaders settled in Paraguay in the 1530s, they reached a land inhabited by three hundred thousand Native Americans, called Guaranis by the Spanish. They lived in fourteen Guarás, ethnic and regional groups within and beyond the borders of the eastern part of modern Paraguay, the portion east of the Paraguay River and north of the Alto Paraná. This area resembles the red-clay region of southern Georgia and northern Florida and its climate is similar. Moving east from the sea-level stretch along the Río Paraguay, it rises to a series of hill chains called *cordilleras*.

The inhabitants of the region at contact were linguistically related to the Tupí-Guarani peoples, who spread over east-central South America from Brazil to Bolivia. They dominated parts of present Paraguay, Uruguay, and Argentina. Guaranis were mainly horticulturalists who supplemented their crops, especially maize and manioc, with hunting, fishing, and gleaning. They developed such rudimentary industrial arts as weaving cotton and fabricating weapons and tools from stones and bones. The origins of the Paraguayan and Argentine people are inseparable.

The Colonial Era

In 1535, Pedro de Mendoza, a Basque noble, led an expedition to the Río de la Plata and founded the first Buenos Aires, the port city that would later become the Argentine capital. The city's first incarnation, however, failed. Hostilities from nonsedentary Native Americans like the Querandí doomed the settlement. The embattled Spanish there found insufficient food to sustain themselves near the Plata estuary, few Native Americans to do the work that they refused to do, and poor prospects for profits. The Mendoza party gradually drifted upriver bringing with them Spanish culture. Some settled at Asunción in 1537. The Carios, the Guaranis of central Paraguay, negotiated alliances with the Spanish newcomers, agreements often sealed with gifts of Guarani daughters to the intruders. To the indigenous leaders, these pacts symbolized a reciprocal relationship of equals. The newcomers thought otherwise. Spaniards assisted Guaranis in local conflicts, especially against their enemies in the Gran Chaco to the west of the Río Paraguay;[29] these were linguistically related groups dominated by Guaycuruan-speaking nomads.

The Paraguayan people were begotten by countless Spanish-Guarani unions and, from the colonial period into the twenty-first century, more

Paraguayans spoke Guarani than Spanish. One invader, Domingo Martínez de Irala, dominated Paraguayan public life in the first decades and installed the authoritarian traditions of Spain. He participated in the overthrow and exile of *adelantado* Alvar Nuñez Cabeza de Vaca in 1545. He fathered children by numerous Guarani mothers, naming many of them in his will. He and his children symbolized the cultural and biological fusions that would create Paraguay. He brought the institutions of Spanish dominance, which were copies and then adaptations of the Spanish originals, including labor systems, ways of government, and the Catholic religion. He awarded some twenty-seven thousand male Guarani Indians to serve three hundred Spaniards in the neo-feudal institution known as the *encomienda*. Possession of this grant was a marker of elite status in Paraguay for more than two hundred years.[30]

Guaranis hoped that the newcomers' technologies would make their lives more comfortable and that European allies would make their lives more secure. They labored for Spaniards. They acquired the tools that revolutionized their ways of work and their lives. When dissident Guaranis concluded that Spaniards treated them not as equals but inferiors, they revolted in 1545. Other indigenous rebellions followed, but all failed. Enough Guaranis had married their interests and their daughters to Spaniards to quell the rebellions, marking the origins of ethnic Paraguayans.

Sexual relationships between Guarani women and Spanish men in the first generation began the process of race mixture, or ethnogenesis, which continues to the present. Guaranis and Spaniards not only produced biologically mestizo, or mixed race, children but also a distinctive, syncretic Paraguayan culture. Its basis was a nearly universal Paraguayan command of the Guarani language, a tradition that continues. Today, more than 90 percent of Paraguayans speak a modernized version of the original Guarani language, infused with numerous Spanish loan words. Only about 50 percent are comfortable speaking Spanish.

Legal and Religious Contexts

Guaranis are perhaps best known as participants in the famous Jesuit mission system of Paraguay. Many Guaranis joined Catholic missions overseen by Jesuits after 1610: Guaranis in Itaty in northern Paraguay and the Mato Grosso beyond, which would become a part of Brazil; those to the south of the Tebicuary River, which runs from east to west about a hundred miles south of Asunción; those in Guairá, later also taken over by colonial Brazilians; and many in modern Argentina. In these areas, the two empires clashed and after independence, these were the sites of border disputes. The first successful missionaries were actually Franciscans, who founded reductions near Asunción, including Altos, Ypané, and Guarambaré.[31] Guaranis chose missions partly to obtain steady supplies of Spanish goods and food surpluses. They also recognized the superiority of the Spanish God. They became Christians. In missions, they gained protection against Brazilian raiders seeking Indian slaves. Other Guaranis lived in encomienda towns like Tobatí and Yaguarón, closer to the center of Spanish government and power, Asunción, than the relatively isolated Jesuit-controlled pueblos. Guarani men fled these encomienda towns[32] regularly throughout the colonial period, establishing a pattern of migration that characterized the upper Plata region. Many rose from the degraded "Indian" status to form the mostly rural Paraguayan society. Between 1767, when the royal government expelled the Jesuits, and 1848, when Carlos Antonio López abolished the legally protected but inferior "Indian" status, racial and cultural mixtures determined the formation of Paraguayan society. Guarani residents of the former Jesuit missions emigrated as those institutions deteriorated in the late 1700s and early 1800s. Most Guaranis fled south toward Uruguay, Corrientes, Santa Fe, and Buenos Aires, but some settled in the Indian towns around Asunción.[33]

Although rebellions in Paraguay occurred in each of the three colonial centuries, the province was securely fastened to the Spanish Empire and its people loyal to the crown. Settler rebellions were responses to perceived local abuses, not challenges to Spanish sovereignty. The political institutions of colonial Paraguay were those common to other regions, including Argentina. Both provinces were administered by royal governors appointed by superior authority—the crown in Spain and viceroys in Lima and, after 1776, Buenos Aires. At times, the Audiencia of Charcas, a judicial and supervisory body located in la Plata in upper Peru (modern Bolivia), made decisions for Paraguay, causing clashes between the audiencia and the viceroy that eventually bred disrespect for law. The royally appointed governor of Paraguay—in the final colonial years called the governor-intendant—was theoretically assisted but in fact often opposed by the *cabildo*, the city council, of Asunción.[34] Native-born Paraguayans, usually called *creoles*, dominated this municipal body until the final colonial decades. In Paraguay, creoles were biologically mestizos. Lines of political authority throughout the empire remained unclear, but colonial Paraguayans, even rebellious ones until after 1810, recognized the king of Spain as their legitimate ruler. In times of strife, which included Indian rebellions, Brazilian incursions, and settler uprisings, loyalty to the Spanish crown was unquestioned. By the late 1600s, Paraguayan pueblos and Guarani encomienda and mission towns voiced their allegiance to the monarch.

Cabildos debated local issues, and those of Asunción[35] were the most important. They oversaw local taxation, land distribution, police and defense, and maintenance of public works. The Asunción council clashed from time to time with the governor and was a focal point of settler-led local revolts. In the uprisings of the 1720s and 1730s—misleadingly called the revolt of Antequera and the *Comuneros*, for example—the Asunción cabildo spoke for the Paraguayan elite. It articulated anti-Jesuit grievances and resistance to burdensome royal decrees. No democracy existed in the hierarchical and ordered society of the Spanish Empire. At meetings of the colonial cabildo, there nevertheless existed opportunity for elite men to express differences on policy matters. A typical colonial dispute occurred in 1775, in which the procurador general, or attorney of the province, León Altolaguirre, objected to the majority decision over the issue of his replacement. He opposed the nomination because the procurador-designate was related to one of the litigants in a pending court case over which he would have to preside.[36] A more important political controversy occurred in that same year. The Asunción cabildo objected to the efforts of Governor Agustín Fernando de Pinedo to abolish the encomienda, the institution that allowed the settler elite to control Native American labor in Paraguay long after it was abolished in the central areas of the empire. Pinedo and his successors ultimately prevailed, but Paraguayans had delayed the process for decades.

The Paraguayan governor exercised civil and military authority. He also made de facto legislative and judicial decisions. His office, as William F. Beezely points out,[37] served as a model for the authoritarians who ruled after independence. Like the powers of the viceroy, the colonial governor's authority was undivided, and the system lacked clear separation among executive, legislative, and judicial functions of government. Most of these powers were vested in the governor, whose conduct in Paraguay resembled that of the viceroy in Lima or later in Buenos Aires. The crown maintained an elaborate judicial system, and it saw the legal rights of elite and Indian alike as important. Spanish kings thought that providing justice to subjects was their most important duty.

The legal system functioned more or less as the crown intended. Local magistrates (*alcaldes ordinarios*) were members of the cabildo elected annually by the *regidores*. Senior members of the council handled local civil and political disputes. They performed their duties as prescribed by the Spanish civil law system, according to inquisitorial fashion, unlike accusatory systems in the English and Anglo-American world. But all accused and civil litigants in Paraguay knew that they had the right of appeal to superior courts, if they could afford it. People used the courts frequently, showing faith in Spanish justice. The expenses of litigation meant that only members of the provincial elite could in fact appeal to distant authorities. During the governorship of Diego de los Reyes y Balmaceda (1717–1721), a Jesuit ally born in Spain, for example, Paraguayan appeals brought about his removal. The possibility of appeal preserved a limited freedom of dissent. Some appeals, like that of Regidor José Cañete to be recognized by the king as the legitimate son of former Governor José de Antequera in the late 1700s, even reached the Council of the Indies, the highest appeals court in the empire.[38]

The Roman Catholic Church stood beside the state in colonial Paraguay. Although some secular clerics came to Paraguay in the early years, the mendicant friars, Franciscans, Dominicans, Mercedarians, and others truly established the Roman Catholic Church in Paraguay. Franciscans like "Alonso de San Buenaventura and Luis Bolaños, founders of the first stable reductions and initiators of the . . . evangelization of the Guarani,[39] were the prime movers of the first Paraguayan missions, or reductions.

The most famous and influential clerics in Paraguay, however, were the Jesuits. Members of the Society of Jesus were well educated, talented, dedicated, and devout. They arrived in 1588 and began their monumental missionary effort among the Guarani in 1609. During the next century, they built a mission complex of which they were justly proud. The Jesuit mission province of Paraguay, not coterminous with the civil province of the same name, was governed from Córdoba del Tucumán in present-day Argentina. The mission province was larger than the civil province, and the jurisdiction of civil and clerical authorities overlapped, at times leading to conflict. Jesuit successes in the missions and their shielding most mission Guaranis from the labor demands of employers in the civil province caused friction. The apparent Jesuit monopoly of the labor of the largest Indian workforce in South America beyond the Andes created settler envy in a labor-starved province. These Jesuit privileges also created hostility on the part of colonial administrators jealous of their authority. Eventually the Jesuit-Guarani mission system encompassed thirty-two Guarani missions, only ten of which lay within the boundaries of the present Republic of Paraguay. Eight were south of Asunción between the Tebicuary and Paraná Rivers and two were in the north-central part of eastern Paraguay.[40]

Many Guarani missions were located in what is now Argentina, the aptly named Misiones province. Part of this region Paraguay claimed before 1870. Other missions were located in present-day Rio Grande do Sul, Brazil. The Jesuit province of Paraguay thus spread over colonial jurisdictions that became the modern nations of Brazil, Uruguay, Argentina, and part of Bolivia, as well as of Paraguay, laying the basis for later border disputes. Jesuits also owned properties in the civil province of Paraguay, including their church and their *colegio* (chapter house) in Asunción and a profitable estate in the lovely town of Paraguarí. In the early eighteenth century on this property, Jesuits held thirty thousand cattle and scores of

African and Afro-Paraguayan slaves. Major players in the local and wider economies, Jesuits bartered beef in this moneyless province for tobacco and sugar. They grew the most profitable market product in the region, *yerba caaminí*, a tea highly prized and widely drunk in southern South America—then and now, hot and cold, sweetened or not. Civil province merchants were jealous rivals of Jesuit enterprises. Centered in Asunción, they had to content themselves with harvesting and marketing an inferior type, mostly wild yerba *de palos*. Their lower profit margins added to their resentment of the black-robed priests. Economic activity occurred within the confines of the Spanish monopolistic system or in defiance of it, an economic authoritarianism that reinforced authoritarian traditions of church and state. The superior marketing skills of Jesuit producers, their relative freedom from taxation, and settler envy of their monopoly of mission labor led to local revolts. These, however, were symptoms of elite factionalism, not disloyalty.

The most famous settler rebellions in Paraguay erupted in the 1640s, 1720s, and 1730s. They brought successful crown repressions, showing the Spanish authoritarianism that laid the foundations for post-independence dictatorships. The best-known colonial uprising was led by José de Antequera y Castro. Appointed governor of Paraguay in 1721 by the viceroy, Diego Morcillo, and by the Audiencia of Charcas, of which he was a member, he replaced Jesuit favorite Diego de los Reyes y Balmaceda. Antequera's anti-Jesuit policies and his disobedience to subsequent viceregal orders caused his removal from office, flight from Paraguay, and imprisonment in Lima. Continuing Paraguayan defiance caused Viceroy José de Armendáriz, the Marquis of Castelfuerte, to intervene in the judicial process. He ordered the Lima audiencia, or court, to find Antequera guilty of treason and heresy. He had Antequera executed in Lima in 1731, even though an initial inquiry had found him not guilty of these charges. This viceregal override of the judicial process was one example of how imperial politics set the stage for *caudillos*.

Revolts of the popular classes in Paraguay, descendants of the original inhabitants, included the Guarani rebellions of the mid-1500s and that of Arecayá in the seventeenth century. The ruling classes suppressed them more brutally than elite-led affairs like the Antequera *alboroto*. No popular movement disturbed Paraguay after the 1600s.

One type of political dispute in the colonial Río de la Plata was jurisdictional. In the 1700s, Paraguayan Jesuits and leaders of the civil province of Paraguay separately petitioned the king, a basis for later Paraguayan–Argentine boundary conflicts. The Society of Jesus asked the king to order that the missions report to governors and bishops in Buenos Aires. Paraguayans insisted that Asunción retain legal authority over several of them. Officials in both Asunción and Buenos Aires at different times exercised legal control over the missions, although the missions remained mostly free from interference by government officials and the episcopal hierarchy. Contrary to charges that Jesuits created "a state within a state" or that the "Jesuit Republic" sought independence from the Spanish crown, however, the missionaries and their neophytes were loyal to the king, although often inconsiderate of local officials. These colonial squabbles over territory and authority emerged as boundary conflicts in the early national period.

The ill-defined southern border had its counterpart in a northern frontier dispute. A clear demarcation between Spanish Paraguay and Portuguese Brazil was never established. In northern Paraguay, border problems with Brazil began in the seventeenth century. Strife was first a product of the Brazilian slave raiders who searched Paraguay for Guarani captives to enslave. Brazilian *bandeirantes* pushed the Paraguayan settlers from the Guairá region, far to the east of Asunción. Portuguese advances reduced the once-huge province of Paraguay, creating lasting resentment in Asunción. Hostilities alternated with commercial interaction between Paraguayans and Brazilians in the Mato Grosso province to the north of Paraguay. Brazilian towns there provided profitable markets for Paraguayan contraband. Spanish and Portuguese Empires vied for the allegiance of the region's Indians, a Guaycuruan group called Mbayás.

Economics and Daily Life

Life in colonial Paraguay was normally undramatic. Its economy was based on subsistence agriculture, although the export of cash crops also brought money and credit to buy consumer goods from Europe. Staple crops included sweet potatoes, manioc, maize, wheat, citrus fruits, sugar, and tobacco. Paraguayans raised livestock, but less profitably than regions to the south—Corrientes, Santa Fe, and especially Buenos Aires—partly because of less favorable environmental conditions and partly because of high transportation costs. The Paraguayan climate, microbes, plants, and insects often made pastoral pursuits in Paraguay a trial, but ranching nevertheless went on. Paraguayan artisans plied their trades in Asunción and in the interior. Guarani villages in both Jesuit and civil provinces of Paraguay specialized in such pursuits as pottery or cart making, while mostly engaging in agriculture.

Economic transactions were barter based. Specie was in short supply, although even relatively humble families hoarded wealth in gold and silver, often in the form of jewelry. Paraguayans usually paid taxes in kind. A little hard currency found its way to the province, and Paraguayans used it to purchase such European merchandise as iron implements and luxury goods. The most valuable Paraguayan export was yerba maté (*Ilex*

Paraguayensis), a tea favored by people in the provinces to the south and west. Exports of lesser value included hides, tobacco, and lumber.

The economy boomed in the late colonial era. Yerba exports increased. Tobacco fed the royal monopoly. A shipyard in Asunción, drawing on the region's superior hardwoods, constructed vessels for river commerce.

Paraguay's ethnic composition was one of a growing racial mixture. It featured widespread Guarani cultural and linguistic survivals. Few Spanish immigrants came until the last colonial decades. Most Paraguayans had both Spanish and Guarani ancestors, with more inclusion of peoples from the Gran Chaco and Afro-Paraguayans than citizens now admit. To call someone a "Guaycurú," the general designation for Chaco-dwelling Mbayás, Tobas, Abipones, and Mocobís, equestrian predators who spoke similar languages, was an insult. Afro-Paraguayans were slightly less than 10 percent of the population.

Countrywide Changes and the Birth of Independence

In the last years of the Spanish Empire, changes occurred. One was administrative. After 1776, the province reported to the newly created viceroyalty in Buenos Aires, not that in distant Lima, Peru, or the Audiencia of Charcas in Bolivia, overturning two hundred years of tradition. Many initiatives of the Bourbon monarchy, especially the reforming efforts of Charles III (1759–1788), changed the Plata region. The results were increased governmental efficiency, greater revenues, and closer political and economic supervision of the local populace. Stricter royal controls also brought increased resentment of the Spanish crown, of its European-born subjects, and of Buenos Aires. The tobacco monopoly, for example, forced growers to sell their produce to the government at controlled prices. It led to an increased contraband trade, especially of cigars of twisted black tobacco. Favoritism of Spaniards in government and business led to more but still modest Spanish migration. Most immigrants came from the Iberian peninsula, but some, like the father of Supreme Dictator Francia, came from Brazil. One prominent Paraguayan rancher and local cabildo member, José Coene, was probably a Jewish immigrant from Flanders (his surname was likely Cohen originally). He of course was Catholic in Paraguay, a subject of a monarchy that outlawed religious toleration. The changing composition of the Paraguayan elite—more from Spain, fewer native-born—can be seen in the changing composition of the Asunción cabildo. There, peninsular Spaniards dominated the city council in the last two or three colonial decades, deepening anti-Spanish sentiment. Spaniards thought themselves more honorable than Paraguayans.

Colonial traditions survived into the 1800s. Of major importance were the yerba trade and economic rivalries within the Río de la Plata region, state intervention in the economy, political and religious authoritarianism, political interference in judicial processes, jurisdictional or boundary disputes, Paraguayan resentment of outsiders, the struggle for honor, and Argentine scorn for rustic Paraguayans.

A consequence of de facto Argentine independence in 1810, Paraguayan independence was set in motion by events in Europe in 1807, when Napoleon Bonaparte invaded the Iberian Peninsula, an aggression that also had a momentous impact on Brazil. Napoleon removed the Bourbon dynasty from the Spanish throne. His armies occupied Spain and Portugal and installed his brother Joseph as the new king of Spain, while the Portuguese royal family fled to Brazil. Few men in Spain or America viewed Bonaparte's rule as legitimate, and his domination was brief. French divisions occupied the Iberian Peninsula, a Spanish loyalist government assembled at Cádiz, anti-French guerrilla warfare swept Spain, and the Braganzas made Brazil the capital of the Portuguese Empire. In Buenos Aires, in May 1810, a group of politically concerned citizens assembled to declare the Platine viceroyalty, the authority to which Paraguay reported, autonomous. They acted, they said, in the name of the exiled king Ferdinand VII; but they created a lasting Argentine and soon a Paraguayan independence. Although the plotters in the port city hoped to include the entire extent of the former viceroyalty in their scheme, leaders in Paraguay denied the claims of the ambitious men in the former viceregal capital.

In Paraguay, the last Spanish governor, Bernardo de Velasco,[41] met with the Asunción elite in July 1810. They discussed the demands from Buenos Aires, which the port city was preparing to enforce with troops. Paraguayans agreed to the governor-intendant's request to remain loyal to Spain and to resist the *porteños*. Argentine leaders sent troops north, and Paraguayans since 1811 have boasted of thrashing the Argentine armies twice, at Paraguarí and Tacuarí in January and March 1811, respectively. They did so without the leadership of Governor Velasco, who fled the battlefield. Owing partly to this dishonorable, shameful act, Paraguayan militia commanders overthrew him on May 14 and 15, 1811.

From that time forward, Paraguay was truly—though not yet officially—independent. Its sovereignty was menaced by Argentines to the south and from the north and east by the Portuguese, although less aggressively. The leaders of the new Argentina, or the United Provinces of the Río de la Plata, as it was known for a time, refused to recognize Paraguayan independence. They were the more serious threat, because they controlled Paraguay's contacts with the rest of the world. They could close the Río Paraná to vessels bound for the landlocked nation to the north.

THE FIRST DICTATOR

A junta, or committee, governed Paraguay temporarily. Because of the unwieldiness of collective rule, Dr. José Gaspar Rodríguez de Francia, the ablest man in Paraguay, a middle-aged lawyer, emerged as the decisive political actor. Between 1811 and 1814, he worked from within and without the new government to establish an independent republic and then to create an authoritarian dictatorship. He was born in 1766 to a Brazilian immigrant father, who came to Paraguay to help Paraguayan tobacco growers improve their product, and a Paraguayan mother from a respected family. The elder Francia became a provincial militia officer and administrator of the Indian town of Yaguarón, where his house later became a small museum. The elder Francia sent his son José to Córdoba, now in Argentina, to study. At the university, he earned a doctorate in theology. Although he had five siblings, he felt no emotional ties to them, nor to his father nor to any of his unknown number of illegitimate children.

Young Francia returned to Asunción and left the priesthood. Having read Jean Jacques Rousseau and other Enlightenment philosophers, he taught for a time at the seminary in Asunción. He built on his university training to become a lawyer. The study of theology and that of law in universities of the Spanish Empire were so similar that changing careers was easy. Francia gained a reputation for integrity and honesty. In Paraguayan historical mythology, Francia devoted his law practice exclusively to defending the interests of society's unfortunates, but in fact his practice was a general one. At the same time, although allegations of African ancestry (owing to his father's Brazilian origins) continued to follow him, he was honored as a member of the elite of Asunción. Provincial leaders several times elected him to important posts on the Asunción cabildo. Francia hated the Spanish-born merchants and landowners who now dominated the province's economic and political life. He "was a fine example of the frustrated creole."[42] His persuasive voice led Paraguayans to refuse to recognize *porteño* claims after May 1810. He failed to recognize either the French emperor's brother or the patriot Council of Regency as legitimate. Like other local leaders, for a time he sided with loyalist Governor Bernardo de Velasco, until Velasco turned to the Portuguese crown for support. When the junta of Buenos Aires sent a force under General Manuel Belgrano to Paraguay to bring the province to heel, Francia applauded their defeat. Not himself inclined to military participation, Francia nevertheless supported Paraguayan victories at Paraguarí, and Tacuarí, triumphs that contributed to the formation of a national identity. In May of 1811, Paraguayan military and civilian leaders deposed Governor Velasco. In June and July, a five-man junta led by Francia declared a conditional independence; but they still referred to their homeland as a province. Paraguay struggled to maintain its freedom against Argentine demands for submission.

In Asunción, politicians played a game of musical chairs. The major issue was the relationship with Buenos Aires. In June 1811, a Congress convened. Francia allied with the military, which he gradually came to dominate, and he achieved total control over Paraguay. He built on inquisitorial foundations to establish an efficient spy system. When he rejoined the government in November 1812, he enjoyed the support of a battalion whose loyalty was to him personally. Gradually, Francia dominated his colleagues and rivals and expelled them from government service. In 1813, Paraguay solidified its independence by proclaiming itself a republic. Paraguayans created a government headed by two consuls (republican and imperial Roman titles), who would alternate in office. Elites were keenly aware of their descent from Rome and were better educated in classical history than in their own. Francia was one consul and he soon eclipsed the other, Fulgencio Yegros, the officer who had led Paraguayans to victory over Belgrano. Francia executed him in 1821.

Francia's government was both innovative and traditional. Many policies resembled those of Bourbon Spain. He was never the proto-socialist that some have claimed. In 1814, he made himself supreme dictator of the republic for a five-year term. In 1816, he made the office a lifetime appointment. He remained in office until his death in 1840. In 1820–1821, he eliminated most potential rivals by jailing or executing them. He ended the privilege of Spaniards and elite Paraguayans. He abolished the Asunción cabildo, and the limited freedom of debate held there also disappeared. He tolerated no opposition. Some men of substance, like Carlos Antonio López, saved their lives and fortunes by withdrawing from public life and avoiding the capital.

The supreme dictator also curbed the authority of the Roman Catholic Church. No atheist, Francia nevertheless disliked the church. He interposed himself between the papacy and Paraguayan priests. Papal correspondence with clerics was channeled through him. Following the precedent of the colonial *sínodo*, a government subvention, he put all the nation's clerics on the state payroll. They answered to him. He abolished the Asunción seminary, a blow to the church and to education. He abolished the regular religious orders and seized their properties. The state itself took possession of them, at Francia's order, rather than Francia personally because he never used the government to increase his own fortune. He was uninterested in personal enrichment. He was not poor nor did he amass great wealth. He did not have personal friends; he chose to live a solitary life. He traded the colonial militia for a standing army loyal to him.

Because of foreign threats, mostly from what is now Argentina, Francia withdrew with his country from the affairs of the region. If Paraguay was never quite the "Hermit State" of legend,[43] its contacts with the outside world were severely reduced. Francia allowed a limited trade with Brazil through Ytapúa and Sâo Borja. Uninterested in foreign contacts or honors, he mostly avoided conversing with the few foreigners in Paraguay. The volume of Paraguay's imports and exports plummeted. Francia "regarded trade, and all other economic activities, as subordinate to . . . the enhancement of state power."[44]

IMPERIAL HISTORY AND REGIONAL RELATIONS

One of Francia's impressive feats was to gather much of the productive capacity of the nation into the hands of the state, especially the state-owned ranches. The Spanish crown had owned some forty ranches, including former Jesuit properties expropriated in 1767–1768. The Estancia del Rey, the King's Ranch, was a prominent owner of slaves and possessor of Indian *encomendados* in the 1700s. Francia nationalized church real estate. He seized in the name of the state the lands of his fallen enemies, mostly in the 1820s. By the mid 1830s, the Republic of Paraguay owned fifty ranches. By 1865, it owned more than eighty.

As William Beezley points out, the Spanish imperial government set the stage for dictators like Francia. It had given extraordinary power to administrators, including viceroys and governors. The lines between the executive, legislative, and judicial functions were unclear. Imprecision and failure to fix responsibility paved the way for the *caudillos* of the national period in Paraguay, Argentina, and elsewhere. Caudillos embodied executive dominance. In Paraguay and Argentina, legislatures were powerless and the judiciary subservient to the executives. In Paraguay, Argentina, and Brazil, the value of honor was at the apex of desired attributes. The honorable people perched on the social summit.

Brazil was part of the Río de la Plata from the beginning. The Brazil that independent Paraguay confronted reached back to 1500, when the explorer Pedro Alvares Cabral claimed it for Portugal. Brazil yielded little of the immediate wealth found in Mexico and Peru. Brazil's early importance lay in its strategic position, flanking the sea route to its valuable Asian possessions and sitting adjacent to Spain's Platine colonies. The Portuguese king controlled his American colony less closely than did Spanish monarchs. Settlers in Brazil established princely plantations. They soon found in contraband trade with Buenos Aires and Paraguay a profitable pursuit, but one that clashed with Spain's notions of proper economic behavior.

In the late 1500s, Brazilian landowners grew cane sugar for export, and the subsequent European demand for sugar made Brazil increase in wealth and size. Owing to the capitalistic nature of sugar cultivation and the growing world demand for sugar, a large workforce was essential. At first, Brazilian plantation owners worked their properties with the labor of often-enslaved Native Americans, but most of the natives of Brazil—few in number to begin with—succumbed to the infectious diseases brought by Europeans and Africans, who began arriving in the 1560s and 1570s. Thereafter, the Brazilian landowning elite and the upper classes of the towns and cities depended on the labor of African slaves. They produced the sugar that brought fortunes to the elites. Brazilians sold slaves in the Plata region for silver from the mines of upper Peru. Slaves in Brazil worked the mines after the discoveries of gold in the 1690s and toiled on ranches and later on the coffee plantations. By 1800, Brazil had received a total of 2.5 million Africans,[45] more than twice as many as in Spanish America. By the early nineteenth century, a majority of Brazilians were black or mulatto, both slave and free.

In practice, Brazil ignored the Treaty of Tordesillas of 1494 between Spain and Portugal, which limited Portuguese claims to the tip of South America jutting into the Atlantic Ocean. Luso-Brazilians (Brazilians of Portuguese descent) plunged into the economy and politics of the Plata region. For a time they were even influential in the Buenos Aires cabildo. Thus Brazil's geographical expansion began early and continued for centuries. By its independence in 1822, it was nearly the size of the present-day country, about equal to the continental United States today.

In 1580, Philip II of Spain took over the Portuguese throne and its empire. Between 1580 and 1640, the dividing line between Spanish and Portuguese territory seemed of little consequence, because one seat of power, held by three kings of Spain named Philip, ruled all of South America. Brazilian settlers pushed west and south. The famous Brazilian pioneers, the *bandeirantes*, searched the interior of South America for Indian slaves. They invaded and reduced the size of Spanish Paraguay. They moved west, engendering hostility to Brazil. Portugal regained independence in 1640. The Braganza family became the ruling family of Portugal and Brazil. Portuguese-Brazilian domination of the South American interior became permanent. Brazil's territorial clashes with Spanish Paraguay were numerous. After taking Guairá, they raided Spanish Jesuits in northern Paraguay. Brazilians menaced the Spanish-Guarani-Jesuit reductions in southern Paraguay and northeastern Argentina as well. After Jesuits organized Guaranis into effective fighting units, mission Guaranis resisted Portuguese incursions.

Another Spanish-Portuguese dispute was over the Banda Oriental, the east bank of the Uruguay River, modern Uruguay. There, Portuguese settlers and smugglers lived. The Spanish objected. It was good cattle country and a natural extension of the economy of the southern Brazilian province of Rio Grande do Sul. It was also an outpost of contraband near the legally controlled but leaky economy of Spanish South America. From the town of Colonia do Sacramento, across the estuary from Buenos Aires, Brazilian merchants traded slaves for silver drawn to the east from the great deposits at Potosí. From the late 1600s into the 1800s, clashes between the Spanish and Portuguese speakers over the Banda Oriental were frequent. Portuguese Brazil annexed the Banda Oriental in 1821, but Spanish-speaking exiles fought to reclaim the province in 1825. Heirs to the two empires, independent Brazil and Buenos Aires, fought a stalemated war over the region from 1825 to 1828. As the Confederation of the Río de la Plata descended into anarchy, a new state, the Oriental Republic of Uruguay, named for the Uruguay River, was founded in 1828 under the tutelage of the British foreign ministry. Uruguay's politics were chaotic.

Napoleon's invasion of Portugal pushed the Braganzas to Brazil. The regent, later King Joâo VI, represented the only legitimate European monarchy ever to reside in the Western Hemisphere. Brazil legally became a kingdom, equal with Portugal, although larger in population and size. Joâo returned to Portugal in 1821, leaving his son Pedro to administer Brazil.

Observing that the independence wars were turning the Spanish American world upside down, Pedro forestalled movements for a republican Brazil in 1822 by declaring it an independent monarchy. He asked Brazilians to write a constitution. When they failed to produce one of which he approved, he issued his own in 1824. Brazil then became a constitutional monarchy, but the emperor was no figurehead. Although Pedro created a functioning legislature and a judiciary, the emperor made important decisions. Pedro I was unpopular. He was Portuguese, not Brazilian, and thus a foreigner. The politically articulate resented his continuing involvement in Portugal's affairs, especially Brazil's assumption of its debts. Brazilians also disliked Pedro's foreign mercenaries—employed in the Cisplatine War, a conflict with Argentina over the Banda Oriental fought between 1825 and 1828[46]—whom he used in Brazil against Brazilians. Opposition grew so strong that in 1831 he abdicated in favor of his son, Pedro II, then five years old. A regency ruled in his name until 1840.

The Brazilian electorate of property owners was small. The main political groups, liberals and conservatives, differed little ideologically. They both represented elite interests. Conflicts in the early years of the Second Empire were usually waged over issues of patronage, while in the background republican and abolitionist movements grew slowly. Brazil's populace included the largest slave society in South America. Brazil's population soon included more free blacks and mulattoes than slaves, but slavery drove the economy. Brazil's economic center shifted from the sugar plantations of the northeast to the gold mines of Minas Gerais and, by the 1800s, to booming coffee plantations in Sâo Paulo and Rio de Janeiro. Slavery followed the economic upturns and depressions.

Brazil's largely black and mulatto people were the object of Paraguayan scorn, fear, hatred, and ridicule. Both López dictators called them "monkeys," a common attitude. The first Paraguayan dictator, El Supremo, was of Brazilian descent, and his policy toward Brazil low key. Paraguayans frequently called Brazilians an insulting Guarani name, *cambá*. Anti-African prejudice survived in Asunción. Racial hostility partly explains how Paraguayan hatred fanned the fanatical fighting spirit against Allied armies of the 1860s, because most were Brazilian.

Although Carlos Antonio López decreed a gradual abolition of slavery in Paraguay, the institution functioned until 1869, when a provisional government replaced that of his son. Between 1840 and the late 1860s, the state itself held several thousand slaves, and the López brothers were active purchasers of human beings, even as Francisco Solano denounced Brazil as a slaveocracy. By the early 1860s, the Brazilian population was between nine and ten million. At that time Paraguay had no more than four hundred and fifty thousand inhabitants.[47]

Paraguayans in the late 1500s founded the cities of eastern Argentina: Corrientes, Santa Fe, and the second Buenos Aires. In northwestern Argentina at about this time, Spaniards founded Salta, Jujuy, Santiago del Estero, San Miguel de Tucumán, and Córdoba. For two centuries, the Argentine northwest was more prosperous than the coast. Wines from Mendoza and cattle, sheep, and mules from Salta and Jujuy supplied the markets of the great silver mining center of Potosí. The littoral cities were poor cousins, surviving on the legal export of hides from the enormous herds of feral cattle that covered the pampas west and south of Buenos Aires. The real profit however, was in the export of silver illegally taken from the mines of Upper Peru, which purchased slaves from Africa. The landowners of Buenos Aires, famously wealthy in the 1800s, were unimportant in the colonial period. The creation of meat-salting plants and other technical innovations after 1800 fed Brazilian slaves and made Argentine plant owners rich. Coastal Argentina developed impressively after 1776. The new viceroyalty included the northern part of modern Argentina; its southern reaches below the effective boundaries of the province of Buenos Aires were dominated by nonsedentary, militaristic Native Americans. They raided and traded with Hispanized settlers.[48] Buenos Aires became the economic and political hub. The Platine viceroy oversaw the modern nations of Argentina, Paraguay, Uruguay, and the southern part of Bolivia. *Porteño* attitudes of superiority and entitlement date from the colonial era.

When porteño leaders established Argentine independence, they demanded that Paraguay follow them. Paraguayans refused. The Argentines sent Belgrano's army to force Paraguayan submission. Belgrano lost and Paraguayans remained separate. Argentines were unable create a government that could govern. Men who desired a dominant central government in Buenos Aires fought those who favored provincial autonomy, the famed Unitario-Federal conflict.

For two decades after 1810, Argentine politics were anarchic; first one faction and then another rose and fell. Briefly, the liberal Unitarians under Bernardino Rivadavia formed a national government and wrote a constitution. In 1829, Juan Manuel de Rosas, a wealthy rancher, innovative businessman, militia officer, and *saladero* entrepreneur, took control of the government of the province of Buenos Aires. He imposed order and provided security for those willing to conform. Allying himself with the Federals, he ruled Buenos Aires from 1829 to 1832 and from 1835 to 1852. He was governor and captain-general of the province, the most famous Argentine *caudillo*. Although he led gaucho armies and effectively commanded irregular troops, he was no gaucho himself but a descendant of elite families. He became fabulously wealthy. He fought leaders of the interior like Unitarian General José María Paz and Governor Pedro Ferré of Corrientes. He eventually subdued these and other provincial opponents. He forged alliances with *caudillos* of the interior. By the 1840s, few Rosas opponents lived in Argentina. Most were dead or in exile in Montevideo, Uruguay, and in Santiago, Chile. Through his terrorist organization, the *Mazorca*, Rosas made himself master of the country.

Although Rosas protected foreign, especially British, merchants resident in Buenos Aires, he defied Britain and France, which blockaded the country. Rosas refused to recognize Paraguayan independence. He never made a serious effort to conquer Paraguay but did squeeze its economy by controlling the lower Paraná River. In Asunción, Francia responded by reducing Paraguay's foreign trade to minuscule levels.[49] Rosas challenged but did not try to topple the government of Carlos Antonio López in the 1840s. He thought of Paraguay as an Argentine province. He and his successors insisted that Misiones and the central Gran Chaco were Argentine, rejecting Paraguayan claims.

Argentines overthrew Rosas in 1852. Opponents included provincial *caudillos* like Justo José de Urquiza of Entre Ríos, who resented Buenos Aires' monopoly of the revenues of the port, the country's largest income source. Other rivals were liberals such as Bartolomé Mitre and Domingo Faustino Sarmiento. Another adversary was Brazil. Rosas fled to England, where he died.[50]

Urquiza headed the new Argentine Confederation, which Buenos Aires refused to join. President Urquiza supported the liberal Constitution of

1853. He recognized Paraguayan independence and allowed Paraguay to restore economic and diplomatic contacts with the outside world, although he upheld Argentine territorial claims.

The economic interests of the leaders of Buenos Aires and their ethnocentrism caused them to reject the Confederation. They threatened to seek independence and waged civil war from 1859 to 1861. Ultimately, Buenos Aires won, joined the other provinces, and rose to national dominance. The liberal Mitre became the first president of a unified Argentina in 1862. As before, the rulers of Paraguay closely monitored Argentine developments.

THE HONOR COMPLEX: CULTURAL COMMONALITY, GENDER APPLICATIONS, LÓPEZ BIRTH YEAR

One legacy of Iberian rule common to Paraguayans, Argentines, and Brazilians was the attention paid to honor. The upper classes insisted that others esteem them and that social inferiors show them respect. Upper-class[51] men and women worried about their reputations and endeavored to demonstrate that they were honorable. Although historians recently have shown that the lower classes absorbed the honor complex, elites insisted that honor was theirs alone. Honor originated in theory from a man's deeds in battle, and he bequeathed it to his heirs, male and female. It was as valuable as real property. Because of its supposed martial origins, theoretically only men could win honor. In fact, men in Spain and Spanish America gained honor in a host of ways, including rewards from superior authority for financial considerations and for non-military service to the crown. Honors included grants or decorations from the king, membership in one of the famous orders, Calatrava, Santiago, or Alcántara, and advancement to noble status. Because of the supposed military origin of honor, women—ideally though not in practice—could not gain or regain but only lose honor. They maintained their honor by living virginal lives before marriage or by fidelity to their husbands afterward. They lost honor by living or dressing immodestly. Improper female behavior was shameful, the opposite of honorable. The honor complex pervaded Latin American society, including Paraguay, Argentina, and Brazil. Most people moderated their quest for honor with practical considerations. Honor was a valued commodity in the society of the Río de la Plata and Brazil to the end of the nineteenth century. In Argentina, honor "was acknowledged and granted protection by the state" as late as the 1887 Criminal Code. Honor "was not just a feeling; it expressed a moral idea that was used to measure social standing and . . . the right of priority."[52]

In nineteenth-century Paraguay, as in Argentina and Brazil, the culture of honor touched most aspects of life. The insistence on the value of honor was universal among the Spanish-speaking upper classes. The Guarani-speaking popular classes, who comprised the vast majority of Paraguayans, incorporated these upper-class values into their own outlook. In most of colonial Latin America, ". . . the culture of honor provided a bedrock set of values. . . ."[53] *Honor*, in the contemporary English-speaking world, means "high regard or respect . . . glory; fame . . . and good reputation."[54] These qualities were also essential to the Latin American culture of honor. A claimant needed public confirmation of his status. Participants in the honor complex strove to avoid shame or humiliation. They envied the success of others and wanted to be envied themselves. Honor, "the basis for pride and precedence . . . materialized when deference was paid or when preferential access to scarce resources was gained because of it."[55] Thus when a man claimed honor, he became a target for others, who aimed to reduce his honor and enhance their own. A proclamation of one's honor was a challenge to his rivals to dispute the claim.

In the Spanish language, the words *honor* and *honra* mean honor; but each has different connotations. Technically *honor* in the Hispanic world of the 1800s referred to a person's status and *honra* to his virtue. In Paraguay, however, people used the words *honor* and *honra* interchangeably. In the 1800s in Paraguay, the men and women occupying the social heights "had the greatest honor-status."[56] They saw a world that revolved around them. Most lived imaginatively in a world where subordinates lacked honor or the right to claim it. Leaders insisted that the whole nation, including the popular classes, must contribute to the nation's quest for honor. The upper classes could lose honor (honra) by base or ignoble acts, because it theoretically "was more reputational than honor." A man (always a man, according to the stereotype) could win honor by demonstrating physical courage, although most inherited it from an honorable father. Another way to gain honor was for the government to bestow it. Once deemed honorable, a man demonstrated his station in life by ostentatious display of wealth. The search for honor was a zero sum game, because while Señor X gained in honor, his neighbor Señor Y's honor declined in comparison.

Women were at the center of the honor complex, although in theory only passively. According to the classical formulation, they could not win honor. But they could lose it through sexual licentiousness—most conspicuously by fornication or adultery, which dishonored the women themselves and their families. A shameful act by one individual stained a whole family. Men recognized a double standard and inhabited a world that honored successful seducers. Other acts dishonorable for women but not for men included dressing immodestly and working outside the home.[57] A tainted or illegitimate birth could damage the reputation of an entire family if publicly recognized, important to Francisco Solano López.

Today the keepers of the national memory of Paraguay reject the rumor of Francisco Solano López's questionable parentage. Public historians thus give the "honorable," not the accurate date of his birth, as on the plaque in the Plaza of Heroes, although their practice is inconsistent. "Honor ultimately depended on brute force,"[58] and the first three dictators monopolized the use of force in Paraguay. The two Lópezes controlled the only printing presses in the nation; under Francia there were none. All three controlled all branches of government. Their ruthlessly effective spy systems, which were structured formally and existed informally, grew from inquisitorial colonial traditions, refined under Francia, and perfected by Carlos Antonio and Francisco Solano López. Spies informed them of what was uttered by important people even in private. Rumors would usually be reported to them sooner rather than later. None of them, of course, could control the attacks on their honor by newspapers and pamphleteers outside the country. Those in Buenos Aires were especially hostile. To the frequent attacks on him and his country by Argentine journalists, Francisco Solano López was hypersensitive. His father, more of a realist, had lived in a culture of honor without its inconsistent values overwhelming him. The son, lacking the qualities of empathy, practicality, and recognition of his own and his nation's limitations, as possessed by his father,[59] took too literally the strictures about honor. Partly because his egotism crowded out realistic considerations, he had few other guides to proper presidential behavior. He lacked a sound moral compass. His own character defects, including the most destructive, a lack of empathy, and his covetousness of worldwide fame, combined with his search for honor to push him to extreme acts. These ultimately produced his own and his nation's ruination, the demographic catastrophe of the late 1860s. In Paraguay as elsewhere in Latin America, elites were ashamed of their indigenous roots; they looked to Europe for cultural models.

In newly independent Paraguay, the culture of honor was neocolonial and very real. One's place in society was tied to one's reputation. Francisco López insisted that others demonstrate frequently and loudly their recognition of his honor. Thus he repeatedly proclaimed how honorable he was. He stood ready to defend his honorable name—by any means available, he said; but these never included personal combat. Although the values of the honor culture permeated Paraguayan society, the upper classes most ardently defended theirs—especially against public attacks. Even the most powerful of the Paraguayan elite, like the family of President Carlos Antonio López, had to contend constantly with murmured gossip and insults. Ignoring the rumors would indicate weakness, which could undermine the family's grip on the nation. "Honor not only helped to order society, it also held the potential to disrupt it."[60] That honor in Paraguay included "a desire to be envied, a desire to be exalted above others"[61] is abundantly clear in the public presence, the posturing, and the proclamations of Francisco Solano López. His life was a quest for "public esteem."[62]

A classic way to display honor, practiced by all the children of Carlos Antonio López, was through "extravagant expenditure on clothing, household furnishings, and . . . carriages."[63] Francisco Solano López spent fortunes on his uniforms and on his homes and their furnishings, a behavior that he did not learn from his father, whose outlook was more reasonable. To demonstrate his honor, Francisco displayed his most prized possession, a fair-haired, alabaster-skinned beauty from Europe, Eliza (in Paraguay, Elisa) Alicia Lynch.

The honor complex was also central to the psychological makeup of the nineteenth-century leaders of Brazil, especially Emperor Pedro II, Francisco López's most dangerous enemy. His hostility to López grew in part from the Paraguayan's affront to his honor, that of a legitimate monarch. He brought the downfall and death of Francisco López.

NOTES

1. During the years when the government affixed the tributes to Francisco S. López, as he usually signed his name, to the wall of the Pantheon, the chief adviser to the Paraguayan government on things *Lopista* was Emiliano O'Leary. He knew the true date of Marshal López's birth. "The hero of Cerro Corá," he says, "was born on July 24, 1826 in the bosom of an extraordinary family." *El Mariscal Solano López*, 3rd ed. (Asunción: Casa América-Moreno Hnos., 1970), 13.

2. Quoted in Siân Rees, *The Shadows of Elisa Lynch: How a Nineteenth-Century Irish Courtesan Became the Most Powerful Woman in Paraguay* (London: REVIEW, an imprint of Headline Publishing, 2003), 3.

3. Lynch's remains now lie mostly ignored in La Recoleta Cemetery in Asunción.

4. George Masterman, *Seven Eventful Years in Paraguay: A Narrative of Personal Experience Amongst the Paraguayans*, 2nd ed. (London: Samson Low, Son, and Marston, 1870), 181.

5. Charles A. Washburn, *The History of Paraguay, with Notes of Personal Observations and Reminiscences of Diplomacy under Difficulties*, 2 vols. (Boston: Lee and Shepard, 1871), vol. I, 471.

6. His knowledge of the Guarani language was impressive. When Belgian scholar Alfred Marbais du Graty published his survey, *République du Paraguay*, López made informed criticisms of the Belgian's errors.

7. George Thompson, C.E., *The War in Paraguay with a Historical Sketch of the Country, Its People, and Notes upon the Military Engineering of the War* (London: Longman, Green, and Co., 1869), 327.

8. Thompson, *War in Paraguay*, 326.

9. Thompson, *War in Paraguay*, 56–57.

10. When in wartime his army was running out of practically everything, López sent wine and sugar to the men in hospitals. The gesture cost little, and the wounded and their families were grateful.

11. *El Semanario*, Jan. 14, 1865.

12. Washburn, *History of Paraguay*, II, 47.

13. Washburn, *History of Paraguay*, II, 29–33; Benítez also edited one of López's newspapers and served as foreign minister until López had him executed.

14. Masterman, *Seven Eventful Years*, 164.

15. Thompson, *War in Paraguay*, 327.

16. Jerry W. Cooney, "Economy and Manpower: Paraguay at War, 1864–1869," in *I Die with My Country*, ed. Hendrik Kraay and Thomas L. Whigham (Lincoln: University of Nebraska Press, 2004), 29.

17. Thompson, *War in Paraguay*, 327–28.

18. Women became increasingly critical of him. After 1865, they comprised an overwhelming majority of the civilian population; Barbara Potthast, "Protagonists, Victims, and Heroes: Paraguayan Women during the 'Great War,'" in *I Die with My Country*, ed. Hendrik Kraay and Thomas L. Whigham (Lincoln: University of Nebraska Press, 2004), 53–54.

19. Thompson, *War in Paraguay*, 29.

20. For readers without access to primary sources, see Chris Leuchars, *To the Bitter End: Paraguay and the War of the Triple Alliance* (Westport, CT: Greenwood Press, 2002), 110–11, 120, 131, 156, 183–90, 207, and 211, for stories of his cowardice.

21. Thompson, *War in Paraguay*, 328.

22. Masterman, *Seven Eventful Years*, 134.

23. Washburn, *History of Paraguay*, II, 49–51.

24. Thomas L. Whigham, *The Paraguayan War, Volume I: Causes and Early Conduct* (Lincoln: University of Nebraska Press, 2002), 247. The author is here being kind, considerate of the sensibilities of modern Paraguayans. He tells the reader about López's fear of battle in a gentle way.

25. Whigham, *Paraguayan War, I*, 247.

26. American Psychiatric Association, *Diagnostic and Statistical Manual of Mental Disorders*, 4th ed. (Washington, DC: 1994), 645–60.

27. Whigham, *Paraguayan War, I*, 419.

28. Jerry W. Cooney, "Economy and Manpower," in *I Die with My Country: Perspectives on the Paraguayan War*, ed. Hendrik Kraay and Thomas L. Whigham (Lincoln: University of Nebraska Press, 2004), 42–43.

29. James Schofield Saeger, *The Chaco Mission Frontier: the Guaycuruan Experience* (Tucson: University of Arizona Press, 2000), 5–7.

30. James Schofield Saeger, "Abolition and Survival: The Eighteenth Century Paraguayan Encomienda," *TAM* 38 (July 1981): 59–85.

31. Louis Necker, *Indios guaraníes y chamanes franciscanos: las primeras reducciones del Paraguay, 1680–1800* (Asunción: Centro de Estudios Antropológicos, 1990); Margarita Durán Estrago, *Presencia franciscana en el Paraguay, 1538–1824* (Asunción: Universidad Católica, 1987).

32. The percent of female fugitives was relatively small, seldom rising above 10 percent. James Schofield Saeger, "Survival and Abolition: the Eighteenth Century Paraguayan Encomienda," *TAM* 38 (July 1981): 59–85. This probably resembles the gender profile of fugitives/deserters during the Great War.

33. In the Archivo Nacional de Asunción, the encomienda censuses in Sección Nueva Encuadernación bear this out, showing that migration was not exclusively to the south and east.

34. Interior towns and villages had cabildos as well.

35. All municipalities, including the legally inferior villas and pueblos, had cabildos.

36. Cabildo elections, Asunción, Jan. 1, 1775, ANA (Archivo Nacional de Asunción, Asunción, Paraguay), SH (Sección Historia), vol. 138.

37. William F. Beezely, "Caudillismo: An Interpretive Note," *Journal of Inter-American Studies* 11 (1969): 345–52.

38. Ann Twinam, *Public Lives, Private Secrets: Gender, Honor, Sexuality, and Illegitimacy in Colonial Spanish America* (Stanford, CA: Stanford University Press, 1999), 265.

39. Durán Estrago, *Presencia franciscana en el Paraguay*, 9.

40. The missions of San Joaquín and San Estanislao located in Taruma were not contiguous with the other thirty missions. There is no good reason, however, for omitting them from the list of Jesuit Guarani missions.

41. Velasco was governor three times between 1806 and 1811, with interruptions of his service in 1807 and 1809.

42. John Hoyt Williams, *The Rise and Fall of the Paraguayan Republic, 1800–1870* (Austin: Institute of Latin American Studies, University of Texas, 1979), 23.

43. John Hoyt Williams, "Paraguayan Isolation under Dr. Francia: A Reevaluation," *HAHR* 52, no. 1 (February 1972): 102–22.

44 Whigham, *Politics of River Trade*, 26.

45. George Reid Andrews, *Afro-Latin America, 1800–2000* (New York: Oxford University Press, 2004).

46. After independence, the area that became modern Argentina had several names. These included the United Provinces of the Río de la Plata, the Confederation of the Río de la Plata, and the Argentine Confederation. For convenience, the area will usually be called Argentina.

47. For a discussion of the population of Paraguay, see the debate between Vera Blinn Reber, "The Demographics of Paraguay," *HAHR* 68, no. 2 (May 1988): 289–319; and Thomas Whigham and Barbara Potthast-Jukeit, "The Paraguayan Rosetta Stone," *LARR* 34, no. 1 (1999): 174–86. See also the earlier article by John Hoyt Williams, "Observations on the Paraguayan Census of 1846," *HAHR* 56, no. 3 (August 1976): 424–37.

48. Kristine L. Jones, "Warfare, Reorganization, and Readaptation at the Margins of Spanish Rule: The Southern Margin (1573–1882)," *CHNPA*, vol. III, pt. 2; *The Southern Margin*, ed. Frank Saloman and Stuart B. Schwartz (Cambridge, UK: Cambridge University Press, 1999), 138–87.

49. Williams, "Paraguayan Isolation under Dr. Francia—Reevaluation."

50. Rosas's remains were eventually returned to Buenos Aires in 1989; Jeffrey M. Shumway, "'Sometimes Knowing How to Forget is Also Having Memory': The

Repatriation of Juan Manuel de Rosas and the Healing of Argentina," in *Death, Dismemberment, and Memory: Body Politics*, ed. Lyman L. Johnson (Albuquerque: University of New Mexico Press, 2004), 105–40.

51. Class is an anachronistic designation, but is used here in its everyday, informal sense.

52. Sandra Gayol, *"Honor moderno*: the Significance of Honor in Fin-de-Siècle Argentina," *HAHR* 84, no. 3 (August 2004): 475–501, quotes 495–96.

53. Lyman L. Johnson and Sonya Lipsett-Rivera, "Introduction," in *The Faces of Honor: Sex, Shame, and Violence in Colonial Latin America*, ed. Johnson and Lipsett Rivera (Albuquerque: University of New Mexico Press, 1998), 1–17, 3.

54. David B. Guralnik, ed., *Webster's New World Dictionary of the American Language* (New York: Warner Books, 1983).

55. Ramón Gutiérrez, *When Jesus Came, the Corn Mothers Went Away: Marriage, Sexuality, and Power in New Mexico, 1500–1846* (Stanford, CA: Stanford University Press, 1991), 177.

56. Johnson and Lipsett-Rivera, "Introduction," 4.

57. Belying the stereotype, Ibero-American women went to court to regain honor.

58. Gutiérrez, *When Jesus Came*, 177.

59. Whether Carlos Antonio López was or was not the biological father of Francisco Solano will not concern us. He recognized Francisco as his son and in every way acted like a father. Thus he is referred to here as the father.

60. Johnson and Lipsett-Rivera, "Introduction," 15.

61. Johnson and Lipsett-Rivera, "Introduction," 15.

62. Mark A. Burkholder, "Honor and Honors in Colonial Spanish America," in *Faces of Honor*, ed. Lyman L. Johnson and Sonya Lipsett-Rivera (Albuquerque: University of New Mexico Press, 1998), 18–44.

63. Burkholder, "Honor and Honors," 30.

2

Los López, Father and Son, Family and Nation

Carlos Antonio López influenced the political outlook of his son, Francisco Solano, who took his father's governing mode as his model. In office, however, the two men displayed markedly different personal styles, meaningful because both were personalistic dictators. The people respected the father and only a few had reason to fear him. The son was more feared and less respected than his father. Their policy differences largely arose partly from their different characters. Many of Francisco's policies were continuations of those of his father. His most important presidential strategies, however, especially his foreign relations, became grotesque caricatures of his father's procedures.

Carlos Antonio López became an absolute dictator in the early 1840s, and his family's privileged position profoundly influenced how his eldest son saw the world. It also determined that the people in Francisco's immediate world treated him with adulation. He spent his early years on his family's rural properties, which were "political states in miniature."[1] His father was one of the "dictatorial masters" of the region.[2] Francisco's pampered status warped his outlook and his approach to adversity. His ego grew to a size out of proportion to his abilities. He never acquired his father's shrewd judgment, prudence, or empathy. He did not need to do so. He learned the form but not the substance of how his father ran the nation. The prevailing culture of honor came naturally to him.

In most other newly independent Latin American nations, *caudillos*[3] or aspirants to power had to work through existing institutions and socioeconomic groups. These normally included the landed elite, the emerging political parties, the Roman Catholic Church, and the army.[4] Most of these institutions were neutralized in the Francia years. In 1840, Paraguay lacked a ruling class, although the López family and their retainers were about to become one. Most other newly independent Spanish American nations had an elite group in civil society with its own power base, usually centered on landed wealth or mining. Its members had numerous clients and dependent peons. Paraguay lacked such a class.

Supreme Dictator Francia had destroyed the power of colonial elite, even though the number that he actually executed was probably fewer than one hundred. Francia's suppression of the 1820 conspiracy alone resulted in his execution of sixty-eight of the conspirators, the heart of a would-be political faction, the imprisonment of hundreds of others, and the nationalization of their properties.[5] Francia also "Paraguayanized" the forty-odd royal ranches. During the supreme dictator's rule, they "were not broken up and sold, as in other parts of Spanish America, but were . . . augmented and made more efficient."[6] Thus, there existed no wealth-producing power base from which ambitious members of civil society could move into politics. Neither was the Roman Catholic Church an important power base as it was in Mexico, partly owing to the supreme dictator's nationalization of its properties. Francia's seizures were the culmination of the alienation of church wealth that began with Charles III's expulsion of the Jesuits in 1767. King Charles appropriated Jesuit landed estates—the valuable mission ranches and farms that formed the Church's major holdings in the region. Francia severed ties between the church and the Vatican, allowing communication only through him. "In 1816, the [Francia] government assumed financial stewardship over the Church," and, at the time, income from church properties made up about 20 percent of government revenues.[7] Since all governments before 1870 prohibited political parties, the army was the only other potential power base. Except for the ineffectual Mariano Roque Alonso, however, it failed to produce successful claimants to office, as it did in many other Spanish American nations, because the first three dictators successfully controlled the military.

THE CARLOS LÓPEZ DYNAMIC

Carlos Antonio López's extension of many of Francia's policies prevented a real ruling class from emerging. With no institutional opponents, the first López controlled the most profitable sectors of the economy including the export trade and land, especially the ranches of the state. He himself took title to many of these enterprises and awarded others to his family. The López family did business under the protection of the state, that is, Carlos Antonio himself. He also converted into state properties the communal lands of the formerly protected Guarani pueblos. He decreed that the Guarani Indians (who, until then, were legal minors) were citizens and abolished their protected status. Now he could draft Guaranis into military service, an obligation from which non-Jesuit Guaranis had been exempt. A few families were quietly prosperous, but we may be sure that they did not offend either Francia or the two López presidents. If anyone posed even a minor challenge to the government, as did the Decoud brothers (see discussion in chapter 3), it was a challenge that did not last for long.

Carlos Antonio López took power soon after Francia died in 1840. At first, a junta or council of army officers made itself into a government. They promised to continue the policies of El Supremo. These soldiers could neither master civilian government nor could they control the nation by force. Politics were chaotic for several months. Francia's secretary, Policarpo Patiño, had hoped to succeed his former chief, but his service to the supreme dictator had brought him infamy. All groups in the country hated and feared him. After army officers arrested him, he conveniently committed suicide in prison.

At fifty-four years of age, Carlos Antonio López emerged from the relative seclusion of his ranch in Olivares, to which he had wisely withdrawn in 1823, to return to public life.[8] His law practice had withered. In 1840–1841, he became active politically, no longer the teacher and lawyer of the late colonial and independence eras. A barracks revolt in February 1841 brought to power Mariano Roque Alonso, an officer then approaching fifty years old. He appointed the more able and better-educated Carlos Antonio López as his secretary and adviser. A group of several hundred Paraguayan notables formed a Congress. They appointed army officer Roque Alonso and López to serve as consuls for three years. Alonso had no government expertise, less talent for it, and little interest in it. Thus, López increasingly dominated Paraguay as Alonso in effect bowed out. As soon as he could, López placed his co-consul at the rear of the political parade. Yet he neither exiled nor executed him. Roque Alonso lived on for another decade.

The first López was provincial in experience and outlook. His gargantuan appetite made him obese, and his corpulence consigned him to a sedentary lifestyle. He never left Paraguay. His great bulk made travel difficult, and he viewed the outside world with distrust. He had not previously belonged to the most respected group. Upper-class men and women gossiped about his undesirable ancestry. Some whispered that the "stain" on the family tree was left by a Guaycurúan ancestor. Although Paraguayans were proud of their descent from Guaranis, "Guaycurú," referring to nonsedentary peoples of the Chaco, was a label of contempt. Another rumor was that the despised López ancestor was African or Afro-Paraguayan.

A hard-working man whose nepotism would distort his government, Don Carlos soon came to favor his eldest son in important matters of state. He saw to his formal education by hiring an Argentine schoolmaster, Juan Pedro Escalada, and a Dominican friar, Miguel Albornoz. He sent him off to Buenos Aires in 1843 for several months to experience life there.[9] Back home, he taught him the ways of government and appointed him to high civil and military offices. These positions were no sinecures. Francisco assumed major responsibilities while still in his teens, and he worked hard at his assignments.

Carlos Antonio and Francisco Solano López were both born into authoritarian worlds, but that of the father was a different ambience from that of his son. In 1787, when the elder was born, Spain still ruled its South American colonies, including the province of Paraguay. Carlos Antonio grew to manhood and passed his maturity in an environment in which a stranger had the final authority. He himself did not rule until late middle age. Until the elder López reached his twenties, the most powerful man in the province was the governor-intendant. Don Carlos passed his thirties and forties in a country ruled absolutely by Francia. He kept a low enough profile to avoid persecution by the supreme dictator, as many other elite or politically ambitious Paraguayans did not. As Francia's abuses cautioned people away from public affairs, Carlos Antonio López curtailed his law practice, which he chose after rejecting his seminary training and his teaching career. In 1819, Francia suppressed the San Carlos Seminary, where López taught; and so he left public life. In 1826, at the age of thirty-nine, he married a pregnant Juana Pabla Carillo. Later that year she gave birth to Francisco Solano López.

Until 1840, Carlos Antonio lived mostly at his and his wife's country properties, surrounded by servants, hired hands, and his family, which ultimately included five children. The boys were Francisco, the eldest; Venancio, his younger brother; and Benigno, the coddled baby of the family and Juana Pabla's favorite. The girls were Inocencia and Rafaela, the latter Carlos Antonio's favorite daughter, who often substituted for her mother on state occasions. Sibling rivalry was an essential ingredient of the López family dynamic, but Carlos Antonio groomed only one son for politics. The father hired tutors to prepare his *primogénito,* his first son, for large responsibilities. Carlos Antonio, as John Lynch notes,[10] was the only Spanish American *caudillo* in the nineteenth century who was able to turn over the government to his son.

Until he was fourteen, Francisco spent his time on his father's estates. There he was the favored son and heir to the family's wealth and position. He expected that all persons except his father treat him with deference, preferably with servility. Employees were "reverent" to all the López boys. The young men led "scandalous and dissolute" lives without adverse consequences, except for Venancio, who acquired a wasting disease.[11] Confronted with no higher authority than his indulgent father, Francisco was never in a position to learn the interpersonal skills that most other boys needed just to survive. Living in the strict world of the Spanish monarchy and the perilous one of Francia, Carlos Antonio had learned patience, judgment, and respect for government officials. He had to discern what other men really felt. He learned when to please some people and when to fear, avoid, and obey others, especially Francia. Francisco, in contrast, lived on the ranch as a boy and in Asunción as a young man. The world was his oyster. He needed to please no person other than his father, and he did that. Francisco usually just gave orders, and people obeyed. His sense of self-importance grew. One habit of his father's that Francisco emulated was working long hours. Most importantly, however, he never had to find out the points of view of other men. Whether he was born without empathy or just never needed to develop it is unknowable. The fact remains, though, that of all the things in life that he lacked, and those were few in the material sense, the inability to empathize eventually contributed the most to his destiny. Francisco's intelligence, diligence, and iron will, in the end, were insufficient to save him from himself.

As his sons and daughters grew to maturity, Carlos Antonio made his properties and those of his wife profitable. Profitability was no easy task in an economy that had been reduced to an autarchy by Francia's policy of isolation. President López awarded his children wealth-producing properties, including urban real estate, productive farms and ranches, and Afro-Paraguayan slaves.[12]

Among elite society in the late 1820s, the rumor spread that Juana Pabla had first became pregnant by her stepfather, Lázaro Rojas Aranda. He was the godfather and the rumored biological father of Francisco Solano. At his death, Rojas Aranda left Francisco his fortune, which further fueled the whispers about paternity. Still, Carlos Antonio was truly Francisco's father in every important way. He groomed him for political leadership soon after assuming it himself.

Isolated by his good fortune, Francisco never had a true friend. From birth, he was surrounded by relatives, servants, clients, employees, and other subordinates, but no real friends. The lack of a friendship between equals warped Francisco's personality. The fissure in his character had a profound impact on his mode of governing. This was clearest in his foreign policy, where he needed the keen and accurate ability to judge other people, ascertain their motivations, and ferret out their hidden agendas.

REGIONALISM AND ISOLATIONISM

Carlos Antonio López had a sense of prudence. Under Francia, the imprudent, the impatient, and the vocal were imprisoned or dead. Even after he became president-dictator in the early 1840s, López realized that he was an important man in Paraguay and nowhere else. For him it was enough. Although he never ventured beyond the borders of his own nation, he could read a map. He understood population statistics. In the 1840s, he ordered a census to be taken, and he learned that his country numbered around two hundred and fifty thousand people,[13] less than a tenth of Brazil's. He concluded that Paraguay should avoid war with that empire. Because of Argentine dictator Juan Manuel Rosas's refusal to recognize Paraguay's independence and his control of the lower Paraná River, Carlos Antonio was unable to travel to foreign capitals—nor did he wish to do so. Nevertheless, he kept himself informed about regional matters. He was an ambitious man, not only for himself and his family but also for his country. He believed that his own success, that of his family, and the nation's well-being were indivisible.

In the early years of his government, Carlos Antonio necessarily concentrated on domestic issues. He founded or renamed and developed towns such as Encarnación, formerly the Guarani pueblo of Itapúa. In modest ways, he improved the nation's defense capabilities, drafting three thousand men into the army, building new frontier forts, and improving old ones. He modernized the police forces of the port cities of Asunción and Pilar. There the kind of trouble caused by sailors could threaten public order and not incidentally the López control of the nation. As part of his intelligence apparatus, a stronger police presence in these key municipalities increased his ability to monitor the activities of the few outsiders who trickled in. President López could record which Paraguayans the foreigners visited, as he perfected Francia's already efficient spy system. He sponsored a modest urban renewal in Asunción and he improved the nation's roads. Reversing Francia's persecution of the Roman Catholic Church, President López, whose brother Basilio was a priest, allocated government revenues for church construction and repair. Like Francia, he treated the peasantry benevolently, respecting their way of life by not interfering with them. Neither did he tax them, owing to the bountiful revenues from state enterprises.

The most striking departure from the policies of the austere Francia was López's seizure of the opportunity afforded by his control of the nation's military and judiciary to increase his own wealth and that of his wife and his children. As president, he took a salary of only 8,000 pesos from the state, a handsome sum in the 1840s and 1850s but far less than he might have demanded. He improved the educational system, although most

Paraguayans remained illiterate, spoke Guarani, and knew little Spanish. In the second decade of his rule, López was able to open Paraguay to the outside world. After a less hostile government took power in Argentina in 1852 and allowed Paraguay access to foreign markets, he imported foreign technical experts to assist in the development of his nation's infrastructure. To mitigate the dependence on foreign specialists, he also sent young men to Europe on state scholarships to learn the skills necessary to defend and to develop Paraguay.

To legitimize his power, López fostered the belief that his rule was more modern than Francia's primitive polity, which it was, and more responsive to public opinion, which it was not. He convened a Congress in 1844. A legislature in name only, it was a rubber stamp designed to give the president's decrees an appearance of legitimacy, much like similar bodies under caudillos elsewhere—including Antonio López de Santa Anna and Porfirio Díaz in Mexico and Juan Manuel de Rosas in Argentina. López himself chose its three hundred members. He had no need to defer to their wishes, nor did he seek their counsel.

In March 1844, Congress met for two days. As López expected, the Congress endorsed all of his proposals and no others. To impress upon the assembled representatives the proper relationship between the executive and the legislature, López himself presided over it, physically demonstrating with his considerable presence its expected subservience. The Congress of 1844 by acclamation named him president with an annual salary of 8,000 pesos fuertes.[14] López stipulated, and thus Congress stipulated, that the president's salary was to be paid in specie, not the "imaginary" pesos used in typical barter transactions in Paraguay for centuries. The legislature also approved a Constitution of 1844, but it had no hand in its creation. López wrote it himself with the assistance of Andrés Gill, a diplomat. Of the president's contribution, a North American observer noted that Paraguay's "whole constitution, civil, political, and religious, is the work of his hands."[15]

This document justified the López dictatorship—and in effect was "a fig leaf of legitimacy to cover the crude realities of his personal rule,"[16] like those of many other Spanish American caudillos—and granted him sole political power. The Constitution called for a Congress to meet every five years, although no subsequent gathering had any authority. Title VI of the document conferred on López the position of the supreme judge in questions pertaining to the affairs of government, making clear that no independent judiciary existed. The code vested all powers in one man, the man who wrote the constitution. The document created "a true legalized dictatorship."[17] The only right that Paraguayans had was the right to petition the government. The basic law of 1844 also legalized prior censorship of the press. There was as yet no press to censor, but López created one the next year when he founded *Paraguayo Independiente*, which he also edited.

A few years after López took power, foreigners began to venture into Paraguay. One was Dr. Alfred Demersay, a French physician. In 1845, he moved from the Mato Grosso province of Brazil to adjacent northern Paraguay. The president denied him permission to visit Asunción. Then the recently arrived Brazilian minister José Antonio Pimenta Bueno, whom the elder López trusted, convinced him to reconsider. López allowed Demersay to visit and when his favored daughter Rafaela fell ill, Demersay treated her. Upon her recovery, the grateful López asked the doctor to conduct of study of the nation. His investigation resulted in the publication of *Histoire physique, economique et politique du Paraguay*. At about the same time, López allowed Juan Andrés Gelly, an expatriate who had for the past two decades worked as an Uruguayan diplomat, to return home. The president found the exile's return useful, especially his knowledge of the outside world. At first President López suspected that Gelly harbored the liberal, or as he labeled them "anarchistic," ideas then circulating in Uruguay. López hated liberals and liberalism. He initially confined Gelly to internal exile in Villa Rica, the nation's second largest municipality. After a time, he allowed him to move to the capital, where he became a presidential adviser. A major service to the nation was Gelly's persuading his chief to modernize the government, military, and infrastructure.

The aforementioned Brazilian José Antonio Pimenta Bueno, who had arrived in Asunción in 1844, also urged modernization. His emperor had directed him to convince Paraguay to favor Brazil and to distrust Argentina. To remain aloof from Argentina was López's wish as well. Francia's Paraguay had maintained off-and-on relations with Brazil, whose independence followed Paraguay's by a decade. In the early 1840s, Rosas in Buenos Aires and the young Emperor Pedro II of Brazil and his advisers developed a tense relationship. Rosas still refused to recognize Paraguayan independence and interfered with its navigation on the Paraná River. He thus closed the door to the lucrative markets for yerba, tobacco, lumber, and hides. Also, Rosas's control of the Paraná River obstructed Brazil's Mato Grosso trade. In the 1840s, President López welcomed Brazilian support. His relationship with Pimenta Bueno was a friendly one, and the senior López took the unusual step of entertaining the foreigner at home.

The Brazilian's efforts bore fruit. In October 1844, Paraguay and Brazil signed a treaty of alliance, commerce, and navigation. The pact also stipulated that the two nations would later decide the issue of disputed boundaries. No boundary settlement materialized until a victorious Brazil imposed one following the War of the Triple Alliance. But the 1844 agreement indicated that if Paraguay were threatened with attack—and the only other likely attacker was Argentina—Brazil would try to prevent hostilities. The agreement, never ratified, drew the condemnation of the porteño dictator. Rosas feared that Paraguay would become a Brazilian protectorate. In any event, Rosas lacked the military power to force Paraguay into joining the United Provinces of the Río de la Plata, and he had other enemies nearby.

Rosas's control of the lower Paraná River caused trouble for López. The two dictators corresponded. Although Rosas usually couched his negative replies to Paraguayan requests in a friendly style, he refused to recognize Paraguayan independence. He granted conditional rights to Paraguayan commerce, but López wanted unconditional rights to send vessels to the south and Argentine recognition of his nation's independence.

In the mid-1840s, Rosas's clash with Argentine opponents tempted López to intervene in Argentine affairs. The leaders of Corrientes province on Paraguay's southern border were restless. They had refused Rosas's invitation to join the Pacto Federal with Buenos Aires, Santa Fe, and Entre Ríos in 1831. When Rosas allowed merchant ships to travel up-river in 1844, authorities in Corrientes seized them. López observed the growing hostility between Rosas's Buenos Aires and Corrientes, and he sided with his provincial neighbor. Corrientes began to act not like a province but an independent nation. In December 1844, Corrientes and Paraguay signed a treaty, an unusual compact between a province and a nation. The dictator in Buenos Aires regarded it as an anti-Rosas alliance of two Argentine provinces. The settlement challenged his position as the sole guardian of Argentine foreign policy. Rosas thus halted all commerce between Paraguay and Buenos Aires and rejected a commercial treaty proposed by López.

The Paraguayan president emphasized two foreign policy issues. One was Paraguay's independence. The other was its right freely to navigate on the Río Paraná. Rosas demanded Paraguay's submission to Buenos Aires. He insisted that the Paraná was not an international waterway, as the Paraguayans and Brazilians claimed but an Argentine river that his government could control as it wished. If Paraguay would concede that it was an Argentine province, he would allow its merchant ships to trade in the lucrative markets to the south. If it would not so agree, he would assault their commerce.

CORRIENTES

In early 1845, the governor of Corrientes, Joaquín Madariaga, asked for Paraguayan help. The senior López blundered into the internal political strife of Argentina; he also sent his oldest son into the conflict, knowing he would be safe. General José María Paz, a Unitarian from Córdoba and an enemy of Rosas, had sided with Corrientes. An able officer, he headed its army. He was joined in opposition to Rosas by a faction in Entre Ríos, an Argentine province. An Entrerriano group pledged to send an army to combat the Rosas forces. In Asunción, Carlos Antonio López broke with his own good instincts. He put caution aside and joined with anti-Rosas forces in Argentina. He did so in part because having a gifted commander like Paz was reassuring.

Rosas influenced public opinion in the region through the press, especially the *Gaceta Mercantil*, his major print voice. López founded his own newspaper, *Paraguayo Independiente*, to get his version of events to the outside world. The periodical was little more than a regularly issued government publicity release. It propounded the views of the Paraguayan dictator and extolled his virtues. It was the official—and only—press voice in Paraguay. The first issue, edited by López, appeared in April 1845.

As López prepared to send troops into Argentina, he reformed his army, then a colonial hand-me-down despite Francia's innovations. The reorganized units failed to impress Argentine officers, who dismissed them as a non-threat. The president organized the small regular army, ordered the creation of a militia, and formed auxiliary units to support them. The reforms gave the president and his son a higher regard for their troops than their abilities warranted. Carlos Antonio asked his people to defend the nation's honor and win glory. The obese dictator insisted that the national motto be repeatedly proclaimed; "Independence or Death" regularly appeared on official documents. By nature inclined toward peace, Carlos Antonio put no great stock in the slogan. In 1845, he nevertheless considered that a state of war existed between him and Governor Rosas.

In June 1845, Uruguay, whose capital of Montevideo was besieged by Rosas's red-clad forces,[18] recognized the independence of Paraguay. Through *Paraguayo Independiente*, López predicted that recognition from other powers would soon follow. Rosas grew angrier. He asked Brazil to withdraw its recognition of Paraguay. Imperial leaders not only refused his request but also annoyed him further. They promised to persuade European and other American nations to recognize Paraguayan independence.

In August 1845, Britain and France blockaded Buenos Aires, a two-year action. The Europeans opposed Rosas's arbitrary control of the mouth of the Río de la Plata. With Rosas apparently pinioned in the south, López sent Paraguayan forces against the porteño dictator. Of immediate concern was the army of Manuel Oribe, an Uruguayan ally of Rosas, whose army, the Paraguayan president feared, was preparing to attack Paraguay.

He thus cast his lot with Corrientes and other anti-Rosas Argentines. Although friendly, Corrientes was as opposed to Paraguay's border claims as the regime in Buenos Aires. In any event, López agreed to a formal alliance with Corrientes in November 1845 and sent the first army outside Paraguay since the colonial era.

The Hopkins Affair

At this moment, what came to be known as the Hopkins Affair began to unfold, as Edward A. Hopkins injected himself into Paraguayan politics and Platine diplomacy. A twenty-three-year-old North American, Hopkins had secured an appointment as an agent of the U.S. government. Having visited Buenos Aires, he thought that he had discovered profitable investment opportunities in the Río de la Plata, especially for himself. Wrapping himself in the Monroe Doctrine, he announced his opposition to such European interventions as those of France and Britain in Argentina. He said that his visit to Asunción was a prelude to United States' recognition. He suggested that establishing a commercial relationship between their two nations would provide a foundation for formal recognition. He also advised the British minister that he, Hopkins, could mediate the escalating López–Rosas dispute. López befriended Hopkins, receiving him "with uncharacteristic ostentation and warmth."[19] Hopkins initially praised President López as an able negotiator, a "remarkable man"[20] with a surprisingly comprehensive view of the world.

At the heart of Hopkins's project was self-interest. His company, eventually capitalized at 300,000 pesos, sought an exclusive concession for steamship navigation and commerce between Paraguay and the world. His brash mediation proposal ended in failure, but he did not give up hope on the project. Hopkins said, "The vegetable kingdom of Paraguay presents the richest attractions . . . to that important class which is devoted to mercantile enterprise." He promised that his investors would profit from the export of medicinal herbs, dyes, and forest resources. The climate was "favorable to all the useful grains and table vegetables [and] delicious fruits."[21] In short, Hopkins found Paraguay attractive for foreign entrepreneurs, especially for himself and whatever partners he could entice. After his mediation efforts collapsed, he left Paraguay for a few years. His return in the 1850s bothered the president; Hopkins's eventual business reverses caused him to change his opinion of López. Hopkins was the first North American observer to record his impressions of López's Paraguay. His relationship with Don Carlos led to conflict between Paraguay and the United States.

The lack of a firm Brazilian promise to support Paraguay also pushed Carlos Antonio López toward a military alliance with Corrientes. He appointed his nineteen-year-old son, Francisco, to command the expeditionary force; young López began his military career as colonel major and soon became brigadier general, highlighting the president's nepotism. The commander in Argentina would be General Paz, who, according to D. F. Sarmiento, "was a European soldier [because he] only believed in bravery as subordinate to tactics, strategy, and discipline."[22] Francisco López thought the priority of those attributes should be the reverse of Sarmiento's. When awaiting Paraguayan units, Paz's army might have been six thousand men,[23] and its objective was to topple the tyrant in Buenos Aires.

The president chose a non-Paraguayan veteran officer as Francisco's chief of staff,[24] which shows that he was then unwilling to place complete trust in his son. Francisco's appointment was unpopular in Paraguay and ridiculed abroad, because Francisco had no military training and no experience. But he was in charge. His mission to Corrientes with the army and his sporadic reading of military history and tactics[25] convinced his already inflated ego that he had talent and experience. What President López's selection of his son truly showed was that he trusted family but not more worthy men for command.

Francisco led four thousand men to Corrientes, but the Paraguay–Corrientes alliance failed. General Paz and Governor Madariaga were jealous of each other, a disastrous civil–military relationship. By the time Francisco reached Corrientes, severe jostling among the three leaders had further disunified the command. When Argentine cavalry forces under Justo José de Urquiza attacked on Rosas's behalf, the coalition splintered. The Paraguayans turned toward home. Paz disdained Francisco López, who returned the Argentine's contempt. The son of a president resented taking orders from a mere general, whose superior command abilities Francisco refused to concede. Paz thought López an incompetent, inferior, and disobedient subordinate. The teen-aged General López expected Paz to respect his rank and his status as heir apparent to the presidency. He saw Paz as disrespectful and arrogant. His father wisely counseled him to moderate his criticism. Francisco had resented Paz's proposal to distribute Paraguayan units among those of experienced Argentine commanders. Francisco took the proposal as an affront to his military ability, surely what Paz intended. Since the distribution would have left Francisco with nothing to command, he refused. To be deferential and subordinate to Paz, as his father had ordered, was painful for Francisco.

After the collapse of the alliance with Corrientes, President López recalled the army. Francisco's initial brush with military life, however, gave him the mistaken belief that he was a talented, experienced commander.

Rosas disseminated the fiction that the Paraguayans had been deceived by his enemies the "savage Unitarians," a useful pose, and he avoided further confrontation. Without armies or allies, the Correntino rebellion collapsed. In 1847, the province repaired its relationship with Rosas.

FRANCISCO'S RISE TO POWER

Although Francisco López's first military experience was thus lackluster, he maintained that he became general in chief in 1845 because "of [his] vast knowledge and superior talent," not mentioning that he was the eldest son of the president. During the march to Corrientes in 1845, according to him, "he gave . . . proof of his conspicuous genius in the rapid organization of a strong and disciplined army."[26]

He did not command a disciplined army. In late February 1846, the young leader faced mutinies in three squadrons, showing his tenuous control of his troops. Mutineers wanted to follow General Paz. Francisco executed them to regain control. The insubordination of Payubre disturbed Carlos Antonio. He resolved to keep his troops inside the nation's borders in the future, which he mostly did. For Francisco, the mutiny drove home a lesson in the exercise of leadership. Later speaking of himself, he bragged, "Marshal López . . . has known how to incarnate in a virtuous people VALOR, OBEDIENCE, and UNION."[27] To Francisco, obedience was paramount. He proclaimed, "Loyalty is a moral virtue and the most precious gift that maintains social relations."[28]

Francisco's arrogance and egotism grew from experience. Until he was fifteen, the young López had lived on the family property at Trinidad, where the rule of his father was absolute. He learned no humility or respect for others from his father's employees there or from the private tutors who taught the López children at home. The other children were also spoiled, but Francisco was the eldest and ablest and the one who counted in the world of affairs. When Francisco studied for a year with Argentine Juan Pedro Escalada, he became certain of his superiority and of the shortcomings of others. During his teens, the first-born son of the *patrón* and president inhabited an authoritarian atmosphere. In the country or in the capital he was the second most powerful figure. His early surroundings readied him for the larger arena into which he would follow his father. Until the day of his death, Francisco knew only privilege and entitlement. From others he demanded deference, not friendships. His nonparticipation in relationships of equals helps explain why he could not cooperate with Paz. Francisco was "indulged as a youth, and accustomed all his life to have his will over all with whom he came in contact."[29] Never did he allow anyone to tell him that his breath was bad or that his clothing was outlandish or that his judgment was faulty, all of which were usually true. Surrounded all his life by sycophants and subordinates, he never made a true friend.

Around the time of the Corrientes march, Francisco began an affair with Juana Pessoa (or Pesoa), a young woman from a respectable family of Villa del Pilar, a river port between Asunción and Corrientes. The relationship lasted into the 1860s, although for López it was never exclusive. He eventually recognized three children of the liaison and gave them his name. To one outsider, his many conquests conducted under his father's protection made him "a licensed ravisher."[30] His brothers were as libertine as he was. Francisco took pleasure in seducing the daughters of upper-class fathers, an essential and ugly feature of the honor complex. Francisco accepted its extreme values but never acquired the leavening of a pragmatism that most others needed to succeed. His "honorable" behavior became a caricature, but it shaped his public posture and policies.

Rumors of his own bastardy followed Francisco throughout his life, and he probably first heard of them at about this time. It was common knowledge that many Paraguayans believed that he was not Carlos Antonio's progeny but the natural son of Lázaro de Rojas, as his mother publicly proclaimed after Francisco's death.[31] Francisco physically resembled his mother's stepfather, his own godfather. [32] The wealthy Rojas had married the widow Carillo; her daughter by her first husband, Juana Pabla, married Carlos Antonio and gave birth to Francisco Solano. If Carlos Antonio did not marry the widow for her considerable property, her wealth was an added attraction. In any event, they married earlier in 1826 and Francisco was born following the wedding in July. Carlos Antonio was a good husband and an indulgent father. Carlos Antonio ignored the whispered gossip, but, as discussed earlier, Francisco was bothered so much that he revised his birth date and proclaimed the false one repeatedly.[33] Although other children followed, two boys and two girls, Francisco remained the only son whom his father thought able enough to be entrusted to conduct affairs of state. He was the most competent, best educated, most intelligent, and the least likeable of the three sons. Although none of the brothers was especially popular, people always deferred to them. Flattery was obligatory.

From his father, "naturally proud and quite sensitive to the least offense," Francisco acquired his sense of honor and chivalry, although the father adjusted these values to the demands of the real world. The son continued to read the books that his father bought him, especially European treatises on geography and military history.[34] His reading of these texts helped convince Francisco of his vast erudition and expertise in military matters. He gained an admiration of Napoleon, common in the 1800s. The Liberator Simón Bolívar was another who admired Napoleon, "although discreetly and not for publication."[35] López gloried in Bonaparte's exploits, as he read about Napoleonic warfare and French military theory and practice.[36] Impressed by the dash and glory of Napoleonic warfare, he missed its essence: a strategy of annihilation carried out by the mass armies of the largest nation in western Europe.

Despite Francisco's shortcomings, his father recognized his strong points and appointed the son to head the army and the war ministry while in his twenties. He was family. His loyalty to his father never wavered. Although Carlos Antonio knew nothing firsthand of the world beyond, his intuitions about foreign relations were usually sound. The opposite held true for his son: The heir presumptive was better read and more widely traveled but never became a good judge of the motivations of the leaders of other nations, especially those of his closest neighbors, Argentina, Brazil, and Uruguay. Francisco was the worldlier of the two but seemed to miss the essence of things, while his provincial father, president from 1841 to 1862, crafted foreign policy skillfully.

Francisco loved material possessions and showing off his privileged status. He lived in an atmosphere of as much privilege and luxury as he could comprehend. He also learned as a boy that the world of politics beyond his family's properties was fearsome and dangerous. He and his family lived safely at the ranch in Rosario but not at the family's Asunción residence in Recoleta. The boy had seen his father avoid public appearances until the death of the supreme dictator.

Francisco never realized that it was a handicap not to have climbed the officer grades by his own merit, which would have been possible during the long period of peace of his father's presidency. He could not have done so in wartime, however, because of his cowardice, which would become manifest later. His brother officers would have seen this quickly. Lacking the constancy needed by wartime commanders, he nevertheless seized control of the army, which would assure him the presidency on his father's death. The appointment also gave his father security. Because of Francisco's control of the army, Carlos Antonio had no fear of a barracks revolt.[37]

Among Francisco and his four siblings, a rivalry developed. Francisco always came first in his father's esteem if not his mother's affections. The father favored the first-born son in matters of politics, diplomacy, and defense. As women, his sisters lacked any opportunities for political participation except by marriage and behind the scenes. Carlos Antonio frequently told Francisco how proud of him he was. The mother, Juana Pabla, pampered her personal favorite, the baby Ángel Benigno, almost always called just Benigno. He and the middle brother, Venancio, envied and feared Francisco. Their suspicions were well founded.

Benigno enjoyed the good life and cared for little else. His father sent him to study at the Brazilian naval academy in Rio de Janeiro, but the experience had little influence on his behavior. Benigno avoided politics and military affairs whenever he could. He held commissions in the army and the navy but resigned them. After spending two years in the beautiful Brazilian capital, he returned home and spent time attending to private affairs, building up his own properties, and carousing. He was especially fond of social functions at the Club Nacional, founded by the López brothers and their sycophants. The two brothers disagreed as they grew to manhood on matters of substance, especially those relating to foreign policy. But Benigno showed neither interest nor aptitude for governing. The portly father favored daughter Rafaela over her sister Inocencia.

As young adults, all the children owned impressive residences in the capital and in the countryside. From their father all the children learned how to enrich themselves using the powers of the state for supremacy in the marketplace. They were all active in commerce, farming, and the raising of livestock. They owned large ranches, plantations, and urban real estate. Owing to their father's power, they profited from the nation's yerba and lumber enterprises. They made money in real estate and moneylending. Their father enabled the children to acquire productive lands from the state and state slaves to work their properties. For these human commodities, they paid prices below market value. Other would-be investors learned that it was unwise to bid against the López family. Francisco took the greatest economic advantage of his position. He gobbled up urban and rural properties himself and through his agents.

Francisco was proud of his education, which was as good as possible, considering that no sophisticated institutions of learning were available. His education was certainly better than that of Rosas in Argentina, although Francisco was less well educated than the Argentine leaders of his own generation, Mitre and Sarmiento, both of whom were intellectuals and authors of influential books about Argentina. Francisco's learning was also inferior to that of Emperor Pedro II of Brazil. Under the best tutors his father could find in Paraguay, Francisco had studied history, mathematics, and Spanish grammar, especially necessary in a land where the most commonly heard language, even in the López homes, was not Spanish but Guarani, Francisco's first language. He learned French tolerably well and, it was said, some English, although his correspondence of the 1850s belies this. Young Francisco had absorbed a smattering of philosophy, Latin, and theology. Observing the last years of the Francia dictatorship, Francisco obtained an education of a sort in politics. He learned the importance of power. His father's judiciousness, caution, and practicality, however, escaped him.

Francisco's firsthand knowledge of the wider world began at seventeen when he accompanied Manuel de la Peña to Buenos Aires. He stayed in the cosmopolitan city for several months, where his views on authoritarian government hardened in the city and province of Juan Manuel de Rosas. It is likely that he formed lasting impressions of Argentines at this time. One of their attributes that he encountered, probably often, was their scornful attitude toward Paraguayans, whom they saw as rustics, inferiors, and barbarians.

When Francisco took real command of the army, he instituted a reorganization to make it more efficient. He had new barracks built, acquired more and better weapons, instituted sterner training methods, and groped toward modernity. His father allowed him to carry out these reforms even though he disliked the cost of military preparedness.[38]

In 1845, in titular command of the army in Corrientes, Francisco addressed the soldiers in a manner prophetic. He spoke mostly of himself. He told the men how great a weight rested on his shoulders. He also showed his creativity. He told them that their offensive was defensive. He assured them of his own courage, although he failed to demonstrate it. He hoped that their patriotism and bravery would earn them all laurels on "the field of honor and glory."[39] Gaining those two distinctions were what appealed to him most about war.

RELATIONSHIPS AMONG LOS LÓPEZ

Francisco had reported from Corrientes that he thought that the enemy hoped to put him in his grave,[40] apparently not recognizing that to Rosas, Paz was the important prize, not Francisco. Although the young man had a veteran officer to advise him, Francisco had considerable autonomy. He promoted sergeants whom he liked to second lieutenant and only afterward informed his father. He also broke in rank a colonel whom he accused of terrorizing subordinates. Because Paz had refused to take his claims to command seriously, the insulted Francisco[41] had rejected an opportunity to learn from the experienced Paz.

One incident illuminates how Paraguayan soldiers were motivated by both national pride and by fear. Corporal Resquín, a man of little talent but of great personal loyalty to Francisco, was an informer. He reported to the youthful General López about mutinous soldiers in three Paraguayan squadrons. Gathering four other squadrons of loyal troops, López had the accused men apprehended. The nineteen-year-old then summarily condemned to death four corporals and promoted Resquín to second lieutenant (*alférez*).[42]

After Corrientes, his liaison with Juana Pessoa bore fruit. Their first son, Emiliano, was born. López later gave him his name and sent him to Europe on a state scholarship, but he never got to know Emiliano, as he admitted in a famous letter.[43] His relationship with Pessoa lasted for at least fifteen years. She continued to bear Francisco's children, even during his more famous affair with Madame Lynch. Both women had other female rivals for Francisco's attention. He never married.

As the first son of the first family, López surrounded himself with people who were in no position to tell him that he was in error, that his judgment was faulty, or that his hygiene was wanting. In fact, his oral hygiene and thus his breath *was* bad, even by norms of the day. Francisco did not bother to maintain the standards of dental hygiene customary for upper-class Paraguayans of his era. By his twenties, his teeth were decaying and by his thirties they were rotting.[44] So many had fallen out by his thirties that people said that he mumbled when he spoke. They often found it difficult to understand him. He embraced an ostentation impressive to Paraguayans but seen as gauche by outsiders. It grew more pronounced after he visited Paris in the 1850s.

The most significant personal defect of Francisco S. López, as he usually signed his name, was his lack of empathy, the ability to identify intellectually and emotionally with another person. It contributed to his faulty judgment of people not under his command. His want of empathy strikes the reader of his letters and speeches. One can find its absence in the seven published volumes of his pre-presidential correspondence. One also sees the omission of this quality in the manuscript letters mostly housed in the Archivo Nacional de Asunción and in the thoughts he expressed in the Paraguayan newspapers of his era, including *El Semanario*, *Cabichuí*, and *El Centinela*. Francisco edited every word of every line of these publications. He often wrote or rewrote their articles. They are authentic expressions of his voice, or at least one of his two most important voices. His private correspondence is more measured. In letters he wrote to Venancio or dictated to a telegrapher who forwarded them to Venancio, he expressed a routine concern for the brother, his mother, and his own children; but he never identified with them or tried to understand what they thought or how they felt. His lack of interest in other people's emotional and intellectual makeup would condition his diplomacy and military judgment. Before he became president, however, this flaw did not hurt the country, because Carlos Antonio oversaw his son's acts and restrained him.

Francisco's numerous illegitimate children did not seem to trouble his countrymen, whose attitudes toward illegitimacy had long been relaxed. A longtime member of the Asunción cabildo in the late 1700s, José Cañete, for example, was the biological son of former governor José de Antequera. This relationship would have prevented him from serving in the prestigious office of *regidor* in Havana, for example.[45] Paraguayans apparently frowned on illegitimacy less than in other countries in Latin America.

Tension between Francisco and Benigno probably began soon after Benigno was born, although we can never be sure. Francisco would have seen that their mother doted on his baby brother. As they grew to maturity, their personal and political differences widened. On matters of policy, Benigno seldom opposed his brother directly, but few secrets were kept in Paraguay. Benigno was reputedly more taken by "liberal" political ideas than his brother,[46] although it could have hardly been possible to have been less inclined to them than Francisco. Benigno wrote to José Berges in 1859 that it was a mistake for Paraguay to become enmeshed in an Argentine dispute, an accomplishment of which Francisco would be proud. Despite their differences, Francisco took Benigno with him to Europe in 1853 and to Buenos Aires in 1859.[47]

All three sons of Carlos Antonio were sexual predators. None married, although they left surviving children. The sisters, unlike their brothers, did wed. Rafaela's husband, Saturnino Bedoya, enjoyed his wife's access to wealth and power, an asset to his career as an auctioneer and businessman. He later found work in a patronage appointment in his brother-in-law's government.[48] Bedoya held a strictly ceremonial post in the government, until he died under the order of his brother-in-law, the president. Inocencia's marriage to soldier Vicente Barrios got him promoted to brigadier general and then to head the war ministry, another ceremonial post.

Like the sisters, on whom political inactivity was imposed by the fact of their being women, neither of the younger brothers was really interested in or participated actively in the affairs of state or in military matters but from time to time held ceremonial appointments. Like Venancio, Benigno was mostly interested more in the pursuit of women and other pleasures of the flesh than in the demanding work of government. As sons of one president and the brothers of another, their positions allowed them grand opportunities for debauchery. At one point, Benigno was allowed briefly to serve as the minister of war without power. Venancio, during the War of the Triple Alliance, commanded a small contingent of troops in the capital and far from the front. The younger brothers' lack of interest in public affairs discredits the later charges that they conspired against their brother.[49]

Unlike their father, who lived a comfortable private life remarkable only for his astounding gluttony, all of his children lived ostentatiously. Although the father's mealtime habits today could be described as an eating disorder, gluttony was in fact a Christian sin, yet it went unrecognized as such. The opulent lifestyles of los López separated them from the masses, who respected and feared but did not like them.[50]

The government of Carlos Antonio López was—by the standards of Paraguayan politics before 1870—benign and paternal. Francisco learned from his father to exercise power himself and never to tolerate disrespect. The case of Bernardo Espíndola is instructive. Espíndola returned to Paraguay from Corrientes. He had accompanied the Paraguayan army to the south, and he wished to thank a man there for his kindness by sending him some *caña*, a rum-like drink made from sugar and the strongest intoxicant made in Paraguay. In order to ship his gift out of the country, he needed government permission. Espíndola made the request in proper fashion, using the official paper. He presented it to the proper functionary. When the bureaucrat denied the request, the irate Espíndola ripped up the official document. Carlos Antonio learned of this act of disrespect through his spies. He ordered Espíndola executed, and he had the order carried out within hours.[51] Executions like these, though, were rare under Carlos Antonio, but for his eldest son they became lessons in how a president should behave.

In 1849, the first President López once again sent a force, this time numbering two thousand men, across the Alto Paraná. It was led by Franz (in Paraguay, Francisco) Wisner von Morgenstern and Francisco López. The character traits for which the twenty-two-year-old López would become famous were already solidifying. The attitudes that characterized his relations with his family, his dictatorship, and his diplomatic and military calculations were clear. His letters to his father show him as respectful, even flattering, but not familiar or affectionate. In a typical letter, he addressed his father as "Most Excellent Sir," "the very Excellent President of the Republic,"[52] instead of "dear Papá." His insistence on formal address was seen in Paraguay as unusually formal.

He was now, thanks to the fortunes of his birth and his own interests, intelligence, energy, and his father's patronage, general in chief of the Paraguayan Army. In that administrative capacity, he was efficient. From Paso de Patria on the southern frontier, young General López reported to his father that forces under Francisco's command had occupied territory belonging to Paraguay. Actually, the land in question between the Paraná and Uruguay Rivers was claimed by both Paraguay and Argentina. He had divided his forces. To head the units camped on the Uruguay River, he (and his father) chose Lt. Col. Wisner von Morgenstern, a Hungarian immigrant and former soldier who was long useful to the López family. Showing how he wished to be seen, young López reported that this effort would show the mettle of Paraguayans to "the civilized world." He longed for Paraguay to be considered a part of that world, especially European nations. He wanted Paraguay to be regarded among the most illustrious of nations,[53] a peculiar notion according to objective criteria when referring to a poor, landlocked nation of three hundred thousand people. But it reveals the aspirations of Francisco S. López for himself and his country.

By 1851, the twenty-five-year-old López was fully in command of the soldiers of Paraguay. He was forging links to officers and men that would ensure his hold on the country when his father died. He was obsessed with proper gradations of respect within the army. His decrees on military protocol showed how his mind worked. For him, military obligations ran up but not down, much like eighteenth-century European armies whose officers were, or aspired to be, aristocrats. He opened his decree by admonishing superiors not to be excessive in speech or discourteous to subordinates. Although he insisted that junior officers must have rights, it is difficult to discover what those rights were. In his understanding of good military procedure, underlings should not complain about injustices. A good officer, López said, should seek the esteem of his subordinates, should provide quick justice, conduct himself in an exemplary fashion, be knowledgeable about his duties, and be brave in the face of the enemy. He warned officers not to become familiar with their subordinates, who must obey their superiors at all times in all places. (Close personal ties might breed loyalties to non-Lópezes.) Subordinates must earn their reputation not by "low adulation," (possibly referring to the constant flattery that he himself demanded) but by their "docility, application, punctuality." They were never to complain of any superior or of any order; he ignored the reality that complaining is a part of army life. Despite never having been a soldier himself, he identified those qualities that made good officers and men. The most essential were absolute discipline, unswerving obedience, and subordination; in the years to come, he would instill these in the forces of Paraguay. Next in importance was the avoidance of unbecoming conduct, including gambling and drunken gatherings. The consequence for disobedience, he wanted his men to know, would be "fatal."[54]

As Francisco López was teaching himself how to be a commander of men in 1851, dissident forces in Argentina prepared to topple the dictator Rosas. They asked for Paraguayan support. The 1845 misadventure had hardened Carlos Antonio López's determination to avoid direct involvement in the politics of his southern neighbor. He had nothing against the leader of the rebel forces, Justo José de Urquiza, the caudillo of the province of Entre Ríos; but the Paraguayan president had contempt for his liberal allies. For President López, liberal political freedoms—voting, free speech, a free press—brought anarchy. In late 1851, Urquiza asked Francisco to lead an army in the movement. General López refused, as President López wished. But his excuse was that his forces were then unprepared to move. Another rationalization was that the request had arrived too late. The younger López also cited the major issues—river navigation and disputed boundaries—that divided the two nations. Yet he asserted his friendship for rebel provinces Corrientes and Entre Ríos,[55] indicating his concern for the issues and his father's policy.

In the early 1850s, López now signed his name as brigadier in chief of the Paraguayan National Army. He would not be thirty until 1856—or, in his telling, 1857. His father delegated to him the power to conduct diplomacy. In 1852, he negotiated with Great Britain. The British government sought a relatively benign statement of friendship and commercial amity. True to his father's wishes, López wanted a treaty of friendship as a prelude to a more meaningful document to protect Paraguayan commerce and navigation in the Plata region. He promised that his country would respect the rights of British merchants.[56]

Recognition from Europe could bring prestige to Paraguay and to the heir apparent, Francisco S. López. The neighbors that would most determine his future, though, were Argentina and Brazil—larger, more populous, and more economically advanced. The connection between a nation's productive capacity and its military power were becoming the determinants of success or failure in war. It was not a lesson that Francisco López wished to learn.

NOTES

1. Charles Gibson, *Spain in America* (New York: Harper & Row, 1966), 211.

2. Gibson, *Spain in America*, 211.

3. *Caudillo* literally means leader or chief, but it is most often used to identify a nineteenth-century Spanish American dictator.

4. William H. Beezley, "Caudillismo: An Interpretive Note," *Journal of Inter-American Studies* 11 (1969): 345–52.

5. Thomas Whigham, *The Politics of River Trade: Tradition and Development in the Upper Plata, 1780–1870* (Albuquerque: University of New Mexico Press, 1991), 162.

6. Whigham, *Politics of River Trade*, 161.

7. John Hoyt Williams, *The Rise and Fall of the Paraguayan Republic, 1800–1870* (Austin: Institute of Latin American Studies, University of Texas, 1979), 57.

8. In 1837, he had come to Francia's attention, never a good thing, and he moved deeper into the background.

9. Julio César Chaves, *El Presidente López: vida y gobierno de Don Carlos*, 2nd ed. (Buenos Aires: Ediciones Depalma, 1968).

10. John Lynch, *Caudillos in Spanish America, 1800–1850* (Oxford, UK: Oxford University Press, 1992), 130.

11. Charles A. Washburn, *The History of Paraguay, with Notes of Personal Observation and Reminiscences of Diplomacy under Difficulties*, 2 vols. (Boston: Lee and Shepard, 1871), I, 390–91.

12. Carlos Antonio formally abolished slavery. He extended the process long enough, however, so that his children had many Afro-Paraguayan men, women, and girls, to exploit. They also worked on the ranches of the state and served in the military. The provisional government that took office in Asunción in 1869 finally abolished the despicable institution.

13. John Hoyt Williams, "Observations on the Paraguayan Census of 1846," *HAHR* 56, no. 3 (August 1976): 424–37; and Williams, *Rise and Fall of the Paraguayan Republic*, 116.

14. Chaves, *El Presidente López*, 44; Thomas L. Whigham, *The Paraguayan War, Volume I: Causes and Early Conduct* (Lincoln: University of Nebraska Press, 2002), 247, says that he earned only 4,000 pesos.

15. Edward A. Hopkins, "Memoir on the Geography, History, Productions, and Trade of Paraguay," delivered to the American Geographical and Statistical Society, Jan. 13, 1852; and in Edward A. Hopkins, Raymond E. Crist, and William P. Snow, *Paraguay 1852 and 1968* (New York: American Geographical Society, 1968), 1–30, quote from 19.

16. Whigham, *Paraguayan War*, I, 66.

17. Chaves, *El Presidente López*, 45.

18. Rosas's aims were twofold. He wished to increase the revenues of Buenos Aires by forcing all trade through there rather than Montevideo, and he wished to crush his Unitarian opponents, who had taken refuge in Montevideo. David Rock, *Argentina, 1516–1987: From Spanish Colonialism to Alfonsín* (Berkeley: University of California Press, 1987), 111.

19. Williams, *Rise and Fall of the Paraguayan Republic*, 146.

20. Hopkins, "Memoir," 19.

21. Hopkins, "Memoir," 16–18.

22. D. F. Sarmiento, *Life in the Argentine Republic in the Days of the Tyrants: Or, Civilization and Barbarism*, trans. Mary Mann (New York: Hafner, 1960[1868]), 163.

23. Sarmiento, *Life in the Argentine Republic*, 164.

24. Williams, *Rise and Fall of the Paraguayan Republic*, 142.

25. His behavior in the field and his later writings and speeches show that he failed to comprehend what he read.

26. *El Centinela*, July 24, 1867.

27. *El Centinela*, May 30, 1867.

28. *El Centinela*, July 4, 1867.

29. Washburn, *History of Paraguay*, I, 471.

30. Washburn, *History of Paraguay*, I, 391.

31. Given the tragic circumstances of the devastation of war and Francisco's recent abuse of her, her other sons, and her daughters, her 1870 declaration should be regarded cautiously.

32. Arturo Bray, *Solano López: soldado de la gloria y del infortunio* (Asunción: Editorial Lector, 1996), 63, 161. Rojas, a man of substantial wealth for Paraguay, bequeathed a handsome legacy to Francisco Solano.

33. The question of which man was Francisco Solano's biological father will never be settled. This work assumes that Carlos Antonio was Francisco Solano's real father because he was the one who truly acted like a father, raising the boy and grooming him to take his own place at the nation's helm.

34. Bray, *Solano López*, 73.

35. John Lynch, *Simón Bolívar: A Life* (New Haven, CT: Yale University Press, 2006), 236.

36. Bray, *Solano López*, 71.

37. A similar stratagem was used in twentieth-century Nicaragua. Anastasio Somoza García (Tacho) appointed his son Anastasio Somoza Debayle (Tachito) to head that nation's armed forces after his graduation from the U.S. Military Academy. Tachito helped maintain his father's hold on the country and ensured that

the family—his brother Luis and himself—would continue their control of the nation after the father's assassination.

38. Bray, *Solano López*, 73–74.

39. FSL, "Proclamation to the Expeditionary Army of Corrientes," December 1845, *Proclamas y cartas del Mariscal López* (Buenos Aires: Editorial Asunción, 1957).

40. FSL to CAL, Paso Bedoya, Jan. 23, 1846, *Proclamas y cartas.*

41. FSL to CAL, H.Q., Camp San Roque, Feb. 23, 1846, *Proclamas y cartas.*

42. FSL to CAL, H.Q., Camp Payubre, Mar. 9, 1846, *Proclamas y cartas.*

43. See chapter 6.

44. Earlier in the century, Simón Bolívar's teeth at the age of thirty-six, according to his aide, Daniel Florencio O'Leary, were "white, regular, and beautiful," because "he took regular care of them," Lynch, *Simón Bolívar*, 22.

45. Ann Twinam, *Public Lives, Private Secrets: Gender, Honor, Sexuality, and Illegitimacy in Colonial Spanish America* (Stanford, CA: Stanford University Press, 1999), 176–78, 185–86, 264–66.

46. This supposed liberalism, if it ever existed, certainly was restricted to the area of foreign policy. The assertion by a few elite Paraguayans at the time and by several historians later that Benigno advocated an open political system, and thus the abdication of the López family, is not credible. Those few who are known to have preferred him over Francisco, in 1862, likely saw him as less ruthless, more pliant, and more afraid of conflict than his brother.

47. Chaves, *El Presidente López*, 217.

48. Francisco would later torture Bedoya. He forced his baby sister to witness her husband's execution.

49. Bray, *Solano López*, 102–3.

50. Bray, *Solano López*, 102–3.

51. Chaves, *El Presidente López*, 271–72.

52. FAL to CAL, H.Q., Paso de la Patria, Dec. 25, 1849, *Proclamas y cartas.* Expressions in the Spanish language are often loftier than those in English, and nineteenth-century males were obliged to respect their fathers.

53. FSL to CAL, H.Q., Paso de la Patria, June 20, 1849, *Proclamas y cartas.*

54. FSL, Decree on Army Morality, H.Q., Paso de la Patria, Feb. 28, 1851, *Proclamas y cartas.*

55. FSL to Gov. Juan Pujol of Corrientes, Paso de la Patria, Nov. 30, 1851, *Proclamas y cartas.*

56. FSL to Charles Hotham, Asunción, Dec. 29, 1852, *Proclamas yAcartas.*

3

Francisco Visits Europe and New Departures for Paraguay

Francisco López toured Europe in 1853–1854, symbolizing Paraguay's opening to the world. A revolution in Argentina provided the opportunity when, in 1852, the dictator Juan Manuel de Rosas,[1] who had refused to recognize Paraguay's independence, was overthrown. He fled to England. His departure opened the way for Paraguay's economic advancement. Argentine liberals, anathema to the López rulers, helped provincial caudillos topple Rosas and allowed development in the upper Plata. The governor of Entre Ríos, Justo José de Urquiza, led the victorious anti-Rosas coalition. Governor Urquiza was a traditional *caudillo*, but he sponsored and later guaranteed the liberal and lasting Argentine Constitution of 1853. The anti-Rosas effort also included Argentine liberals like Bartolomé Mitre and Domingo Faustino Sarmiento. Both completed military service and wrote books about Argentina that are now classic texts. Each was president during Argentina's war against Paraguay and Francisco Solano López. The Argentine opposition to Rosas in 1851–1852 was also helped by Brazil and Uruguay; it was customary for Platine nations to intervene in the domestic affairs of their neighbors.

Urquiza permitted Paraguay's reconnection with the world, opening the Paraguay–Paraná river system. As in the colonial era, Paraguay enjoyed regular access to foreign markets. The real Asunción leaders of the 1850s were but two men: President Carlos Antonio López and his son Francisco Solano. Only their opinions mattered; they held power and refused to share. Together they sought material progress. For the father, the first objective was to expand the nation's commerce. What Paraguay

offered buyers in foreign, mostly regional, markets included yerba, tobacco, lumber, and hides.[2]

The López family dominated the exploitation and marketing of these
products. Carlos Antonio and his immediate family were active merchants, ranchers, plantation owners, and slave owners. They were landed
proprietors and holders of urban real estate. Even the women—Francisco's mother, Juana, and his sisters, Rafaela and Inocencia—conducted
business ventures in which the profitability depended on Carlos Antonio's power. They traded in paper money, buying torn bills "at a discount
of six pence in the dollar, and by their connection with the government
they changed it at the treasury for new paper at the full value."[3] They
were also pawnbrokers who "lent money on jewelry . . . and anything
they liked they kept, without reference to the owner's wishes."[4] In a typical transaction, Francisco bought a ranch in Catiaguá from the state for
12,000 pesos. This was a bargain price even if he actually paid the money,
an accounting that none dared request. His brother Venancio purchased a
state ranch near San Joaquín and bought Afro-Paraguayan slaves from the
government. At public auctions and markets, other potential purchasers
refused to bid against the López family because they feared reprisals. The
youngest brother, Benigno, bought from the state the ranch of San Ignacio
for 12,000 pesos and purchased urban properties in desirable locations in
the capital. The libertine baby of the family also obtained from the state a
twelve-year-old female slave and other Afro-Paraguayans, still legally
chattel despite Carlos Antonio's imperfect emancipation edict in the
1840s. Like their brothers, Inocencia and Rafaela learned the lessons of
avarice from their parents.[5]

ON THE HOME FRONT: TREATIES AND DIPLOMACY

Though personally rapacious, Carlos Antonio and Francisco Solano
López together oversaw Paraguay's security and independence. The son
cared more about the nation's prestige and his own reputation abroad
than the shrewder father. Francisco longed for favorable notice by European nations, Britain, France, Prussia, and others. He hoped, impracti-
cally, to lead Paraguay into their company. To begin, he had to raise his
own profile and his nation's image in southern South America.

An early indication of the emergence from Francia's isolation was the
arrival in Asunción of diplomats from Britain, France, Sardinia, and the
United States in 1853. All recognized Paraguayan independence and
signed agreements promising friendship, commerce, and navigation.
Francisco López, then twenty-seven, performed diplomatic service on his
father's behalf. He negotiated and signed pacts, but only his father ap-

proved them. Paraguay granted the signatory nations permission to send their vessels up the Paraguay River to Asunción and on the Alto Paraná River to the newly founded city of Encarnación, although Paraguay lacked dominance over the Paraná River south and east of its confluence with the Río Paraguay. As long as the European and North American powers obeyed Paraguayan laws, subject to the whims and prejudices of the president and his eldest son, citizens of those nations could live, travel, and work, a release from Francia's xenophobia. Unlike Paraguayans, who needed permission to leave the country, foreigners could come and go as they pleased. Treaties with Britain, France, and Sardinia were eventually ratified in London, Paris, and Turin, ceremonies that provided a rationale for Francisco's European trip.

Rapid commercial and industrial growth followed the reestablishment of the export economy, now connected to lucrative foreign markets. The government sponsored the development of land and river transportation.

In the 1850s, Paraguayan relations with the United States hit snags. One was the Hopkins affair (see chapter 2) and another was the *Water Witch* conflict. The first of these disputes in part grew from the failure of Edward A. Hopkins to understand the gap between law and behavior in Paraguay. The gulf did not hinder the nation's economic growth. Nor did it interfere significantly with the profits of foreign investors and merchants, as long as they secured the goodwill of the nation's president, not depending on statute law. The second was a misunderstanding that brought violence and heightened Paraguayan concerns about national honor.

TO EUROPE: RAILROADS, NAPOLEON, AND PARAGUAYAN DEVELOPMENTS

To demonstrate the new openness, Francisco López must travel to Europe, he and his father decided. The father seldom went anywhere even inside the country owing to his considerable bulk and trusted his son to represent him faithfully. Even had Carlos Antonio wished to see foreign sights, dictators who leave their nations risk being overthrown when abroad. Francisco would serve as his father's emissary to the outside world and would concentrate on modernization. His most important European mission was to purchase arms and munitions to increase national security, although his ostensible objective was to ratify the treaties just signed with Britain, France, and Sardinia and to negotiate an agreement with Spain recognizing Paraguayan independence. Francisco was also to seek the industrial goods necessary to speed development. For him personally there was probably no more important goal than to see the wonderful places about which he had read, especially in France, where his hero Napoleon Bonaparte had won glory. Also on Francisco's itinerary was Rome because his father wanted the pope to appoint an auxiliary bishop for Paraguay, specifically, Carlos Antonio López's brother, Basilio, who had been the vicar general of Paraguay since 1844. Another hope, ubiquitous and unfulfilled in most independent Latin American countries, was to attract European immigrants. Francisco wanted skilled Spanish colonists to develop his own nation.

Modern military technology was Francisco's primary concern. Up-to-date arms could increase the security of a small nation with unfriendly neighbors. The principal purchase was to be a modern steam warship, the centerpiece of Paraguay's river flotilla. In addition, López had to recruit British sailors to operate the vessel and to teach Paraguayans how to do so. He also aimed to engage engineers and builders who could teach Paraguayans to construct modern ships. Many other innovations, like the construction of a railroad and installation of telegraph lines, in fact, had military applications. His recruitment was successful. Most technical experts hired by López came from the United Kingdom, and they contributed to Paraguay's growth and development in the late 1850s and early 1860s. Others came from France, Spain, Italy, and the German areas.

Carlos Antonio made his eldest son minister plenipotentiary with complete authority to negotiate with foreign governments and businesses. His was no paper title. Francisco, the formal head of the delegation, in fact made all major decisions. He relied on Juan Andrés Gelly, a Paraguayan with non-Paraguayan diplomatic experience, as an adviser. His youngest brother, Benigno, was titular secretary of the traveling delegation, although Gelly performed the secretarial chores.[6]

Francisco left Paraguay June 12, 1853, with a ten-man retinue. His party interestingly included his brother Ángel Benigno. That this pair traveled together suggests a less hostile relationship between them before 1862 than some historians allege. The delegation also included Lt. Colonel Vicente Barrios, soon to be Francisco's brother-in-law, and cronies Lt. Rómulo Yegros, Capt. José María Aguiar, Pedro Eguzquiza, Carlos Saguier, and 2nd Lt. (Subteniente) Paulino Alén. All brought servants. Francisco and Gelly were the indispensable men. The latter knew Europe. He had gained international experience while serving as an Uruguayan diplomat in Paris in 1839 when he was in exile from Francia's regime. Gelly had also lived in Argentina and Uruguay. In 1845, Carlos Antonio brought him back to serve his fatherland. He contributed to its progress at home and abroad as a diplomat and as a writer. His survey of Paraguay's politics and economy was published in Brazil in 1848 and in Asunción 1849. It was critical of Francia and praised Carlos Antonio.[7] Gelly gained the confidence of President López, accepting at face value the portly dictator's guarantee of his personal safety. Gelly thought well of Francisco. Led by the son of the dictator and the experienced diplomat, the party headed for Europe, including England, France, Spain, and Italy, although their international experiences began at Buenos Aires and Rio de Janeiro.

Leaving the neighboring capitals,[8] the Paraguayans arrived in London September 19, 1853. While Gelly oversaw the details of the most important negotiations and correspondence,[9] Francisco, universally recognized as heir to the presidency, made the key decisions. He would not be upstaged by a family employee. They avoided the British industrial centers of Liverpool and Manchester because of the outbreak of cholera.

In London, López fortuitously found his way to the British firm of John and Alfred Blyth and Co. of Limehouse. Although he and his later publicists boasted of his mastery of English, the language remained a mystery to him; he conducted business in French and Spanish.[10] He arranged for the Blyth enterprise—a Bechtel of the 1850s—to build a steam warship, later named the *Tacuarí*, which would provide new firepower for Paraguay on the Platine rivers. It could also carry cargo, passengers, and mail. Blyth and Co. was to buy or build smaller ships to serve as packets between Asunción, Buenos Aires, and Montevideo. The firm was also an employment agency, because the technical experts whom they advised Francisco to hire contributed to the modernization of Paraguay's shipyards, where Paraguayans themselves eventually would build steamships. When finished, the *Tacuarí* further pumped up López's pride in himself and his nation, which he was coming to believe were one and the same. He imagined that the new ship inflated Paraguay's military reputation. Through the Blyth firm, he hired engineers, physicians, telegraphers,[11] and naval experts, including masters and machinists. He offered them attractive salaries. They came to work and to teach Paraguayans how to use and repair modern technology, an early example of import-substitution industrialization. Francisco also arranged for Blyth to devise a scholarship program to provide young Paraguayans opportunities to acquire new skills. These young men were to travel abroad on government scholarships. Sixteen would study English, French, German, and Italian, and another nine were to learn such practical skills as mechanical engineering and naval construction.[12] One was Juan Crisóstomo Centurión, who finished a five-year course in England the year before López declared war on Brazil. Fourteen years younger, he served the future marshal personally in the Great War of the 1860s as secretary, soldier, publicist, and inquisitor. He wrote a moving and honest four-volume chronicle of the conflict.

The most prominent of the several hundred mostly British specialists hired by the Lópezes was William Whytehead, who accepted a client–patron relationship with the young war minister. Ultimately, López and his father brought two hundred and fifty foreign technical experts to

Paraguay, ostensibly for peaceful purposes. Innovations like the railroad and the telegraph would also bolster the nation's military potential.[13] The experts would help construct a railroad, build and direct modern ship-yards, run an arsenal, and oversee the modernization of the army, navy, and public health system.[14] At the same time, the two dozen youths whom the Lópezes sent to Europe to study were an early example of a South American nation's quest for technology transfer. They were sup-posed to return to help develop the nation, teaching their countrymen new skills.

Francisco's star expert was William K. Whytehead, an engineer who re-turned with Francisco to Paraguay on the *Tacuarí* in 1854–1855. Whyte-head became the nation's chief engineer. Able, loyal, and well educated, Whitehead founded an arms industry. For a decade, he served both pres-idents López faithfully. He settled into Paraguay and was comfortable there. He corresponded with Francisco in French, although his Spanish was competent. With the largest salary in Paraguay next to the presi-dent's, 400 pounds a year, Whytehead lived well. He employed an Eng-lish servant family and two *peones* or servants from Paraguay.[15] As head of the arsenal, which manufactured munitions, he was in almost daily contact with Francisco, who was minister of war and the navy before his father's death. Francisco relied on Whytehead's expertise for many years, until 1863, when he withdrew his favor, which caused Whytehead to grow despondent. (The López family honor was at stake. See chapter 4, Military Growth, Increasing Paranoia.)

When he was in Britain, López rode railroads and decided that Paraguay should have one. Before he left England, the Count of Claren-don arranged for him to meet Queen Victoria on the Isle of Wight. On De-cember 5, 1853, he received an audience with Her Majesty. Traveling by railroad from London to Southampton, he rode the royal yacht. The queen was cordial to him, he told the Paraguayan foreign minister, and she wanted him to tell his father of Britain's interest in his country. Queen Vic-toria said that Paraguay could count on the good offices of her govern-ment, Francisco stated—however, the United Kingdom and Paraguay at-tached different meanings to the queen's routine statement of goodwill. Francisco made the 120-mile round trip by rail in twelve hours,[16] an im-pressive mobility that could strengthen Paraguay's economy and power in the Plata region.

The railroad, which Francisco coveted, was built under the guidance of such foreigners as Captain George F. Morice,[17] formerly of the British navy and the commander of the *Tacuarí* and other vessels. George Thomp-son, a civil engineer who made vital contributions to Francisco's war ef-fort in the 1860s, contributed engineering insight during the railroad's construction. He later directed the building of earthwork forts and fortified positions for gun emplacements. Thompson would go on to provide a memorable account of his years in Paraguay, of Francisco López, and of the war in which he served as a senior officer until surrendering his unit to the Allies in late 1868. With his father's approval, Francisco helped upgrade the practice of medicine and public health in Paraguay. He hired physicians through Blyth and Co. Medical experts in Paraguay included physicians William Stewart, Frederick Skinner, and pharmacist George Masterman, who also left an account of his years in the country that detailed his impressions of the young dictator. They and others first received their salaries in gold and in paper currency and, after 1858, in silver and paper. In 1866, Francisco paid them only worthless paper notes. By then, Francisco had taken personal possession of all the gold in the country and could have compensated them in hard currency had he so wished.[18]

For payments to the Blyth firm, the López governments allocated the profits from the sale of yerba mate, a government (and thus López family) monopoly. Francisco had the Blyth brothers deposit state funds and also keep another account, drawn on the same source, in the Bank of England for his personal expenses.[19] From Asunción in March 1856, for example, he sent the Blyth brothers 12,500 ounces of gold, about 6,800 pounds sterling. Because the regional demand for yerba was high, profits were large. Although the López family seldom distinguished between state and family funds, yerba sales and other exports paid for the nation's development and López luxuries without the government's having to resort to taxation. Paraguayans also sold timber and tobacco downriver. Francisco's attempts to develop a European market for yerba and tobacco proved futile. As president, Francisco sent five thousand pounds of yerba to the Prussian army without charge, a gesture either wacky or creative depending on one's view of him. He hoped that German soldiers would acquire a taste for the tea and create a new market.[20] The only outlet to markets was the Paraná–Paraguay river system, and Buenos Aires authorities always held a potential chokehold on all exports. As a gesture of friendship, Francisco sent Alfred Blyth two "tiger" (probably jaguar) cubs, telling them that they would be a "rarity" in London.[21] What he expected Blyth to do with them, he did not say.

On December 16, 1854, Francisco reached Paris. He hoped to present his credentials to the emperor as soon as possible.[22] Although a recent biographer of Elisa Lynch calls Paris of the 1850s "a squalid city,"[23] it was full of glamour for Francisco. He was overwhelmed by most things French, especially *Les Invalides*, the French monument. Stories of Napoleon Bonaparte and his fame inspired Francisco to the end of his days. He met Emperor Napoleon III, the nephew of the Corsican dictator-emperor, in early January 1854. Francisco reported that the emperor showed him more than a little respect,[24] stretching the truth. A ceremony in Paris on January 30,

1854, formalized the treaty between Paraguay and France signed earlier in Asunción. The meetings between López and Napoleon III were official, not personal. The luxury of the emperor's court and the apparent military might of the Second Empire awed Francisco. The formalities between the French emperor and Francisco later became the myth of a warm friendship after twentieth-century hagiographers fashioned the post–Liberal Era López legend.[25]

Francisco and Eliza

When he arrived in Paris, the young López was seen as short (possibly 5'4"), pudgy, but neither attractive nor unattractive physically. Non-Paraguayans noted his atrocious breath, recently underscored by a female biographer of Eliza Lynch, whom he would soon meet. The residue of his habitual cigar smoking increased his halitosis. He learned to dress like a military dandy. The generous funds from his father—and Francisco's willingness to spend the money on himself—made him attractive to certain women. He sought the pleasures that Paris offered in abundance, including French cuisine and the fine wines to which he would become physically addicted.

According to legend, one of his party, Captain Brizuela, introduced him to Eliza Alicia Lynch, a gorgeous woman, then by her own unreliable account eighteen years old. She was certainly older than that. According to a funeral message from her son Frederico, she was then twenty-two. Eliza knew more about the world, French manners, wines, and culture than was likely for an eighteen-year-old Irish woman, married at fifteen and isolated for three years in Algeria, as her own version insisted. She might have been as old as twenty-eight in 1853, according to her many later, especially female, enemies in Asunción. When she met Francisco, she was separated from her French army surgeon husband, a man named Quatrefages. She had left him in Algeria with a visiting Russian, who took her to Paris. Her own version was that she left because of illness and the heat of North Africa. Some said and López believed that she was the most beautiful woman in Paris. From 1854 until his death, she was Francisco's lover and closest companion, although in Paraguay she discovered that she was not his only lover. Francisco would father children by other women over the next ten years; but Lynch, his favorite, was useful to him for the rest of his life. She bore him five sons and a daughter. She schooled him in matters of taste and the culture of polite society, to which she never belonged.

By her own telling, she was born in County Cork, Ireland, in 1835. Her family was honorable, she said. She argued that on her father Frederick Lynch's side of the family she was closely related to two bishops and many magistrates, all nameless. On her mother's side,[26] she was related to an admiral who had fought under Lord Nelson at the Battles of the Nile and Trafalgar. Her uncles were officers in the British army and navy, an improbable claim. That her Catholic uncles could have reached high rank more than two decades before the revocation of the Test Act is unlikely. According to Lynch, her parents took her to London when she was twelve years old. They sent her to "one of the best schools" in the city, a school that she failed to name. On June 3, 1850, when she was supposedly fifteen (and more likely nineteen), she married Lt. Xavier de Quatrefages, a surgeon with the French army. She accompanied him to Algeria. According to her, three years in Africa ruined her health and she had to leave. The more credible story is that she left Algeria for Paris with a lover, who then abandoned her. She then went to live in England, she said, with her mother and her sister, who was then married to William Boyle Crooke, a British naval officer. Because her father had died, her tidy story continued, her mother moved to Paris to live with a sister. Eliza joined her mother and the four women of the Strafford family. The Strafford husband and father was absent, according to Lynch-Quatrefages, attending to official duties in Dublin. A recent Lynch biographer says, "her mother took her from the dying peasants of Ireland to Paris." Her own version was that shortly after separating from her husband she met Francisco S. López. Her enemies charged that she had really been born in 1822 and that she lived in Paris as a "woman of ill repute." More benignly, some said that she was a courtesan, which she also denied.

In any event, when Eliza met López in Paris in 1854,[27] she was a beautiful, blonde, blue-eyed young woman with a gorgeous complexion. She was also a skilled linguist, perfectly at home in English and French. She would later master Spanish and Guarani. She introduced Francisco to expensive wines, jewelry, clothing, carriages, and house furnishings.

The never-married couple conceived their first child, Juan Francisco, nicknamed Panchito, in France, and Lynch gave birth to him in Buenos Aires in 1855. The second child, a daughter, Corina Adelaida, was born in 1856 and died young. Lynch and López produced four more sons: Carlos, Frederico, Enrique, and Leopoldo. All the children went by the name Lynch in the 1850s and early 1860s. Only Enrique would participate significantly in the public life of post-war Paraguay. Today his descendants are members of the Paraguayan upper class, using the name Solano López, an address unused by Francisco, to identify their descent from the heroic marshal.[28] Although Lynch herself never reached the top of society even in Paraguay, she remained beside Francisco throughout the War of the Triple Alliance, facing its dangers with "an abundance of that courage of which [López] was so greatly in want," exposing "herself where the danger was greatest."[29] It certainly took courage to leave Paris for Paraguay.

Since we have yet to find her baptismal or school or other local records, we can speculate that Lynch-Quatrefages, at the end of her life known in Paris as Lynch-López, was a cultured courtesan from Ireland in her twenties when she met Francisco. Without doubt, she captivated him. She was beautiful and appeared cultured. Francisco was besotted. At the end of his European sojourn he brought his fair-haired beauty to Paraguay. It is often said that he made this decision over the protests of his brother Benigno; the youngest brother allegedly argued that because she was married, Lynch would be scorned by Asunción society.[30] The story of the rift between the two as beginning in France over Eliza is curious, because all of the López boys kept mistresses. Some of the women, like Francisco's Juana Pesoa (or Pessoa), maintained long-term relationships with one or another of the brothers. Lynch was indeed married. In Asunción, polite society scorned her until Francisco came to power in 1862. That Francisco had a mistress or that the totally foreign and exotic Eliza (in Paraguay, usually spelled Elisa) was his mistress did not themselves cause "proper" society to think the relationship outrageous. Rather it was the public nature of their alliance and Elisa's achievement of wealth and status that angered the Paraguayan and resident foreign women who saw themselves as social arbiters in Asunción. Refusing to be shut away, Elisa plunged into the Asunción social scene and became the hostess of the most brilliant salon in the country. At her houses, women eventually came for sewing bees, to read foreign magazines and newspapers, to attend recitals and plays, to eat French cuisine of "up to eight courses," and to see "what may have been the only grand piano in Asunción."[31] Within a few years, she became a "new queen of fashion," and she "set an example that the more wealthy tried to imitate."[32] Her parties and dinners were occasions where the English-speaking community gathered. She was one of the British modernizers of Paraguay. That she was spectacularly greedy made her a focus of envy.

Francisco knew that hostility to Elisa would make little difference to him if his father had no great objection. The heir apparent first son of the president-dictator was invulnerable to criticism. Criticizing him was dangerous to one's health and liberty. After the death of his father in 1862 and Francisco's assumption of power, Elisa's enemies fell silent for seven years—when his rule ended.

Francisco's primary aspiration remained the strengthening of the armed forces, as Carlos Antonio hoped, to deter attacks by her larger neighbors. His first agenda item for military development—the steam warship to protect vital river commerce and deter aggression—was now under construction. Even though his father had delegated to Francisco power to sign contracts, use credit, and raise capital from merchants and bankers,[33] it had taken Francisco more than just money to buy a warship.

For a vessel of war in 1853, he needed and obtained the permission of the British government. It would be ready in eight months' time. An able negotiator, Francisco hired an independent inspector to examine the finished product. He bought a 428-ton vessel that could travel 12 miles per hour and the contract called for the ship to be built for 4,000 pounds sterling, or 20,000 pesos. In the mid-1850s, the *Tacuarí* was a state-of-the-art warship. By the time that Francisco readied it for combat a decade later, though, it was obsolescent, outmoded by Brazilian ironclads.

Francisco's audience with Queen Victoria had been an important event,[34] at least important to Francisco. He had met European royalty. He was treated courteously by the monarch of the most powerful empire in the world. The audience convinced him that national and thus personal mobility was possible if he could find the key.

In December 1853, after López and his party left London, he wrote the Paraguayan foreign minister. He told Sr. Varela to pass this information on to his father. He did not write directly to his father—possibly because it was not part of protocol, and Francisco was a formal man. He addressed others by their honorific titles and expected them to reciprocate. As long as there were rules to follow, the young Paraguayan diplomat performed ably. Francisco was Envoy Extraordinary and Minister Plenipotentiary of Paraguay with full powers to negotiate.[35] To write directly to the president of the republic would have been to avoid proper channels and show disrespect for the presidential office that Francisco intended to occupy. The European, especially the Parisian, experience left an indelible impression. Its impact can be seen today in the heart of Asunción—in the National Pantheon and the Municipal Theater,[36] both designed by Italian architect Alejandro Ravizza, who also built grand homes for Francisco López and his brothers and sisters.

López met Napoleon III in a public audience, and the emperor received his diplomatic credentials. He bragged that Napoleon was respectful to him. Although López knew that such courtesies were customary, he intuited that Louis Napoleon was sincere. Francisco attended a reception for diplomats accredited to the French government. At this gathering, the emperor paused before the diminutive Paraguayan and introduced him to his wife, Empress Eugénie (originally Eugenia, since she was Spanish), an introduction that López desired desperately. Francisco insisted that the introduction honored the supreme government of Paraguay, his father, whom Francisco's letters flattered. One reason for the parental tributes might have been to sweeten bad news. Francisco was having difficulty prying loose funds from the British banking firm Baring Brothers. He also confessed that because of war rumors, which would soon erupt into the Crimean War, he was having difficulty buying the weapons that he wanted.[37] He also had trouble hiring sailors for the new warship. The

British government, which was preparing for war with Russia, was reluctant to grant the Paraguayan requests,[38] and López was troubled.

Nevertheless, the young Paraguayan loved Paris, not least for its sensual pleasures, including especially Lynch, and the French wines to which he became first accustomed and then addicted. Despite his fondness for Paris, he wanted to finish his work and return to Paraguay. He worried about new tensions in Paraguayan–Brazilian relations. His sense of self-importance swelling, he by now thought himself indispensable to the government and the nation. He insisted that Paraguay should demand the respect that it deserved. He hated Brazilian slights.[39] He was also keenly aware that his father was aging. He was in his late sixties and suffering from gout and his obesity. If Carlos Antonio expired while Francisco was abroad, his ambition to rule Paraguay might be thwarted.

On January 30, 1854, López finalized the diplomatic objective that brought him to France, the ratification of the treaty of friendship, commerce, and navigation. He took credit in the name of the nation, not his own, specifying that he was a representative of his father's government.[40] As a gesture, Napoleon III made Francisco a Commander of the Legion of Honor,[41] for which he had had only to show up. This award pleased Francisco so much that, as president, he would create a similar society of honor in Paraguay. But he did not try to persuade his father, who cared little for flashy symbols, to create it. The routine honors accorded Francisco profoundly impressed him. The French court dazzled him. He delayed his departure from Paris until he could formally take leave from the court and the emperor.[42] In France as in England, López "picked up a great deal of superficial knowledge and some polish." But it was the French mystique of honor in battle that most impressed him. He would later enjoy ". . . playing the Napoleon of South America."[43]

López and his party moved on to Italy, where they spent March and April 1854. There, Francisco saw King Victor Emmanuel of Sardinia, who awarded him the Sacred and Military Order of Saints Maurice and Lazarus, another routine honor that further inflated the ego of the young minister.

He went to Rome and tried to see the pope. As it turned out, the pope was too busy to meet him. Thus, Francisco settled for a talk with his subordinate Cardinal Antonelli and got the auxiliary bishop for Paraguay. The young López overlooked the pope's refusal to see him because the main purpose of the side trip was to find an honorable job for his Uncle Basilio. This office would add dignity to the family name.

Most had heard that a racial "stain" tainted the López family. One rumor identified the blot as African ancestry. Another identified the objectionable ancestor as "Guaycurú," a group of linguistically related nonsedentary Chaco peoples including Mbayás, Payaguás, Tobas, and others, disdained by most Paraguayans of Guarani descent.[44] Calling someone a "Guaycurú" remained a serious challenge to one's honor. In 2002, a Paraguayan told the author how her contemporaries used the term as an insult during her childhood in the 1960s. Another educated and well-traveled Paraguayan remarked that a prominent Paraguayan intellectual was not to be trusted, "because he's a mulatto, you know."[45] Thus, whatever the López ancestry, racial prejudice existed in Paraguay and Francisco wished to quash rumors of racial inferiority.

After Italy, López led the Paraguayans to Spain.[46] In Europe, he enjoyed exercising the power of the purse, his own, his father's, his country's. In Madrid, however, he encountered a setback: He failed to secure a Spanish treaty recognizing Paraguayan independence. One possible reason for the Spanish delay was that Spaniards still smarted from the loss of their American empire. Although they had recognized the independence of other former colonies, it was a bitter pill. They thought that their empire had benefited Americans.[47] A more important reason why the treaty of recognition was delayed, according to López, was that Spain demanded that children of Spanish citizens residing in Paraguay be given the right to choose their citizenship, Paraguayan or Spanish, upon reaching their majority. López opposed granting anyone such a right, since he was not a supporter of legal rights anyway. He incorrectly maintained that persons born in "all civilized nations" were citizens of that nation and that nation alone, although this was untrue. Both Lópezes insisted that anyone born in Paraguay was a Paraguayan and nothing else.[48] An additional problem was that the Spanish government demanded payment for the properties confiscated from Spaniards after independence.[49] Although the proposed treaty was eventually revised (after Francisco returned home) on terms more favorable to Paraguay, Francisco left Spain before signing it, meaning that he could not bring Spanish colonists to Paraguay. Instead, he contracted with a French firm to deliver one thousand French families to Paraguay, an enterprise about which his father was unenthusiastic and that turned out disastrously.

Returning to Paris, López again delighted in the French capital and the company of Eliza Lynch, who pursued both wealth and comfort avidly with him for the next fifteen years. She wrote to him in French in June 1854, addressing him as "Mon Pancho." Following her tender greeting was a request for money.[50]

Francisco, however, never let slip his attention to matters of state. He appraised in person the steam warship, the *Tacuarí*, which now weighed in at 448 tons (20 tons over the estimate) and was ready to sail. Its final cost ran upwards of 150,000 pesos and it had 200 horsepower engines. It could steam 16 miles per hour even with six large artillery pieces. In November 1854, the ship left London for Bordeaux, where it picked up the

Paraguayan delegation. George F. Morice, formerly of the Royal Navy, commanded it until 1856. The vessel made successful voyages between Paraguay and Europe and completed many others to Platine cities, especially Montevideo and Buenos Aires, before the calamitous war. In 1854, it returned to South America with the Paraguayans and British technical experts. The most distinguished expert was the aforementioned Whytehead, editor of *The Engineer*, who would direct the Paraguayan arsenal, the shipyards in Asunción, and the ironworks at Ybicuí. The father and son López hired more than two hundred foreign specialists, most British but including French, Swedish, Italian, and German technicians.

Francisco decided that his now pregnant mistress, Eliza, could not accompany him on his voyage home. Instead, he had her follow him on a later ship.[51] The *Tacuarí* stopped at Lisbon, the Madeiras, the Cape Verde Islands, and finally reached Pernambuco, Brazil, in mid-December. On December 23, 1854, it anchored at Rio de Janeiro. Two days later, López spoke with Dom Pedro II, the young Brazilian emperor. López tried to convince him that the Argentines wished to gobble up Paraguay in order to reconstitute the old viceroyalty. The Argentine threat, he argued, forced Paraguayan leaders (him and his father) to remain watchful. Then he visited Montevideo, where he told Uruguayans that both small countries faced a common menace. He said that Uruguay and Paraguay had a similar interest in survival, because Argentina and Brazil threatened them both.[52] He then returned to Asunción.

López recalled his European experience frequently. The Napoleonic myth would misguide him for the rest of his life, as he misread Bonaparte's way of war. López concluded that "Bravery and nothing more than bravery made Bonaparte great . . . ,"[53] although the Paraguayan was wrong. He thought himself Napoleonic. The real Bonaparte was a victorious general for so long because was an able, innovative, sometimes brilliant commander, well schooled in the art of war by academic training and experience. Napoleon's way of war, given France's advantage as the most populous nation in Western Europe, could not have been copied by tiny Paraguay; but López would direct conscription more ruthlessly than the French leader ever imagined.

BACK HOME: THE *WATER WITCH* AND HEAD-OF-STATE CHANGES

Francisco returned to a Paraguay in conflict with the United States. In 1854, the USS *Water Witch* arrived as part of a scientific mapping expedition. Its captain, Thomas Jefferson Page, squabbled with Carlos Antonio López over the rights of Americans, specifically those of Edward A. Hopkins, who at times represented the United States in an official capacity. He still believed that Paraguay offered opportunities for enrichment. For a time, López was Hopkins's patron, and the North American started "a cigar factory in Asunción and a brick factory at San Antonio,"[54] but he fell afoul of President López. Hopkins, "a man of liberal ideas," thought that Paraguay would move toward democracy after the overthrow of Rosas in Argentina in 1852.[55] He was wrong. Moreover, Hopkins behaved arrogantly toward Paraguayans, and his air of cultural superiority more than his republican ideas caused his misadventure. He offended the elder López, who expelled Hopkins in 1854. His businesses were ruined. Hopkins demanded monetary compensation. Lt. Page, who had come to investigate Platine waterways, took Hopkins's side. López had his newspaper denounce Hopkins for deliberately mixing his duties as American consul and private businessman—ironically, a mixture of government and private business that was familiar to the López family.[56]

López declared vessels from the United States unwelcome. The Americans argued that the Alto Paraná River, which Page was surveying, was an international waterway, touching Argentina and Brazil as well as Paraguay, but Paraguay claimed sovereignty over Misiones province and thus dominion of the left (south) bank of that river. In February 1855, Paraguayan gunners at Fort Itapirú on the Alto Paraná opened fire on the *Water Witch*. Paraguayans claimed that the Americans had ventured into Paraguayan territory. "Relations between the . . . United States and Paraguay entered a period of tension"[57] because Paraguayan fire killed an American sailor and wounded others. Ultimately, a U.S. threat of naval intervention brought President Urquiza of Argentina into the dispute, and he offered to serve as mediator. American diplomat James B. Bowlin accepted, and the dispute was settled by arbitration. Paraguay indemnified the family of the dead American sailor. This forced apology was a Paraguayan humiliation.

This episode further convinced Francisco López that his nation must become more powerful. Only military victories could recover the lost honor. In the late 1850s, he increased the lethality of the Paraguayan army and navy. In 1857–1858, he purchased shoulder weapons for a large military force. His understanding of ordinance was imperfect, as evidenced by the fact that the few rifles and many smoothbore, flintlock muskets that he acquired were not standardized. By 1858, he still suspected hostile intentions by the United States. He did not fear the large nation, telling one correspondent that it would suffer "fatal consequences" if it got mixed up in Paraguay. The U.S. Congress had authorized President Buchanan to use force if necessary. Francisco said, "The Yankees were always faithful to the old system," preferring "the force of cannon before reason and justice."[58]

Lack of standardization in military technology created problems in the war years of the 1860s, but the problems brought imaginative Paraguayan solutions. From England, Francisco purchased iron and bronze artillery pieces beginning in the 1850s. Now that he placed Whytehead at the arsenal, he had other artillery forged. At the new iron works of Ybicuí, some 120 to 150 laborers worked alongside a few dozen specialists, mostly newly trained Paraguayans. By the late 1850s, Francisco employed British artillerymen as instructors.[59]

Francisco's first priority remained the military, but he tried to improve the manners of the elite when not at the office or at headquarters. With his brothers, he founded and guided the activities of the Club Nacional, located some two hundred paces from his primary Asunción residence. Guided by his father's presence and his caution, he performed his duties loyally and competently. In 1855, for example, Carlos Antonio granted Francisco full powers to negotiate a new treaty with the Empire of Brazil. Unlike his son, Carlos Antonio never met Emperor Pedro II, never visited Rio de Janeiro, and in fact never left Paraguay. Despite these handicaps, he was a shrewd judge of the motivations of Brazilian leaders.

That year, one of Francisco's priorities was to negotiate a settlement of the long-standing Brazilian–Paraguayan boundary dispute. He also wanted a treaty of commerce and navigation, but the navigation issue was too complex to solve peacefully. Each side denied the other's basic premises. On the one hand, Paraguay demanded of Argentina the rights to navigate the Paraná; on the other, Paraguay was reluctant to grant Brazil those rights on the Río Paraguay, especially above Asunción. President López feared the expansionist inclinations of her gigantic neighbor. Francisco questioned the cardinal principle of nineteenth-century Brazilian diplomacy, *uti possidetis*, holding that a country owns a territory by actually possessing it, not merely claiming that it does. He did not object so much to the principle, which many South American nations observed, as with the Brazilian interpretation of it. The not unreasonable Paraguayan assertion was that possession was demonstrated by *official* occupation over a long period of time and also by the formal founding of towns and forts. Francisco pointed to the former Spanish Fort Borbón, presently Olimpo, on the west bank of the Río Paraguay as an example of such occupancy. He denied the rights of unofficial possession and claimed it as mere physical settlement of individuals, such as those of Brazilian pioneers who were moving into the disputed region to farm and ranch. Thus, Francisco did not quarrel with *uti possidetis*. What he disputed was the Brazilian reading of it,[60] which favored the empire's expansion at Paraguay's expense. The Brazilian emperor's lack of respect for his country aroused Francisco's ire.[61]

More than his father, he was stung by criticism of his nation and his father's corrupt and authoritarian government, especially those he read in newspapers published in Buenos Aires. Leaders and citizens of the port city felt superior to Paraguayans, many of whom worked there in menial jobs. The widely known fact that the López family monopolized and enriched itself from the yerba trade was one issue that the Argentine journalists criticized. Another was the Whytehead-directed arsenal, which manufactured weapons for the Paraguayan military and luxury objects for the López family. One article reported on a bronze bed made there for Juana Pabla Carillo. The ornamental ironwork that decorated the mansions of Francisco López came from the arsenal, as did the fans for Madame Lynch's house and balconies in the homes of brothers Venancio and Benigno.[62]

When it became obvious in the late 1850s that Francisco S. López would be the next Paraguayan ruler, and more likely sooner rather than later, it appeared that he had prepared himself well for the position. He was widely read for a Paraguayan, and he was well traveled. Neither reading nor travel, however, brought him the ability to understand points of view other than his own. He was unable to appraise accurately the motivations of the leaders of rival nations. He failed to comprehend their arguments when they conflicted with his own, and he failed to understand the origins of the claims or the outlook of the men who held them. He thought, for example, that Argentine leaders still hungered to re-create the viceroyalty of the Río de la Plata. He failed to grasp that Argentine political goals had evolved. He believed that *porteño* leaders still sought to absorb Paraguay and that it was a major agenda item. He feared becoming a vassal state. Leaders of the Argentine Confederation at that time were not prepared to go to war to incorporate Paraguay. They faced pressing domestic issues. With Uruguay, or as it turned out with one Uruguayan faction, Francisco concluded, Paraguay shared a common interest in survival against expansionist and interventionist Brazil and Argentina. He argued to them in 1854 that the present "equilibrium," an equilibrium whose duration was truly brief and whose origin unclear, should not be destroyed by Argentine efforts to bully Paraguay and Uruguay.[63] He failed to indicate when the supposed equilibrium had begun, because historically no equilibrium that involved Uruguay had ever existed. Uruguay's existence dated back only to 1828. Before that, it had been a favorite battleground between its Spanish- and Portuguese-speaking neighbors since the 1600s. After Uruguayan independence, Brazil had intervened there militarily more than once, and the siege of Montevideo by Rosas's Uruguayan proxies was prolonged from 1839 well into the 1840s. Neither action—the Brazilian intervention or Rosas's siege—bothered the elder López or Francia nor induced them to hitch Paraguay's wagon to Uruguay's team.

The younger López found himself in a precarious situation. By talking with the Brazilian emperor, he had conspired against Argentina. He then conspired with Argentina against Brazil, suggesting that if it dominated Uruguay and Paraguay, it would subjugate Argentina.[64] In 1856, he concluded that Uruguay was the "Gordian knot" for all four nations.[65] He then began to worry about an offensive alliance between Brazil and Argentina's now President Urquiza. He feared their simultaneous invasion of currently autonomous Buenos Aires and Paraguay. He was suspicious of diplomatic talks between Uruguay and Brazil.[66] These developments focused his upgrading his nation's military. In fact, when his sister Inocencia married Col. Vicente Barrios in September 1856, Francisco remained at the fort of Humaitá[67]—a demonstration of his concern with military issues and his lack of concern with personal matters that deeply touched other people, including his siblings.

He fiercely desired world recognition. He wanted to be a great man. To increase his nation's and his own stature, Francisco thought, he must improve his image in the great port down the river. He employed journalists in Buenos Aires to flatter him, his father, and their nation. The price was high. On one occasion, he balked, refusing to pay the 150 oz. in gold demanded by one journalist for pro-López propaganda. Instead, he made a counteroffer. Francisco proffered 200 arrobas of high-quality yerba, indicating that it could be sold on the open market for a sum equal to the writer's demand.[68]

In 1858, Francisco López suspected that a military alliance between the Empire of Brazil and the Argentine Confederation was then in place, although it was not. As proof, he pointed to the Brazilian minister, José María da Silva Paranhos, who had just arrived in Asunción. Paranhos carried a copy of a Brazilian–Argentine agreement about river navigation, the lifeblood of the now booming Paraguayan economy and, though Francisco paid little attention, just as essential to the agriculture and commerce of Brazil's Mato Grosso province. Francisco, told by his father to negotiate with Paranhos, thought that the Brazilian–Argentine agreement offended national honor and, by extension, his own. He was also angry, inconsistently, that Argentine journalists took payment from Brazil for favorable articles in their newspapers, just as they accepted them from him.[69] Nevertheless, Francisco signed an innocuous treaty of friendship with Paranhos, which was "clearly and decisively forced by Brazil" on Paraguay.[70]

It is unclear precisely when in the 1850s Francisco developed the notion that Uruguay was the "Gordian knot" holding together the politics and diplomacy of the Plata region and that Paraguay's and Uruguay's interests were intertwined. He had tried to persuade Uruguayan officials of this on his return from Europe. Although no executive before or since has thought[71] that Uruguayan affairs were essential to Paraguay's security, Francisco saw Brazil's intervention there as an insult to his nation and himself.

In his personal life, he partied, rode around on horses (and increasingly in carriages, as he grew fatter), and found sexual outlets for his tremendous energy. Francisco and Elisa continued to produce children together. Some Paraguayans referred to her as La Lynch, and she was still captivating. Ensconced in Paraguay as consort to the next president, she set about changing domestic habits by her example. About this far-off place she had originally known nothing, except that it *was* a country, and one to which her short, pudgy lover was the de facto heir. Her knowledge of the country grew. She set about becoming rich by bestowals from Francisco and his assisting her acquisitions of land and money until the allies killed her lover in 1870. One historian's charge that her "education was superior and will stronger than his [López's] own"[72] must be weighed carefully. She *had* spent more time in Europe than Francisco. She was a better party conversationalist than he. Unlike him, she listened when people talked. But no evidence suggests that her limited formal education was superior to his. The criticism of Lynch's origins and conduct and greed arose from the public nature of her relationship with Francisco and from envy of Lynch's prominent position, her ostentatious wealth, and her presumed political influence over Francisco, which was in fact limited.[73]

In her own way, Lynch contributed to the modernization of Paraguay. She convinced Francisco, once her "mon cher Pancho,"[74] to reorder Paraguayan social relations on French models. She encouraged the giving and attending of formal, nonfamily dinners with printed invitations. She convinced Francisco to make Paraguayan society more elegant. She decorated his residences with expensive tapestries, silk curtains, paintings, furniture, and figurines from European artisans. Neither before nor after he was president, however, did Francisco hold social events at home. For entertaining, he used the new Club Nacional. He used Lynch as a social surrogate. In her residence, more elegant than those even of the favored classes in Paraguay, she displayed fine "bronzes and porcelains, French tapestries, and oriental rugs" and hung oil paintings for the first time.[75] Francisco funded all of these luxuries through the revenues of the state. Women followed her lead. They changed their hairstyles. They began to use cosmetics popular in Paris. She brought her own hair stylist, Jules Henry, to Paraguay. She convinced William Whytehead, the López family's chief technical expert and for a time her friend, to import sewing machines from England. By 1863, women's use of sewing machines was common. Under her influence, four photographers' studios, one run by a woman, were operating in Asunción. She encouraged the serving of

French cuisine. She also contributed to the possessing classes' growing taste for champagne, of which she drank much. She spent five hundred pesos a month on food prepared at the Club Nacional. After López became president in 1862, invitations to her social gatherings were an indicator of where you stood in the eyes of the government. Since the 1850s, the English speakers had formed an expatriate community. Their social events were usually dinner parties followed by whist and chess and they revolved around Lynch, their social leader.[76] Whytehead, for example, attended her functions regularly. She then dropped him from her guest list in 1864. His absence from her parties showed the engineer's fall from official favor.

López approved of her innovations, and he added his own. These included the splendid but gauche uniforms that he had tailored in Paris. They also included the expensive French wines that he now drank with lunch and dinner, although he bought cheaper vintages to serve his guests. Lynch was influential partly because of the glamour attached to her British and French backgrounds. And "her youth, beauty, boldness, and elegance . . ."[77] charmed most men. In her salon, she received notable foreigners. At Francisco's urging, she held dinners at her homes that Francisco could not or would not hold in his. Like his father, Francisco remained suspicious of foreigners. Lynch, on the other hand, socialized with English speakers like herself. Many were now residents and earned handsome salaries. Before he fell afoul of President López, Charles A. Washburn, the American minister in Asunción, was a frequent guest at her soirées.[78] His relations with López early in his posting were correct. Later they would be rancorous.[79]

The Club Nacional was located in the center of Asunción a stone's throw from Francisco's principal residence. Social and political events intertwined at the club—property of the government and de facto property of los López. The López siblings held balls and banquets there, and Francisco encouraged local and visiting merchants and diplomats to join. To refuse brought a precipitate decline in one's fortunes.

To live on his salary as war and navy minister would have bankrupted Francisco López. In 1855, his salary was 2,000 pesos a year, a huge sum, multiples of what the engineer Whytehead freely agreed to work for, to leave home for, and to travel to an unknown place for, to live in relative luxury. Lynch's food budget was 6,000 pesos a year. At times, she dined with Francisco alone, and both drank French champagne at these quiet meals. She drank copious amounts of it without ever appearing drunk.[80] After she followed Lopez to the front in 1865, she and their children continued to enjoy comfortable quarters. There she increased her social status, holding dinners for the marshal's Paraguayan sycophants and the declining number of foreign dignitaries who visited. To attend a function by a member of the López family ". . . was a patriotic duty."[81] The new mode of entertaining, a part of Paraguay's modernization effort, lasted until 1864 in Asunción.

Once, in the 1850s, Francisco's actions exceeded his father's wishes, a rare occurrence. The outcome was a minor disaster. A plan was hatched by the López father and son, certainly at Francisco's urging, to attract European immigrants.[82] The president wanted to bring farmers from Spain. Instead, he attracted some four to five hundred gullible French citizens without the necessary skills. They accepted Francisco's offer of more assistance than the president was willing to allocate. Francisco promised them fertile land on which to live and grow crops. The government would, he assured them, furnish animals and farming implements. They would pay no taxes and would be exempt from military service for ten years. The Lópezes sent the French not to eastern Paraguay, where crops grew well, but to the Gran Chaco to the west of the Río Paraguay, where conditions were harsh and the land poor. There even Native American inhabitants of the region had failed as farmers. The French colony failed. Francisco López had seen in their arrival a display of his skills as an international operator. For his father, immigrants were at best a Chaco barrier against the hostile Guaycurúans there and possibly an argument in favor of Paraguay's claim to sovereignty in the region. The French, whose colony came to be known as Nuevo Bourdeaux, or Burdeos, soon wished to go home. The senior López "was less than lavish with . . . support," and the colony "was spewing its dismayed settlers throughout Paraguay."[83] The elder López arrested many of them, charging breach of contract.[84] As the colonists begged to be allowed to leave, their government took their side. A brief war of words between Paraguay and France ensued, and the pitiful colonists, after some government persecution, finally departed.

Soon an internal security measure of President López and Francisco escalated into an international incident that sabotaged relations with the United Kingdom. In 1858, the government arrested several men and charged them with conspiring to assassinate the president. That they had so intended was doubtful. Who would kill Carlos Antonio to get Francisco, the obvious successor? One of the accused was James (Santiago) Canstatt, a merchant. He had a British father and an Uruguayan mother and claimed dual citizenship. The British government defended his rights and insisted that he be tried "according to the laws . . . of civilized nations,"[85] impossible in a nation like Paraguay, without an independent judiciary. In court cases of interest to the López family, their decisions stood. During the Canstatt case, as at other times, they commonly referred to one or another "constitutional principle" decreed by Carlos Antonio López, who sentenced Canstatt to death. The Lópezes also arrested the brothers Decoud. One brother, formerly a business agent for López, had embezzled funds and fled south to safety. Father and son resorted to "vicarious punishment," a favorite tactic. It would be "carried by his successor, the younger López, to a refinement of cruelty. . . ."[86] One of the Decouds, Carlos, had been engaged to a woman whom Francisco coveted. The maiden disdained his advances, dishonoring his family. It was widely believed that the government persecuted young Decoud at the insistence of Francisco, who liked to deflower young women of the best families of the nation, not a breach of the honor code. His position made him unaccustomed to rejection. Thus the Lópezes had the Decouds executed, "perhaps the only great atrocity committed during the reign of López I."[87] But Canstatt's fate rested on British power. The issue stirred the diplomatic pot in 1859, and we shall return to Canstatt presently.

One of Francisco's proudest triumphs came from his alleged skill as a diplomat, although his diplomatic instincts were erratic. His advocates boast of his success as mediator in Argentina in 1859, of which he himself often crowed. The background is that in 1852, two Argentinas emerged, because Buenos Aires city and province refused to join the new Argentine Confederation. That polity was headed by Justo José de Urquiza. The confederation's major problem was its frictional relationship with Buenos Aires, which was disinclined to share the customs revenues. Distrust also resulted from *porteño* leaders' hostility to Urquiza, partly because he had for been allied with Rosas and partly because he was so provincial; his rusticity clashed with the polished sophisticates of the port city. But the main contention was economic. In 1859, the two sides went to war. The first phase of the civil war was mainly one battle, Cepeda, won by the Confederation. Urquiza's forces could defeat porteño armies but were unable to dominate the city and province for long. Both sides agreed on many of the main issues. They all wanted a unified Argentina. They wanted to modernize the country.

The first family of Paraguay was unpopular in Buenos Aires. Porteño newspapers, for example, condemned the government's or the López family's monopoly of the trade in yerba maté. Francisco López took offense to one newspaper account that charged that that Paraguayan commerce flourished but that the Paraguayan people failed to benefit, maintaining that only the ruling family did—this was an overstatement because the whole country was on the move.

The strongest Argentine criticism focused on the rulers' tyranny. The despotism of the father was not a fact that Francisco wished publicized. The leaders of Buenos Aires, the newly victorious liberals, had expelled their own tyrant in 1852, although they declined to bring the masses into politics. Their partisan press, including *El Orden*, *El Nacional*, and *La Prensa*, regularly denounced the Paraguayan rulers. Porteño criticism humiliated Francisco. Moreover, the port city's leaders permitted the 1858 founding of an anti-López association of exiles, the Sociedad Libertadora del Paraguay. Although Carlos Antonio censored opposition propaganda, he was unable to stem the insulting references to him and his family in the Buenos Aires press.[88] Unlike his eldest son, he did not let it distract him.

ARGENTINE–PARAGUAYAN RELATIONS

Before the battle of Cepeda, President Carlos Antonio López offered mediation. Confederation President Urquiza, himself a former *caudillo*, requested and received an armistice from Buenos Aires. He and his opponents in Buenos Aires eventually accepted the Paraguayan proposal. Unwilling to leave the country himself, Carlos Antonio appointed his thirty-three-year-old son to negotiate. Francisco hoped to distinguish himself in Buenos Aires. He left Asunción aboard the *Tacuarí* on September 27, 1859. He stopped at the Argentine city of Paraná to consult with Urquiza, then absent, and sailed on to Buenos Aires.

Francisco first negotiated a truce. He confronted the hostility of porteño leaders to the Urquiza government. Some porteños had thought that a military victory over the Confederation was possible and negotiations superfluous. They were wrong. On October 23, 1859, Urquiza's forces virtually annihilated those of Buenos Aires, and the leaders in the port city agreed to talk.[89]

Hoping to unify the nation peacefully and aware that he needed porteño cooperation, Urquiza refused to inflict further damage on Buenos Aires. He could have done so, since his forces had reached the outskirts of that city; but he spared it from destruction. Given the physical proximity and ideological similarities of the contending forces, Francisco López's job as mediator was made easier than it might have been, had they been more widely separated. Nevertheless, Francisco worked effectively to bring the two sides together. He achieved a modest though temporary success in the talks of November 1859. López's pleas to recognize their common identity fell on receptive ears. He proved a patient and a persuasive negotiator. He negotiated the Treaty of San José de Flores, in which both Argentine factions agreed that Buenos Aires was an integral part of the Argentine Confederation. The Republic of Paraguay was the guarantor of the treaty—a guarantee that was only symbolic, though, given Paraguay's distance and isolation.

Francisco's mediation brought merely a pause in the Argentine conflict, but leaders on both Argentine sides agreed that he had contributed to the peaceful resolution of their differences.[90] Among the porteño leaders who rendered formal thanks to López was Bartolomé Mitre, the future president of a legally unified Argentina. Francisco basked in Mitre's praise in 1859.

López judged his mediation in 1859 more crucial than did Argentines. The rhetoric of their congratulations and praise of his efforts in 1859 was fulsome and sincere, but formal.[91] He felt his participation in the negotiation was a special honor to his father. The settlement was a "glorious" experience for him.[92]

López took leave of President Urquiza, with whom he had developed an amicable relationship. The Paraguayan called it friendship. Urquiza invited him to visit his home in Entre Ríos, but events forced Francisco to decline—namely, the Canstatt problem resurfaced. As Francisco and his party sailed from Buenos Aires, the British navy took possession of the *Tacuarí*, held the warship for ransom, and pursued Francisco in retaliation for Paraguay's persecution of the British subject, James (Santiago) Canstatt. Thus, Francisco hurried home without the *Tacuarí*. Urquiza had intended to reward Francisco more fittingly, he said, and he praised his meritorious service in the Argentine cause. Urquiza, a veteran of many battles, presented his personal sword to Francisco. Flattered, Francisco saw it as an omen. He was bursting with pride at his achievement on an international stage. It inflated his ego. He imagined that important people throughout South America were singing his praises, which brought him elation.[93]

In early 1860, Francisco judged that the Agreement of San José would bring Argentina a lasting peace. His diplomacy, he congratulated himself, had produced "a very great outcome." Accepting Urquiza's sword, Francisco dissembled, telling the Argentine leader that his thanks were the only recognition that he wanted.[94] Francisco proudly displayed a commemorative gold medal honoring him for aiding Argentine unity. Symbols of honor were highly sought after trophies.

When Urquiza completed his presidential term, he retired to Entre Ríos. Francisco still called him a friend.[95] He actually spent little time in Urquiza's company. In fact, neither party received lasting benefit from Francisco's treaty. It provided only a pause in the conflict that ended with the military victory of Buenos Aires in 1861.[96]

After the British warships escorted the *Tacuarí* into port, the British impounded the vessel, demanding that the Lópezes free Canstatt—actions that were indeed violations of international maritime law. But the mightiest power in the world prevailed. López father and son were unwilling to relinquish the *Tacuarí*, the pride of the nation and symbol of its modernity. Thus, Carlos Antonio freed Canstatt. He had to indemnify him for his business reverses before Paraguay recovered the *Tacuarí*. The Lópezes were humiliated and dishonored. Francisco denounced the British government's act as insulting. He sarcastically voiced the hope that the British foreign office would learn some international law. He was stung, especially by the opinion of British officials that Paraguay was a nation of barbarians. This shame was the antithesis of the honor Francisco longed for. The barbarian image was what he hoped by force of his will to surmount. López had some knowledge of how the British government worked, but he hoped that Her Majesty's government would find "an honorable occasion" to reverse its protection of Canstatt. At the same time, he continued to purchase favorable notices of himself and his father in the British press. He urged that his name and his nation be praised not just in any old newspapers but, instead, in the most prestigious periodicals.[97] He had little success.

A new development, the Hortelano affair, added fuel to the shame-induced outrage that burned within Francisco. In Argentina in 1860, a young man named Benito Hortelano had counterfeited Paraguayan bank notes, and the Argentine authorities arrested him. Porteño leaders merely confiscated Hortelano's possessions. Their failure to punish him severely increased the López father's and son's hostility to the haughty liberals of Buenos Aires.[98]

After the Battle of Pavón in 1861, a porteño victory,[99] Buenos Aires increasingly dominated Argentina. Its favorite son, Bartolomé Mitre, became president in 1862. Argentines had conducted new negotiations to unify their country, and these nullified the agreements made on Francisco's watch. He judged the Argentines' behavior "offensive." They had altered the terms of his treaty. The refusal of Argentina to challenge the British seizure of the *Tacuarí* was, he thought, a gratuitous insult to him.[100] He was right.

Francisco's correspondence at this time is revealing. Characteristically the letters center on his own importance and the impact of events on him. First-person references clutter the letters. Historians who spend their time reading correspondence between leaders of the Hispanic world, including monarchs, are struck by Francisco's excessive use of "me," "I," and "my." Critical readers of his correspondence without any other knowledge of his character would judge him at least an outlandish egotist.[101] Francisco proclaimed his honor, feeling correctly that he needed to remind others of it. Honor was still a zero-sum game. He told one Argentine that the Paraguayan government (his father) had "honored" him by appointing him mediator in the Argentine dispute. In a neutral setting, such an appointment *would* have been an honor. The reality here was that nepotism led to the choice.[102] Francisco's assertions of honor and the necessity for others to recognize it grew more frequent as he grew older. It was a value system to which he clung in the absence of other personal qualities such as pragmatism and common sense and empathy.

THE YOUNGER FACE OF POWER

As his father's health declined in the early 1860s, Francisco increasingly ran the government, made easy by his control of the army and his father's trust. After returning from Buenos Aires, Francisco was clearly his father's heir, although fearful Paraguayans preferred the weak, unambitious Benigno. It thus fell to Francisco and not his father to offer an appointment to Argentine Carlos Calvo to head the Paraguayan legation in Paris and London, proposing a salary of 6,000 pesos a year plus expenses. Calvo, whom Francisco addressed as "my true friend," was not truly a friend because Francisco was incapable of true friendship. ·

On the eve of his presidency, therefore, the young Francisco was experienced. He had familiarized himself with every aspect of the Paraguayan government. He had not only worked in military and foreign affairs, his special areas of expertise he thought; but he also oversaw the nation's economic development and technical modernization.[103] His background prepared him to become more tyrannical than his father and caused him to perceive that his ability was great in military and foreign affairs, where he had knowledge but lacked understanding.

In the last decade of Carlos Antonio López's presidency, his family continued to plunder the state for personal profit. In the late 1850s and early 1860s, Benigno López bought numerous slaves from the government. He purchased *libertos de la república*, slaves who were supposed to be freed when the men were 25 and the women 24 years old. In 1856, he bought from the Minister of Hacienda four male slaves between the ages of 15 and 30 for 360 pesos. In 1857, he purchased from a government ranch four female slaves along with their two *liberto* children, for which he paid 400 pesos. Only minions of his father and brother could collect the money, if they dared. He outright disregarded the tradition of freeing the slaves at a certain age. In August 1860, the state sold Benigno another slave, a thirty-five-year-old man, for the measly sum of 100 pesos. In October 1860, Manuel José Carraula, a private citizen, sold Benigno a twenty-five-year-old woman and her two daughters, both *libertas de la república*. The youngest López purchased a slave couple in their twenties and their two children from José Rafael Zabala in November 1860. In November 1864, Benigno, who could today be labeled a pedophile, bought a twelve-year-old girl for 54 pesos.[104]

The family ownership of human beings is a way to judge the distance between Francisco López's pronouncements and reality. In a few years, Francisco would motivate troops by condemning Brazilian slavery. His own racial prejudice against Afro-Brazilians was as strong as his criticism of slavery. Because Afro-Paraguayans never quite reached 10 percent of the nation's population, chattel slavery of them was not as conspicuous as in Brazil. Still, neither the first nor the second President López actually abolished the abominable institution, although the father decreed its gradual elimination. Seeing slavery in their own country, however, Paraguayans understood what it meant when Francisco told them "that the Brazilians wished to enslave them."[105] Francisco himself employed slaves.

Benigno's plundering of the property of the state exemplified the family's business practices. When a López family member wanted something, he or she could "buy" it from the government. The López clan paid whatever price that they thought would keep up appearances. Benigno, in November 1858, bought one hundred oxen from state farms, whose managers were employees of his father. In May 1859, he bought sixteen good horses and a hundred young bulls (or steers). The following September he obtained twenty-five mares tamed to ride or drive. In 1860, the military commander of the upriver town of Concepción was ordered to deliver to Benigno two hundred hides, until then state property. Benigno's business dealings with his father's government also included *cal*, or limestone, three hundred fanegas of which he obtained in 1861 (a fanega is about 1.5 bushels or 55 liters). The records of these transactions list no payment at all.[106]

By the early 1860s, no Paraguayan doubted that Francisco would head the country. Carlos Antonio was well into his seventies, grossly overweight, and unwell. His brothers knew that Francisco was not a man to trifle with. He demanded that even they be obsequious, and they complied. Even before he claimed the presidency, he insisted that they address him formally and in more respectful terms than they did each other. Writing to Francisco eight years before he became president, Venancio addressed his older brother as "my esteemed brother." At the same time, he called Benigno "my dear brother,"[107] showing that Venancio feared offending his older brother.

In the year before the death of Carlos Antonio López, Francisco, as minister of war and the navy, escalated his concern about national security to an obsession. He controlled its military absolutely. Many of Francisco's efforts to upgrade the nation's land and naval forces were in fact competent. The increase in strength might deter aggression, the president hoped. Carlos Antonio, however, never dreamed of using Paraguayan forces offensively against his larger neighbors. In fact, he warned Francisco against it. He believed that only diplomacy would serve.

In January 1862, Francisco was haunted by the Brazilians moving south from the Blanco River into the disputed region between the Apa and Blanco Rivers. He sought detailed military intelligence. He worried about military effectiveness and feared a Brazilian surprise attack. He pondered sending mobile forces north for better intelligence. He was troubled by

Brazilian ships that stopped at Asunción and passed on to the Mato Grosso. He fussed over the deserters who fled to Brazil.[108] López was hard working, demanding, and detail oriented. His best military attribute was his talent for organization, even if in some of its particulars like weapons procurement he was neglectful. He paid attention to the particulars of troop strength, recruitment, and the morale of noncommissioned officers. He was his own intelligence chief and head of logistics. He provided his troops with chaplains and hospitals. He had his soldiers in the north pursue bandits, mostly Brazilians, he thought, who were persecuting "our Indians with blood and fire."[109] They were more likely renegades with little national allegiance of any kind. He dispatched a Scottish doctor, William Stewart, in charge of public health, to attend to the ravages of an epidemic.[110]

What annoyed López the most, as he was poised to become the nation's absolute ruler, was Brazilian penetration. He thought that Brazilian exploration parties, largely cavalry units, were a threat. He expected a surprise attack on the Apa River. If any observation post was attacked, he ordered in September 1862, the forces there must vigorously resist. The subordinate commanders were to report to him immediately developments in the north. In case of a firefight, his client Francisco Isidoro Resquín "should have no scruple" about crossing the Río Apa after Brazilians to win a victory.[111] No one yet knew it, possibly not even López himself, but he was preparing to attack Brazil.

NOTES

1. Legally Rosas was only the governor of the province of Buenos Aires, but he controlled other provinces through alliances with caudillos of the interior.

2. Thomas Whigham, *The Politics of River Trade: Tradition and Development in the Upper Plata, 1780–1870* (Albuquerque: University of New Mexico Press, 1991), 69 ff.

3. George Thompson, C.E., *The War in Paraguay with a Historical Sketch of Country, Its People, and Notes on the Military Engineering of the War* (London: Longman, Green, and Co.), 9.

4. Thompson, *War in Paraguay*, 9.

5. Julio César Chaves, *El Presidente López: Vida y gobierno de Don Carlos*, 2nd ed. (Buenos Aires: Ediciones Depalma, 1968), 218–19.

6. R. Antonio Ramos, *Juan Andrés Gelly* (Buenos Aires: Asunción, 1972), 417–19.

7. Juan Andrés Gelly, *El Paraguay: Lo que fue; Lo que es; Lo que será*, prólogo de J. Natalicio González (Asunción: Editorial del lector, 1996). Gelly said that Francia and his henchmen thought up "ways to mortify their compatriots, to vex them, and to ruin them," 40.

8. The city of Buenos Aires was the capital of Buenos Aires province.

9. Ramos, *Gelly*, 417–22.

10. From Paraguay, Francisco addressed Alfred Blyth as "Mon cher ami," not "dear friend," as he would have done had he mastered English. FSL to Alfred Blyth, Asunción, Feb. 25, 1856; Juan A. Livieres Argaña, ed., *Con la rúbrica del Mariscal: Documentos de Francisco Solano López* (Asunción: Escuela Técnica Salesiano, 1970), Tomo III, 1856. Francisco's alleged mastery of English is belied not only by his inability to write simple letters but also his inability even to copy English words faithfully—spelling John as Jhon and Witch as Wicht.

11. The chief telegrapher, however, was not British but German, Richard F. E. von Fischer-Truenfeld. He did not come to Paraguay until 1864.

12. FSL to J. and A. Blyth, Asunción, June 1, 1856, *Con la rúbria del Mariscal*, V.

13. Ricardo Caballero Aquino, "Introduction," to Josefina Plá, *Los británicos en el Paraguay, 1850–1870* (Asunción: Arte Nuevo, 1984), 11–13.

14. Plá, *Británicos*, 25.

15. That they were actually in servitude to work off a debt is doubtful, but several sources use that designation.

16. FSL to Benito Varela, Paraguayan Legation, London, Dec. 8, 1853, ANA/CRB, 828.

17. Sometimes the name is rendered Morris and elsewhere Moore. In Paraguayan works, it remains Morice.

18. Plá, *Británicos*, 48–84.

19. FSL to Alfred Blyth, Asunción, Feb. 25, 1856, *Con la rúbrica del Mariscal*, III.

20. FSL to Egusquiza, Asunción, July 6, 1864, *Proclamas y cartas del Mariscal Francisco Solano López* (Buenos Aires: Editorial Asunción, 1957).

21. FSL to Alfred Blyth, Asunción, Aug. 18, 1856, *Con la rúbrica del Mariscal*, III.

22. FSL to Varela, Paris, Dec. 22, 1853, ANA/CRB, 837.

23. Siân Rees, *The Shadows of Elisa Lynch: How a Nineteenth-Century Courtesan Became the Most Powerful Woman in Paraguay* (London: REVIEW, an imprint of Headline Publishing, 2003), 5.

24. FSL to Varela, Paris, Jan. 7, 1854, ANA/CRB, 858.

25. Ramos, *Gelly*, 424.

26. Her mother was one Corinne Schnock.

27. Elisa A. Lynch, *Exposición y protesta que hace Elisa A. Lynch* (Buenos Aires: Imprenta de M. Biedma, 1875), 6–9; Rees, *Shadows of Elisa Lynch*, 5–9, 312; see also the novel written in French by Henri Pitaud, *Madama Lynch*, 4th ed. (Asuncion: Talleres El Gráfico, 1978) and translated into Spanish. This edition was dedicated to the "Excelentisimo Sr. Presidente de la República del Paraguay General of the Army Don Alfredo Stroessner" in a prologue written earlier by Juan O'Leary. Other novels that romanticize the Lynch–López relationship include María Concepción L. de Chaves, *Madame Lynch y Solano López* (Buenos Aires: Artes Gráficas Negri, 1976); and William Barrett, *Woman on Horseback: The Biography of Francisco López and Eliza Lynch* (New York: Fredrick A. Stokes Company, 1938), which despite its title is fiction.

28. Solano López is *not* how Francisco identified himself.

29. Charles A. Washburn, *The History of Paraguay, with Notes of Personal Observations and Reminiscences of Diplomacy under Difficulties*, 2 vols. (Boston: Lee and Shepard, 1871), II, 397.

30. One biographer says, "It was the first clash with Benigno. Neither of the two would forget that unpleasant and bitter scene." Arturo Bray, *Solano López: soldado de la gloria y del infortunio* (Asunción: Editorial Lector, 1996), 84. If this dispute occurred, it would help explain Francisco's future persecution of his brother; but later events, including his choosing Benigno to accompany him to Buenos Aires in 1859, cast doubt on an unending feud between the two brothers beginning in 1854. Francisco's real hostility to his brother and Benigno's fear of Francisco likely began in 1862 or after, with rumors that some Paraguayans preferred Benigno to Francisco.

31. Rees, *Shadows of Elisa Lynch*, 83–85.

32. Washburn, *History of Paraguay*, I, 442.

33. Ramos, *Gelly*, 429.

34. Letters of FSL to Benito Varela, Secretary of State and Foreign Relations of Paraguay, London, December 8, 1853, ANA/CRB 828, 829, and 830.

35. FSL to Varela, Paris, December 22, 1853, ANA/CRB, 837.

36. In June 2005, the theater was not in use.

37. FSL to Varela, three letters of January 7, 1854, ANA/CRB 858, 859, 860.

38. FSL to Varela, Paris, Feb. 22, 1854, ANA/CRB, 880.

39. FSL to Manuel Moreira de Castro, Paris, January 22, 1854, ANA/CRB, 865.

40. FSL to Varela, Paris, Feb. 7, 1854, ANA/CRB, 873.

41. Ramos, *Gelly*, 428.

42. FSL to Varela, Paris, March 7, 1854, ANA/CRB, 884.

43. Thompson, *War in Paraguay*, 12.

44. George Masterman, *Seven Eventful Years in Paraguay: A Narrative of Personal Experience Amongst the Paraguayans*, 2nd ed. (London: Samson Low, Son, and Marston, 1870), 60.

45. Personal communications, Asunción, February 2002.

46. Ramos, *Gelly*, 424–26.

47. The continuing symbolic importance of the empire to Spaniards can be seen in Antonio Feros, "'Spain and America: All is One': Historiography of the Conquest and Colonization of the Americas and National Mythology in Spain, c. 1892–1992," in *Interpreting Spanish Colonialism: Empires, Nations, and Legends,* ed. Christopher Schmidt-Nowara and John M. Nieto-Phillips (Albuquerque: University of New Mexico Press, 2005), 109–134.

48. FSL to Chancellery of Madrid and Secretary of State of Spain, n.p. [1854], *Proclamas y cartas*.

49. Ramos, *Gelly*, 426.

50. EAL to FSL, Paris, June 5, 1854, ANA/CRB, 929.

51. Ramos, *Gelly*, 429–32.

52. Ramos, *Gelly*, 433–36.

53. *El Centinela*, Aug. 8, 1867.

54. John Hoyt Williams, *The Rise and Fall of the Paraguayan Republic, 1800–1870* (Austin: Institute of Latin American Studies, University of Texas), 164.

55. Chaves, *El Presidente López*, 232.

56. Chaves, *El Presidente López*, 234.

57. Chaves, *El Presidente López*, 237.

58. FSL to Nicolas Calvo, Asuncion, June 11, 1858; and FSL to Alfred Blyth, Asunción, September 21, 1858, both in *Con la rúbrica del Mariscal*, V.

59. Plá, *Británicos*, 90–92.

60. FSL to Pedro Ferreira de Oliveira, Plenipotentiary of Brazil, Asunción, Apr. 17, 1855, *Proclamas y cartas*.

61. FSL to Lorenzo Torres, Asunción, June 25, 1857, *Proclamas y cartas*.

62. Plá, *Británicos*, 133–34.

63. Ramos, *Gelly*, 435–37.

64. FSL to Facundo Zuviria, Asunción, Feb. 24, 1856, *Con la rúbrica del Mariscal*, III.

65. FSL to Lorenzo Torres, Asunción, Feb. 24, 1856, *Con la rúbrica del Mariscal*, III.

66. FSL to Carlos Calvo, Asunción, March 22, 1856; FSL to Buenaventura Decoud, Humaitá, April 1, 1856, both in *Con la rúbrica del Mariscal*, III.

67. FSL to Buenaventura Decoud, Humaitá, September 6, 1856, *Con la rúbrica del Mariscal*, III.

68. FSL to Hector Varela, Asunción, Apr. 20, 1856, *Proclamas y cartas*.

69. FSL to Félix Egusquiza, Asunción, January 1858, *Proclamas y cartas*.

70. Chaves, *El Presidente López*, 290.

71. Williams, *Rise and Fall of the Paraguayan Republic*, 198.

72. R. B. Cunningham Graham, *Portrait of a Dictator: Francisco Solano López* (London: William Heinemann, Ltd., 1933), 102.

73. Juan Crisóstomo Centurión, *Memorias o reminiscencias históricas sobre la guerra del Paraguay*, 4 vols., (Buenos Aires and Asunción: Imprenta de Obras de J.A. Berra/Imprenta Militar, 1894–1902), I, 344, charged that it was crucial. He said it was she who caused the downfall of the man and his nation, but he admitted that his leader's egotism was boundless; *Memorias*, I, 359; and II, 337. Masterman wrote, "she could really do with him as she pleased," and was herself the person who "made his desire of military glory . . . the ruling passion of his life," *Seven Eventful Years*, 59, 92; Washburn surmised that Lynch tried to amplify "the natural cowardice of Lopez [sic]" to magnify her own importance; *History of Paraguay*, II, 397. The present author believes that she influenced him to do on matters of political and military importance only what he was already determined to do.

74. EAL to FSL, Paris, June 5, 1854, ANA/CRB, 929.

75. Plá, *Británicos*, 244–45.

76. Plá, *Británicos*, 104–6, 245–48.

77. Plá, *Británicos*, 248.

78. Plá, *Británicos*, 146, 237, 240–44.

79. Washburn's *History of Paraguay* is full of bile. It reveals the author as a complainer and a hard man to like. Unlike his successor Martin McMahon, however, Washburn was able to see much of Paraguay and to meet Paraguayans who were not ardently pro-López. He generally disdained Paraguayans, although he made the Casal family an exception. What McMahon was able to see in six months in 1868–1869 was not Paraguay but only a tiny portion of a burned-over battlefield. A defense of McMahon and by implication a denunciation of Washburn by a former U.S. diplomat is Arthur H. Davis, *Martin T. McMahon: Diplomático en el estridor de armas* (Asunción: Arthur H. Davis, 1985). I had the good fortune of consulting it in the library of the now privatized Centro Cultural Paraguayo-Americano and was directed back to it by Professor Barbara Ganson.

80. Masterman, *Seven Eventful Years in Paraguay*, 58.

81. Plá, *Británicos*, 41–45, 247–48; Chaves, *El Presidente López*, 220; and Washburn, *History of Paraguay*, I, 440–41.

82. Argentina and Brazil, both of which welcomed significant numbers of European immigrants, were exceptions.

83. Williams, *Rise and Fall of the Paraguayan Republic*, 193.

84. Williams, *Rise and Fall of the Paraguayan Republic*, 193.

85. Washburn, *History of Paraguay*, I, 395.

86. Washburn, *History of Paraguay*, I, 403.

87. Thompson, *War in Paraguay*, 13.

88. Chaves, *El Presidente López*, 273–76.

89. Bray, *Solano López*, 87.

90. Bray, *Solano López*, 91

91. Bray, *Solano López*, 94.

92. FSL to Carlos Tejedor, Nov. 16, 1859, *Proclamas y cartas*.

93. FSL to Salvador María Carril, Paraná, Dec. 19, 1859, *Proclamas y cartas*.

94. FSL to Nicolás Vásquez, Asunción, Jan. 2, 1860; FSL to Urquiza, Humaitá, Jan. 26, 1860; both *Proclamas y cartas*.

95. FSL to Urquiza, Asunción, Feb. 5, 1861, *Proclamas y cartas*. That Urquiza was still governor of Entre Ríos and as captain-general of the province head of its military might have influenced López's profession of friendship.

96. The Battle of Pavón was itself indecisive. Mitre and Buenos Aires could claim victory because Urquiza decided not to continue the fight.

97. FSL to Carlos Calvo, Asunción, letters of July 20 and Aug. 20, 1860, *Proclamas y cartas*.

98. Bray, *Solano López*, 104–5.

99. Pavón was a tactical draw. But because Urquiza led his army back to Entre Ríos in the interests of peace, it was a strategic victory for Buenos Aires.

100. FSL to José R. Caminos, Asunción, July 20, 1861, *Proclamas y cartas*.

101. FSL to Carlos Tejedor, Buenos Aires, Nov. 24, 1850 [1859], *Proclamas y cartas*.

102. FSL to Tejedor, Buenos Aires, Nov. 28, 1859, *Proclamas y cartas*.

103. FSL to Carlos Calvo, letters of Jan. 17 and Apr. 20, 1860, *Proclamas y cartas*.

104. Records of the transaction apear in ANA/CRB, 1206.

105. Masterman, *Seven Eventful Years*, x.

106. These transactions are found in ANA/NE, vol. 2745.

107. Venancio López to FSL, August 9, 1854; Venancio to Benigno López, October 1854, both ANA/CRB, 949.

108. FSL to Resquín, Comandante de Villa Concepción, Asunción, Jan. 3, 1862; ANA/SE, Vol. 2834.

109. FSL to Resquín, Commandante de Villa Concepción, Asunción, April 21, 1862, ANA/NE.Vol. 2834.

110. FSL to Resquín, June 5, 1862, ANA/NE, vol. 2834.

111. FSL to Resquín, September 4, 1862, ANA/NE, vol. 2834. This volume contains twenty-four letters from Minister López to Resquín written between January and September 1862.

4

⚜

López's War: Diplomacy, Combat, and Honor

THE STATE OF THE REGION

Platine diplomacy, especially among Paraguay and its two large neighbors, Brazil and Argentina, connects the presidencies of Francisco Solano López and his father. It also separates them because of the two men's differing national strategies and tactics. Carlos Antonio López made a success of his reversal of Francia's isolationism after the fall of Rosas in Buenos Aires in 1852. Paraguay benefited from its reconnection of his nation to the world.

For the first two rulers after 1840, the primary issues with Argentina remained national independence and freedom of navigation on the Paraná and Paraguay Rivers. The next issue was with the disputed borders to the south. On its southeastern frontier, Paraguay claimed Misiones province, to the east of Corrientes province, as did Argentina. Also undetermined was the location of the border in the Gran Chaco; both nations claimed territory between the Bermejo and Pilcomayo Rivers.

Paraguay's policy on navigation rights on the Paraná and Paraguay Rivers was logically inconsistent, arguing one position with Argentina and another with Brazil, not an unusual occurrence in the foreign affairs of any nation. Paraguay claimed the right to travel the Paraná River free from Argentine oversight. For reasons of security, though, the same leaders wished to deny full navigation rights to Brazilian ships sailing north past Asunción, a reversal of its Argentine policy. Brazil, of course, wished to send whatever ships it chose, including warships, to the Mato Grosso, on the northern border of eastern Paraguay, just as Paraguay did in sailing on the Paraná through Argentina. The overland journey from Brazilian commercial and political centers to the Mato Grosso took months owing to the nearly impassible terrain. Brazilians sought guaranteed freedom of transport on the Paraná and Paraguay Rivers, both of which touch Paraguay, Brazil, and Argentina today. These waterways were essential to the transportation systems of all three countries, and large merchant ships could ply them. River navigation was the only practical way for the empire to reach the Mato Grosso, and the only way for producers there to send their goods to market. Paraguay, in effect, wanted veto power over Brazilian ships going north. López father and son feared not only Brazilian warships on the Río Paraguay but also the establishment of stronger military bases there. The Paraguay–Brazil border dispute over territory between the Apa and Blanco Rivers tilted toward Brazil because of its size. The dispute was an outgrowth of claims by both Portuguese and Spanish empires. Neither controlled it effectively. Until the late 1700s, the Mbayá Indians, a nonsedentary, militaristic, equestrian group, dominated the area and raided Portuguese and Spanish outposts. After the 1760s, the Mbayá nation, never a cohesive political unit, plummeted demographically. Its northern bands formed economic and political ties with Brazil, while those of the south began to settle around such Spanish centers as Concepción, about 150 miles north of Asunción, and the mission of Belén. They merged into the larger Guarani-speaking populace of the region. Their former home and hunting areas invited exploitation by land-hungry Paraguayans and Brazilians.

In Argentina, Justo José de Urquiza recognized Paraguayan independence in fact in 1852, formally in 1856, without settling boundary disputes. Santiago Derqui was named the next president of the Argentine Confederation, and Urquiza returned to his power base in Entre Ríos. There, as events of the coming years would show, his power was waning, although Francisco López ignored this. Nor would the Paraguayan ever comprehend Urquiza's commitment to a unified Argentina. Derqui lacked Urquiza's leadership ability and the military backing of Entre Ríos's forces, widely believed to be devoted to Urquiza. After the Argentine civil war ended at the Battle of Pavón in 1861, Bartolomé Mitre and other liberals of Buenos Aires, heirs to the Unitarian enemies of Rosas, dominated the national government of a legally unified Argentina. But the nation was still in the process of formation. The porteños had won the civil war at Pavón in 1861 partly because of Urquiza's reluctance to prolong the conflict. He defeated porteño armies, but his military victories never brought him control of the province.[1] Mitre was elected president of an Argentina still divided by strong regional loyalties. During Mitre's presidency (1862–1868), Argentine relations with Brazil became less stressful.

Francisco López in the 1860s saw the declining tensions between the two dominant Platine powers as a threat and an insult. Brazilians were inferior, he thought, different in language, in ethnic background, and in customs. Paraguayans scorned and feared them. They considered the Brazilian character deformed by its heavily African population. Carlos Antonio López himself scorned Brazilians. His son encouraged artists to draw racist caricatures of them. Fearing Brazil more than Argentina came naturally to the López dictators,[2] a turnabout from the tolerant policy of Francia, whose father was Brazilian.

Relations between both López presidents and Urquiza were cordial until Francisco attacked Argentina. During the pleasant period, on one occasion, Urquiza sent gifts to all the male members of the López family. Their presents to him in return included high quality yerba and distinctive ponchos. When Urquiza asked Francisco to be his daughter's godfather, Francisco was honored by the request, although not honored enough to attend the baptism. He inconsiderately excused himself from the baptismal ceremony, pleading the press of official business. He therefore had less personal capital on which to draw when he asked Urquiza to side with him against Mitre than he imagined. López father and son professed concern for Argentine welfare and posed as neutrals in its regional political disputes. But they preferred provincial caudillos like Urquiza to porteños like Mitre, whose liberal agenda included opposition to dictators like los López. The Argentine press publicized the iniquities of Paraguayan policy, especially the ruling family's monopoly of the yerba trade. Critics attacked Carlos Antonio and Francisco Solano, the only men whose opinions counted, the only two who could make crucial decisions. The López duo believed correctly that the liberal factions of the port city after 1852 threatened their interests. From his father, Francisco inherited a distrust of porteños,[3] and he found his own reasons to dislike them.

By 1860, Carlos Antonio had turned over most government functions to his eldest son. Now in his seventies, the gout-ridden dictator's "obesity had reached such extremes that he could hardly walk. . . ."[4] Nevertheless, the old man's caution checked Francisco's impetuosity. In routine matters, Francisco made most decisions of state. Although he had controlled the military since the mid-1850s, he never challenged his father's authority.

The Lópezes feared that Mitre wished to restore the boundaries of the old viceroyalty, like earlier Argentine leaders. Mitre denied that restoring the viceregal domain was his goal. It was nevertheless his duty to maintain the security of Argentine borders. He sent an expedition to the Corrientes–Misiones region to regain the territory, which he claimed that Paraguay had usurped. He and other Argentines believed it to be part of their nation.[5]

Because of its location, Buenos Aires held a potential chokehold on the lucrative export sectors of the Paraguayan economy. Argentine disapproval never stopped the López family from enriching itself at the nation's expense. Except for his gluttony, the elder López was not a man of excesses. He did not crave luxury but his children did. They ordered Felix Egusquiza, their factor in Buenos Aires, to buy them fine clothing, wines, fancy carriages, and household goods from Europe. Times were good in Paraguay until 1864, and their conspicuous consumption did not halt the nation from growing richer. Merchant ships of foreign registry called at Asunción in increasing numbers until the outbreak of war.

Francisco was proud of his small but growing river fleet. A few ships could even sail to Europe and back. In 1857, the navy had consisted of four modern ships. The largest and most modern was the multipurpose *Tacuarí*, the wooden side-wheeler built in Britain. Others were assembled in Asunción under English direction, and British machinists served on them.[6] Shipbuilding was an early attempt at import-substitution industrialization. López "inaugurated a new stage in regional shipbuilding."[7] He made regular investments of state funds after 1855 to modernize the shipyards and build steamships. López's policy, however, only pushed dependency back a step or two. The country continued to rely on more advanced nations for the essential machine tools. Even though assembly of ships greater than five hundred tons occurred locally, the essential machinery and machine tools that produced them still came from England. The new vessels were dual-purpose ships. They exported primary products, especially yerba, in return for finished goods. They were also armed, and they were supposed to increase security by guarding the riverine approaches to the nation. The worldwide ironclad revolution in warships of the 1860s made them obsolete as fighting vessels, even on the rivers bordering Paraguay.

FRANCISCO'S EARLY RULING YEARS

The economic prosperity of Carlos Antonio's dictatorship lasted into the first two years of his son's. Nevertheless, Francisco's military mobilization, beginning in the 1850s and advancing markedly in the first two years of his presidency, would have beggared the country, even if López had not turned to war. Francisco López drafted so many men into the armed forces that Paraguay became "overmobilized,"[8] doing critical damage to its economy. Its standing army became larger than either Brazil's or Argentina's. It is probable that López believed the population, on the eve of the war, was twice its actual size, a dangerous miscalculation. The last good census was taken in the 1840s.

With little bloodshed, the elder López had overseen the economic growth of the small republic. Although his rule was authoritarian, he was not especially cruel and his caution and sound judgment moderated the impulsiveness of his eldest son. Two episodes, however, recalled the suppression of political opponents by Francia and previewed his son's full-scale resurrection of the policy in the 1860s. One was the execution of Carlos Decoud, Francisco's rival in a love affair. Another was the sad tale of Pancha Garmendia, a beautiful maiden after whom Francisco unsuccessfully lusted. One night he had surreptitiously entered her bedroom, hoping to conquer his prize. Instead, she made a scene. Her outcries kept her virtue intact. Her rejection of his "infamous proposals"[9] shamed him, a blow to his honor. He persecuted others who courted her. In the 1860s, she was a virtual prisoner in her home, afraid to venture out.

Some Paraguayans credit Carlos Antonio with establishing the stability that could prepare the way for democracy. The respected historian Julio César Chaves was one. In fact, however, the authoritarian governments of Paraguay were only good for the succession of more authoritarian governments. However, the father did oversee economic growth and a rise in the standard of living of many Paraguayans.

Before he died, the father reminded his son and heir of the threat of larger neighbors. He warned him that the only viable way to deal with greater powers, Brazil especially, was peacefully, by diplomacy, not war. On August 15, 1862, the dying Carlos Antonio named Francisco vice president and temporary successor. A Congress would be called to make a permanent choice. The fact that Congress would choose Francisco was a foregone conclusion. Both father and son covered their authoritarianism with a veneer of legality. In the case of his successor, Carlos Antonio cited Article 5 of a law that he had promulgated in 1856, giving the president the power to name an interim ruler, reinforcing an earlier edict.[10]

On September 10, 1862, Carlos Antonio López died.

The day after his father's death, Francisco Solano López told the nation that he had accepted his father's will. He had assumed the vice presidency, a heretofore nonexistent office. He called his father's administration "wise and prudent." Significantly, Francisco decided that his father's greatest service to the nation was his garnering "abundant glory for his country and his memory."[11] Accolades were more important to the son than they had been to the father. What made Francisco the new president was neither his training nor experience nor intelligence but power. Force determined his attainment of absolute political and military power. He controlled the army, and the army monitored Congress. This body, like legislatures in other Spanish American states in the 1800s, lent an air of modernity to his decrees. Congress had no regularly scheduled meetings and was not elected by the public. The president selected the legislators.

The executive controlled all of the votes. Even the representatives' speeches were written by López or a López speechwriter, of whom Francisco employed several during his presidency, including Natalicio Talavera, Juan Crisóstomo Centurión, and Fidel Maíz. They carried out his every wish and put his whims into words. Still he himself edited their copy. He trusted no one.

In 1862 and 1863, it became clear that any tendency toward integrity or independence could be fatal. In Congress, Deputy Florencio Varela issued a lonely voice of protest over the nepotism of the succession, citing a decree of Carlos Antonio's. Francisco sent him to jail. Then and later a few dissident voices whispered that Benigno might have been a better president than Francisco; what this really expressed was fear. Benigno had neither aptitude nor inclination for government. He had none of the training for office that Carlos Antonio provided Francisco. He was simply less feared.

When Father Fidel Maíz, head of the Seminario Conciliar, whispered to an acolyte in the imagined privacy of his rectory that Benigno might have been the better choice, the López spy system, which reached into the priest's quarters, reported Maíz's offense to the president. López sent him to prison, where he endured suffering and torment. Father Maíz later remembered a good relationship with the pre-presidential Francisco López. That earlier relationship was such that even after López took formal power, the new president chose Maíz, Paraguay's most learned and distinguished cleric, to officiate at his father's funeral. The priest's downfall was but two months away.[12] Francisco López approved Maíz as rector of the seminary, a good post but less grand than what a man of his gifts deserved. There were also other objections. Earlier Madame Lynch had asked Maíz to baptize one of her and Francisco's children, and Maíz agreed, although conditionally. In the eyes of the church, all were illegitimate. The priest insisted that he perform the baptism in the cathedral, while the baby's parents wanted the ceremony held in Lynch's home to avoid gossip about their irregular, and, according to Catholic doctrine, sinful, relationship. Thus, Francisco turned to Presbyter Manuel Antonio Palacios to perform the sacrament. Palacios was an intimate of López whose sycophancy was boundless. His deficiencies in Christian understanding can be understood by one example: He said, "Noah had only two sons, Cain and Abel."[13] Not gifted but ambitious, he dutifully performed the ceremony at home. This favor and Palacios's continuing toadying to Francisco would help elevate him to head the bishopric, with Francisco's backing, denying any promotions of the more meritorious Maíz, then in agony in prison.

The spy system grew from colonial inquisitorial procedures, and Francia had increased its efficiency.[14] As Francisco established his personal power, Maíz feared the new president's arbitrary exercise of it. The priest knew Francisco well and perceived that he lacked a sense of proportion. He had reached a position of power as a teenager, brigadier general at eighteen and head of the Ministry of War and the navy before he was thirty. Maíz had wished, he later reflected, for a separation of powers among the executive, legislative, and judicial branches of government. If true, he must have known that such a system was impossible in Paraguay in 1862. When he uttered careless words in private, a young cleric-spy reported them to the president. López ordered Maíz removed as rector, handcuffed, and imprisoned incommunicado and in solitary confinement. Insisting on a facade of legality, the new president arranged for Maíz to be tried in a kangaroo court. He appointed Father Palacios to preside over the trial of a rival of whose talent he was jealous. López always made a show of legality when torturing and executing. In fact, the law was merely what Francisco and his father before him had said it was. Father Fidel Maíz was accused and convicted (the two being one and the same thing) of being a secret Protestant, a ridiculous notion. The show trial also sentenced him to excommunication for possessing works by such dangerous authors as Voltaire, Rousseau, and Victor Hugo.[15] That the priest survived and was released after four years was only the result of a lucky break. Because of his erudition, Francisco needed him. Maíz had sensed in late 1862 that Francisco, whom he had known most of his life, was a menace to the nation. López kept him confined but alive, in case he needed his intellect and erudition. Maíz's suffering would break him to Francisco's will. Maíz would later return the favor to Bishop Palacios; he would officiate at his trial and execution (see chapter 5). He later recalled that someone close to the Marshal-President had warned him of the bishop's jealousy, but the priest needed no such advice.[16]

Francisco's puppet priest, a sycophantic dunce, became bishop in 1865 with Francisco's backing. He carried out López's insistence that priests violate the sanctity of the confessional. He made them report any rumors of subversion revealed during the sacrament. López sent a number of priests to prison. Since López believed torture an efficacious way to root out conspiracies and conspirators, the president and his bishop-servant employed brutal measures.[17]

Members of Congress knew that Francisco controlled the only power base in the country, the army. Francisco was on good terms with the rank and file, who knew their place but liked his bantering with them. This typical male banter was formulaic; it conveyed no sense that he had any interest in their thoughts, except insofar as they mirrored his own. He had also rewarded key officers who had demonstrated their loyalty to him with their posts during the seventeen years during which Carlos Antonio had groomed Francisco to take his place. The first López was thus the only Spanish American *caudillo* of the nineteenth century who was able to impose a second generation on his nation.[18] Francisco was the only caudillo to inherit his position.

Holding on to the presidency was as important as formal appointment, but López had been preparing for the succession for years. Men loyal to him held all key posts. López picked only loyalists for the Congress of 1862, the twelfth such meeting since independence. On October 16, 1862, one month after his father's death, the puppet members named him president for ten years. This ritual added an appearance of legality and modernity to a process that was in fact one of brutal force. He insisted on the public subordination and enthusiastic veneration of him. When he called Paraguayans a free people, he meant that they were free to respect him and free to display ostentatiously their subordination to him, or else suffer serious consequences. He also meant that they were not ruled by non-Paraguayans, which they could appreciate.

The new president was thirty-six years old. Generally healthy, he was gaining weight. He exercised a little, enjoying dancing and horseback riding and occasionally fencing, although little of an aerobic nature. He seldom walked more than a couple of hundred paces. He was routinely religious but less intense about his devotions than he would later become. He drank much wine at meals and brandy afterward, but those around him did not consider him drunk at that time.

Like his father and other Spanish American caudillos, López believed that he embodied the will of the people. He could intuit their will without consulting them. He told them, "your representatives" had elevated him to the "supreme majesty of the republic." In this capacity, his first duty was to maintain "order, justice, and morality." In Francisco's mind, justice and morality depended on order. He counseled them to obey his decisions. Commanding the army for so long, he thought of himself as a military man, posing as one elevated to the presidency from army ranks. Paraguayans were supposed to see his own conduct as an example, especially his obedience to and respect for his father. He expected his subordination and obedience to Carlos Antonio subsequently to be rendered to him by all others. He demanded their support,[19] and they responded.

López was skilled in the mechanics of government. Although his formal education was scattershot, he had read widely. He loved history. "He was . . . apt to learn, of quick perceptions, and . . . had naturally an excellent memory."[20] His reading, however, never caused him to grow intellectually or morally or to see the world from perspectives other than his own. One author asserts that López read the military theoretician Antoine Henri Jomini.[21] If so, he never grasped Jomini's main point, which was the importance of keeping an army concentrated. López was surrounded by sycophants. He found their praise of him justified. His father had not been so deceived. Francisco's private persona was more measured than his boastful public pronouncements. As a judge of other men, he was at best average; he could, however, discern creativity in others. This faculty enabled him to exclude men of talent from his government and military. They were potential threats. He knew that his people were patriotic and obedient. López grew irate when someone disobeyed his order, and he was normally unforgiving. His personality was authoritarian. Thus, he persecuted those who were less than enthusiastic about his presidency, like Father Maíz, who spent years in prison, and Deputy Varela, who died there.

MILITARY GROWTH, INCREASING PARANOIA

At the outset of his presidency, Francisco confined his brother Benigno, a potential rival, to internal exile, essentially house arrest, on his rural estate. The president worried that his brother was more popular than he. He was certainly less feared. Benigno's handful of supporters thought him less competent but less dangerous. Benigno, as the baby of the family, was spoiled by his parents, even more than Francisco. As his elder brother demanded respect from his siblings and others, he also craved the respect of the outside world. He yearned for the esteem of European leaders and sought honors from the leaders of neighboring countries, which were seldom forthcoming. When he encountered disrespect toward him or his nation, he acted impulsively.[22] The Brazilian and Argentine leaders' disdain was provocative.

Following his inauguration, López held a splendid gala at the National Club to congratulate himself. He appeared in a flashy blue and red military uniform tailored in France. He impressed nationals by such ostentation, as Latin American caudillos commonly did; but foreigners saw the uniforms modeled on those of French generals as gauche, in the way that peninsular Spaniards looked down on creoles, white Spaniards born in America. He displayed his medals, many of which he had awarded himself, in the same fashion. Francisco would publicize Napoleon III's congratulatory letter to him upon his becoming president. The note from France, however, was formal and formulaic, indicating no personal relationship between the emperor and the new dictator. It was certainly written by Louis Napoleon's clerks in response to Francisco's informing them of his promotion. Francisco penned announcements to the heads of all the major world powers and other Latin American countries. Proclaiming one's honor was essential to the honor culture.

Francisco quickly organized his government, filling posts with men of modest ability without personal ambitions, men who could not threaten him. The new vice president was a loyal family retainer, Francisco Sánchez, then sixty-seven, also minister of the interior, who did much of the heavy lifting of government when Francisco went to the front. As foreign minister, he chose the reasonably able and subservient José Berges. Ironically, in downtown Asunción today, streets named for López and Berges, whom he later executed, run parallel. As the titular head of the war ministry, Francisco appointed his sickly brother Venancio. The president intended to make all decisions about military policy and strategy personally. Francisco would replace his first treasury minister with a López in-law, continuing his father's approach. The second President López also created two new national holidays, July 24, his birthday, and October 16, the day he became president.[23] To dance and sing and praise the president on these days was mandatory for all. Public parties were ordered for every town. Francisco usually supplied the food and drink.

In 1862, the nation was at peace. It was becoming prosperous. Since independence, the internal peace was unique in the troubled Plata region. Although Paraguay had experienced limited industrial growth, seen for example in the arsenal, the shipyard, and the ironworks at Ybicuí,[24] the new markets for agricultural and pastoral pursuits brought the government enough revenues to finance military and military-related development. The new president allocated most government revenues to his military, the arsenal, and such enterprises as the railroad. Tracks would run from the capital to the new encampment that López founded at Cerro León and past Lynch's country house. Of course, he also spent government revenues on his own creature comforts.

López's work schedule was intense. He was tireless and attentive to detail, and he involved himself in every aspect of the government. His lack of sound judgment could override his basic intelligence because he was impetuous. His emotional reactions to troublesome situations often overcame the rational part of his nature. His best technocrat, William Whytehead, for example, created a row with Venancio in mid-1863, when he had slighted Venancio's mechanical expertise. The charge was true. Whytehead was a first-rate engineer and an expert in technical matters. Venancio was not. But Francisco decided that the chief engineer of the state had insulted his family's honor. Francisco stopped consulting Whytehead,[25] whose resulting emotional decline was compounded when he was crossed off Lynch's guest list. He ended his disgrace by suicide in 1865.

One example of López's industriousness-to-a-fault is the attention he paid to the young Paraguayan men studying in Europe on government fellowships. From his desk in Asunción, Francisco tried to micromanage their studies. In the same way, he took time to read carefully and criticize competently the work of Alfred du Graty, *La Republique du Paraguay*, published in Europe and commissioned by Carlos Antonio. Francisco was upset by du Graty's mistaken usage of Guarani, Francisco's first language, which he had spoken at home since childhood and with his mother, with servants, and officers and soldiers all his life. As a result, he decided that only a Paraguayan could write a Guarani grammar.[26]

1864: Uruguayan–Brazilian Dynamics and Perceived Insults

Francisco increased his army strength. Its size would have eventually beggared the country even without the war of the 1860s, a case of over-mobilization. He perfunctorily took the measure of his neighbors and found them hostile. They were not friends, but nations do not have friends, at best only allies. Argentina and Brazil claimed territory that López thought Paraguayan. He believed Brazil to be his principal threat. His judgment was more right than wrong, because Brazil would supply most of the allied troops in the great war of the 1860s. The Brazilians, however, were making no plans for offensive war against him; but President López assumed that they were, accepting rumors that fitted his pre-conceptions.[27] The Brazilian emperor Pedro II ". . . was certainly a man of peace, not favoring an expansionist policy."[28] Like López, however, he thought that he and Brazil were the same and that his honor and that of his country were interchangeable. One noted historian said that López was not so much worried about Argentina and Brazil expanding into Paraguay as he was that the two would block his own expansion. The diplomatic conflict was "a sounding board for the voice of Francisco Solano López."[29] Nineteenth-century Brazil kept expanding, although customarily avoiding military force. The imperial government did see Uruguay, its little neighbor to the south, as an irritant. Francisco objected to Brazil's involvement in Uruguayan politics, asserting it would set a precedent that Brazil could use against him. The politics of the two small Platine nations, which shared no common border, were different, though—notably in their relations with the Brazilian Empire. In Uruguay, Brazil was determined to influence events. Its stake there was connected to its own stability, exemplifying the adage that all politics is essentially local. Brazil had sent troops into Uruguay, the Banda Oriental, several times since independence because that eastern republic's chronic unrest was an irritant to imperial stability. There was colonial precedent. Brazilian interference in the region was manifest as early as 1680.

López reopened negotiations with Brazil. He wished to settle two crucial issues: river navigation and the border question. The disputed region north of the Río Apa was important to him. In addition, he saw a third problem: Brazil's failure to respect his warnings to cease intervening in Uruguay. On a personal level, this neglect irked him the most, and he found it increasingly meaningful in the coming months. In the same way, he took unofficial Brazilian movement into the disputed region of Apa-Blanco personally. His father had been right. A diplomatic settlement offered more hope than a military one but no opportunity for glory.

López also felt that Argentina was defying him by its periodic involvement in Uruguay. Before Uruguay's independence in 1828, the United Provinces of the Río de la Plata (the future Argentina) and the Brazilian Empire fought for control of the Banda Oriental. Despite the settlement, both intervened militarily in the buffer state in the coming decades. After the *Tacuarí*-Canstatt affair in 1859, the president-in-waiting also grew hostile to the British government, whose protection of Canstatt he found insulting, which it was. Britain's seizure of his prized *Tacuarí* and withdrawal of its representative from Asunción infuriated him. He lectured the British on international law, about which he cared little; but on this occasion he was correct. The British government had acted extralegally if not illegally to settle a human rights issue.

In Uruguay, Argentine President Bartolomé Mitre covertly supported his ally Uruguayan Colorado leader Venancio Flores's filibustering expedition, which began in April 1863. Brazil also supported Flores, because the then Uruguayan President Bernardo Berro was at odds with the Brazilian settlers who dominated the northern third of the country. Brazil's long tradition of involvement in the Banda Oriental included two interventions in the 1850s. Argentine dictator Rosas had conducted a lengthy siege of Montevideo, the Uruguayan capital, where his exiled opponents conspired against him. Brazil had helped Flores become president of Uruguay in 1855, although he was unable to hold onto the office. Flores's political leanings were ostensibly liberal, although ideology was irrelevant to the conflict.

In 1864, López commanded the largest army in the Plata region. He knew that he was strong, at least for the moment. He warned Argentina to remain neutral in the Banda Oriental. He expected other Platine leaders to heed his directives. Personally, he had seldom encountered any other response besides subordination. He became choleric when he observed foreigners behave disrespectfully to him and his country, a rudeness that never happened to a López in Paraguay. The largest standing army in the region stood behind his threats. He wished to change Paraguay from a poor, weak nation to an influential one. Then his voice would count more in South America. He thought that he could achieve this by force or the threat of force. López referred to the government in the abstract, *el gobierno*, as if it were something apart from him; but in fact he meant himself. The government *was* Francisco López. As he worked to achieve a border settlement with Argentina, he insisted that the Argentine representatives meet with him in Asunción, not in the Argentine capital. He argued that Asunción was closer to the disputed borders than Buenos

Aires.[30] The Argentine rationale for Buenos Aires, proximity to documents, was similarly flimsy.[31]

In fact, though, Buenos Aires was unsuitable for the reason that if López left Paraguay, he would have to place political and military authority in another's hands. If he sent diplomatic representatives to Argentina, he must delegate authority, giving them power to make decisions, a power that he refused to share. No underling would negotiate for him unless, like Berges, he could be counted on to follow López's orders to the letter. His letters to President Mitre written at this time are respectful. They contain none of the boastfulness of his newspaper editorial-articles or speeches. His self-involvement, though, is clear in both kinds of documents.

López spread his spies (*piragüés*) through the capital and around military centers. It remained a two-tiered system, with formal and informal components. As in the Buenos Aires of Juan Manuel de Rosas, servants in Asunción homes reported on the opinions of their patrons. As the months passed, López governed in an increasingly erratic manner. Like his father, the younger President López scorned the liberalism preached, and less often practiced, by the leaders of Buenos Aires. The greater freedom of the press in Buenos Aires, however, offended him. Newspapers there sullied his honor and enraged him. He saw dissent as anarchy, not a manifestation of a healthy society.[32] He never comprehended why the Argentine government did not stop its newspapers from printing stories offensive to him. Even after he sent his armies into Argentina, he demanded that Argentines halt public expressions dishonoring him and his country. His inability to grasp the motivations of others remained a failing until the end of his life.

In 1863, López wrote Mitre insisting that the interests of Paraguay and Argentina were similar. To settle their disputed boundaries must involve some sacrifice by each. He was willing, he said, to appoint a plenipotentiary to Argentina if Mitre would reciprocate.[33] On this question, as on all other important ones, Francisco nonetheless could not delegate authority. He was unwilling to reduce his personal authority by a smidgen. Mitre had named Valentín Alsina, a liberal (*septembrista*) politician who spoke for the interests of Buenos Aires, as the Argentine plenipotentiary, and López had no quarrel with the man, only with his choice of location. Alsina refused to go to Paraguay, undoubtedly at Mitre's urging. López argued that only a handful of Paraguayans were capable of carrying on such delicate negotiations. He wanted all of them in Asunción where he could direct them. On the other hand, the president said, Mitre had in his employ many able men other than Alsina.[34] In retrospect, it is difficult to see how López missed the implication that his contention was uncomfortably close to the criticisms of Paraguay circulating in the port city. Mitre and López finally met again in 1866, but the issue was very different.

In 1864, López pretended that Paraguayan–Argentine relations were amicable, suppressing his anger over Mitre's support for Flores in Uruguay. Argentina's fortification of the island of Martín García, resulting in its military domination of the Paraná delta, threatened López. In Uruguay, whose cause he made his own, or at least that of its Blanco government, he maintained that the Argentine action was "humiliation."[35] The humiliation that most disturbed him was his own and not Uruguay's. At times, López expressed fears of Argentine annexation of Uruguay,[36] unlikely in view of the British guarantee of Uruguayan independence. López cited the rights of small nations under international law, which he insisted protected Uruguay.

Although concerned about Argentina, López worried more about the Brazilian diplomatic mission then in Montevideo. He denounced imperial hostility to the Blanco government and Brazil's intent to control the Uruguayan–Brazilian border. He called the empire's policies "immoral."[37] The Uruguayan Blancos, the faction in power in the early 1860s, could resist neither of its larger neighbors effectively. In desperation, they turned to López for support. Brazil felt responsibility for the welfare of Brazilian residents of northern Uruguay and worried about the resumption of regional unrest in its southern province of Rio Grande do Sul. The Uruguayan government could not even subdue the Argentine-backed Uruguayan exiles then fighting under Flores. Thus, the reed at which they clutched was López and his militarized republic. Concurrently López was demanding that he and his nation be accorded a weightier role in regional affairs. He insisted that his goal was to maintain a balance of power, or "equilibrium" as he called it. That no enduring regional equilibrium was ever truly established proved no barrier to his declaration that one existed. Balance of power was his issue. Establishing the principle, he thought, could give him the stature that he craved and a role more consequential than Paraguay's small population warranted. The government in Montevideo knew of López's large army. Its emissaries hoped to drive a wedge between Argentina and Paraguay. This might not be difficult, given the porteños' long-standing scorn for the López family. What the Uruguayans really wanted was not an empty proclamation from López. They did not care about international law. They wanted his armed intervention. They wanted his powerful army not for national but for partisan advantage.[38]

In that fateful year of 1864, the Uruguayan government, hoping to relieve the pressure from Brazil, begged López to intervene on its behalf. Francisco ordered his foreign minister, José Berges, to inform the Brazilians that Uruguay had requested his mediation and that he had agreed. A distinguished British historian of an earlier generation said, "Berges did not seem to realize that mediators are not appointed by one of the two contending parties but by two."[39] It seems more likely, however, that the problem was not one of López's ignorance, as Horton Box alleged, but Foreign Minister Berges's need to obey his president. Berges's message expressed López's aggressive position. The president was angry that Brazil ignored his mediation proposal. The slight was a personal offense to López.

Posturing was essential to Francisco López's governing style. He took his poses seriously and expected others to do so as well. While foreigners paid little attention, Paraguayans had no choice but to comply with his wishes. Every year of his presidency, he ordered the whole nation to celebrate his birthday. He insisted that celebrants commemorate the occasion exactly as the government, that is, as he himself wished. He directed the national holidays that he dedicated to himself, although he maintained that the fiestas were voluntary demonstrations. He insisted they play the parts that he had written for them. In September 1864, for example, he addressed the ladies of Asunción, whose "spontaneous" expressions of support were usually led by his sisters. He told the women how happy he was that they had honored him on his birthday of July 24, which in fact he had made a national obligation. He praised the bravery of the females, and he lauded their faith in him and their patriotism.[40] He cared little about what anyone else thought. He told them what to think. Since so few Paraguayan women were literate, we have little documentary evidence of their feelings at the time.[41] That Francisco's words were heeded by most is born out by the fact that one of his own brothers refused to comment on public affairs until the official position on an issue appeared in *Semanario*, Francisco's personal pulpit.

In September 1864, he learned that the Brazilian government had ignored his warning to revise their Uruguayan policy. He orchestrated a demonstration of "popular" support for his policy in downtown Asunción. He had people repeat his pretense that this gathering was spontaneous, sincere, and eloquent. He insisted that Paraguay—meaning himself—could not tolerate Brazilian disrespect. He hoped that the empire would moderate its offensive policies. He warned that "my voice will not go unheard. . . ." He advised, prophetically it turned out, that "the triumph of the nation's cause" might force great sacrifice on its children.[42] He then concluded that the nation's cause was holy. God was on the side of Francisco López. He declared that Brazilian intervention in Uruguay was serious enough to interrupt the prolonged peace his people enjoyed, although such interventions had occurred in the 1850s without any impact on Paraguay. He was publicly irate about the foreigners' view of Paraguayans as barbarians. He concluded that it was time to show the world Paraguayans' worth. He would act like Napoleon. Paraguayans must seize what their military power and their nation's progress entitled

them to.[43] Victories on the battlefield would demonstrate that Paraguay—
and he—had joined the ranks of civilized nations.

Brazil as Enemy

Toward the end of 1864—which was springtime in Paraguay and autumn
in the northern hemisphere—López again asked Justo José de Urquiza to
use his influence on Paraguay's behalf. For six months, he misread the patriotism of the former Argentine president. Urquiza was earlier an enemy
of Mitre and still no friend of his. López's lack of insight into Urquiza's
outlook, however, made him ill equipped to understand Urquiza's position. As López readied his forces to attack Brazil, he wrote to Urquiza that
he, López, who boasted of his contribution to Argentine political stability,
would break apart his neighbor to the south. He hoped that Governor
Urquiza would lead Entre Ríos to break with Buenos Aires and bring Corrientes along. Urquiza should reform a nation from the other Argentine
provinces, excluding the port city and its province.[44]

Despite his professions of support for the Uruguayan Blancos, López
refused to help them materially. The Argentine-backed Flores force was
poised to take power. López refused to subsidize the Blancos. That would
bring no glory, no honor. He refused their request for four thousand
Paraguayan soldiers. Such an expedition would fail, López knew. He
would need twenty steamships to transport such a force, and he could not
gather sufficient vessels. Furthermore, no relief effort could pass the Ar-
gentine-held island of Martín García. Nor could it match the ocean-prac-
ticed navy of Brazil. To López, Brazil was now "the enemy."[45]

As he decided such issues as war and peace, he fretted about trivial
matters, including his yerba shipment to Prussia. He admired that state
because of the gentlemanly character of its Hohenzollern monarchy, by
definition honorable. Unsuccessful with Prussia, he decided to send yerba
to the French army in Algeria,[46] where not coincidentally, Madame Lynch
had lived.

Francisco López's navy was small, but his offensives of late 1864 and
early 1865 would bring him new ships, the Brazilian *Marquês de Olinda*
and *Anhambay* and two Argentine vessels.[47] He had also acquired foreign-
built craft, including the *Pulaski*, *Cavour*, and *Ranger*. They strengthened
his naval arm, possibly adding to a false sense of security. While larger
than before, the Paraguayan fleet was never strong enough to meet the
Brazilian navy on anything like equal terms. Moreover, the Brazilians
could acquire new vessels as needed. López never could.[48]

López, angered by Brazilian interference in Uruguayan affairs, was
ready to act in the spring of 1864. His concerns were not new. His correspondence of the 1850s reveals an aggressive posture toward Brazil. Many

Paraguayan biographers assert that he wanted peace. He had, however, enlarged his army past any size necessary for peacetime. Since May 1864, he had tried to obtain arms from Europe. With an army already large for a nation of 450,000 people—close to one-fifth of the population—he redoubled his mobilization effort.

In October 1864, he exploded at the Brazilian rejection of his diplomatic initiatives, especially his mediation offer. The Brazilian envoy to Uruguay, José Antonio Saraiva, had in August told the Blancos they must succumb. The Brazilian rebuff offended López's honor, but Brazil had no interest in Paraguayan mediation. Its representatives would not renounce imperial objectives in Uruguay, which they saw as necessary to the tranquility of Rio Grande do Sul. The Uruguayan Blancos in July 1864 had renewed their efforts to obtain Paraguayan help. The feud with Flores and the looming conflict with Brazil were intertwined. The Blancos had argued that the danger to the Uruguayan government was identical to the threat facing Paraguay. The claim was a stretch, but López accepted its logic.[49]

In fact, the situations were quite different. Nineteenth-century Brazil was expansionist, but it did not have to contend with a large group of influential and troublesome subjects living in Paraguay, as it did in Uruguay. It had no unruly province on the Paraguayan border, as it did in Rio Grande do Sul. The Farrapo rebellion—a separatist effort of ranchers from Rio Grande do Sul that festered in the 1830s and 1840s—was recalled by Brazilian policymakers, who considered the Blanco policy a stimulant to unrest in Rio Grande do Sul. In the 1860s, the Brazilian government was more stable and stronger than two or three decades earlier. Unfortunately, "López's perception of his nation's neighbors . . . lagged several decades behind a swiftly advancing reality."[50]

López's logistical efforts were also out of tune with his temperament. His hero Napoleon had observed that an army traveled on its stomach, emphasizing the importance of logistics, one of the many sound Napoleonic principles that Francisco ignored. In August 1864, Francisco had urged his agent in Buenos Aires, Egusquiza, to allocate 2,000 pounds to buy modern rifles. The Paraguayan leader had made insufficient effort over the previous decade to obtain standardized weapons, a terrible oversight. Acquiring enough rifles or rifle muskets would have been easy if Francisco had started standardizing several years earlier. With better planning, it might have been possible. Now it was not.

On August 4, 1864, the Brazilians insisted that Uruguayans meet their demands. When the news reached Asunción, López's response was the fateful ultimatum of August 30. He denounced Brazil for rejecting his mediation. Through Foreign Minister Berges, who took no action without the president's approval, López insisted that Paraguay would not permit Brazilian forces to occupy any part of Uruguay, not even temporarily, although it had done so in the past and his own father had paid little heed. The realities of Platine geography meant that he was powerless to prevent it. Brazilian forces in Uruguay would upset his "equilibrium of the Plata," the balance of power that López had convinced himself was necessary to the security of his nation. Unlike Francia and his own father, the young president made a connection between the fortunes of Uruguay and Paraguay, a link "that better minds had previously (and have since) failed to discern."[51]

Brazilian leaders viewed López's intrusion as insolent. Desiring an expeditious settlement to their Uruguayan problem, they sent in their forces, because delay would disserve the many Brazilians in Uruguay. With no Uruguayan–Paraguayan border and with the Argentines in control of the river approaches, the Brazilians knew, it would be somewhere between difficult and impossible for López to aid the Uruguayans. López was pushing Argentina and Brazil, suspicious of each other well into the nineteenth century, into the same camp and eventually a military alliance.[52]

In 1864, López was increasingly bitter about the unflattering characterizations of him in the porteño press. That he felt dishonored was what the writers intended; he let them get his goat. His offer to mediate the Uruguayan problem was "treated with contempt and ridicule by the Argentine newspapers," whose journalists thought Francisco López "a brutal tyrant, and his people . . . ignorant and submissive savages."[53] He frantically sought more arms, shoulder weapons, and artillery. He had never standardized of his weapons, partly because Paraguay bought what was available. That he had purchased arms of many types and calibers would make more difficult the problems facing his forces. But he was emotionally ready for war.

On the Eve of Battle

The *casus belli* for Francisco S. López was Brazil's invasion of Uruguay on September 14, 1864. Brazil's disrespect was manifest. López concluded that a war would bring him prestige and honor if only his forces could acquit themselves with courage and dash. He likely had no intention of fighting a protracted war.

As President López prepared to fight the Empire of Brazil, he continued to appeal to the old caudillo of Entre Ríos to join him. López, who had run a personalistic government in Paraguay, now played on Urquiza's personal feelings, which he misread, and to his thwarted ambition. He recalled the rivalry between Urquiza and Mitre, president of a new Argentina, different from what he had seen in 1859. It was a state well along in the process of formation. For Urquiza to ally with López against Mitre would destroy his major accomplishment, the unification of Argentina. Francisco thought that the feelings of affection and ritual kinship of his compadre Urquiza for him would be persuasive. In truth, López had failed to cultivate the garden of friendship with Urquiza. He had not helped the relationship when he declined Urquiza's invitation to attend the baptism of 1859. In any event, national interest would have trumped a personal friendship even if Francisco had known how to be a friend. Events demonstrated that Urquiza's Argentine patriotism overrode his rivalry with Mitre.

Urquiza sent an emissary to ask López to respect Argentine neutrality. López had no wish to hear advice contrary to his instincts. López's enmity toward both Mitre and Brazilians by 1864 was already great; he imagined already consummated the Argentine–Brazilian military alliance that the Paraguayan dictator's attacks would soon bring about.[54]

On September 14, 1864, Brazil sent twelve thousand men into Uruguay, triggering a wrathful response from López. Brazil's disrespect had dishonored him. His sense of personal and national honor was gigantic, and his goal—international acclaim for himself through his country—must be decided in battle.

Francisco severed diplomatic relations with Brazil. In November 1864, he initiated hostilities. First, he sent warships up the Río Paraguay to seize the Brazilian *Marquês de Olinda*. The ship was anchored at Asunción and contained cargo, including weapons, passengers, and the governor-designate of the Mato Grosso. Francisco debated with himself for hours about which course to take before he ordered the vessel seized.

López wrote to his subordinates in measured tones. His letters do not show the braggart or the man out of touch with international reality that one finds in his public pronouncements. Neither his public nor his private voices revealed exclusive insights about the man. They displayed different aspects of a complex character. By December 1864, he was plunging ahead with war against Brazil. Apparently, he intended a short war to force Brazil and the world to respect him through the actions of his loyal, patriotic, and honorable followers. He might have concluded that the blood of his brave soldiers and sailors would wash away the stain of the Brazilian rebuff. He thought so in 1864: A short, successful war could elevate him to heights greater than the small size and relative poverty of his landlocked country had consigned him.[55]

López had no immediate intention of attacking Argentina, but he had little experience with those who defied him. His privileged background had given him no opportunity to develop interpersonal skills necessary for understanding those who ignored his wishes. Because his father alone among nineteenth-century caudillos was able to choose his son as his successor, we have few good comparisons. López was unable to fathom the leadership of Brazil or Argentina. Thus, the Uruguayan representatives who visited Asunción in 1864 could trifle in the fault lines of his character. They pushed him toward a military action that he had long contemplated, although he neither saved the Blanco government of Uruguay nor dispatched the troops they requested. Uruguayan entreaties possibly helped distance him from geopolitical reality, namely that Brazil was almost twenty times the size of Paraguay in population and wealth. Even more crucial, it had access to European sources of military hardware. It possessed superior warships that his nation did not.

By this time, the industrial revolution had truly revolutionized warfare. López could tongue lash, could frighten, could exhort his people into a war effort whose totality was then hardly imaginable; but he could neither outproduce Brazil nor duplicate its access to foreign markets. Neither did he grasp the likelihood that an attack on Brazil would offend Pedro II's sense of honor. "Pedro II was extremely protective of the country's honor, which he equated with his own."[56] The Brazilian emperor was a royal personage. His family had sat on the Portuguese throne since the 1600s. His commitment to the honor complex was equal to the Paraguayan dictator's, and the resources at his command were vastly greater.

1865: Misunderstandings and Botched Plans

For the past decade, López had spent most of his working hours as war minister and army commander, both under his father and for the first two years of his presidency. As he militarized his nation, he put more men into service than the country's economic structure could tolerate, inevitably leading to overmobilization. If his enemy's will did not slacken promptly, the strained economy would eventually collapse.

López's logistical preparations were extensive but erratic, his war plans incomplete. Although "dedicated to the task of military procurement,"[57] he lacked a comprehensive design for outfitting the Paraguayan army. By the standards of the day, he had failed to build a modern army, although it became a suicidally effective one on its own soil. As the size of his army swelled toward 20 percent of his nation, officer quality declined. Poorly trained officers could not train men adequately. Woeful was López's military aptitude, though he thought otherwise. He never understood his idol the Corsican's insight that the objective of war should be the destruction of the enemy's army and his will to fight. Francisco failed utterly to perceive that Emperor Pedro II would see an attack by a gnat-like neighbor as an affront to his own and his nation's honor. Unfortunately. the emperor's disdain for the Paraguayan dictator intensified his determination to respond decisively.

Misunderstandings abounded. In late 1864, Paraguayan agents in Montevideo and Buenos Aires, Juan José Brizuela and Felix Egusquiza, failed to make clear to President López the meaning of developments in the south. They were not especially competent diplomats, for López seldom employed superior people. These men knew, like all civil and military officials, that it could be dangerous to report unpleasant facts to López.

Mitre in Argentina and Pedro II in Brazil also miscalculated. Like the emperor, Mitre thought little of López and of Paraguayans. He had no inkling of how intrepidly they would fight for their country. Mitre hoped that they would rebel against their tyrant, a grave miscalculation that ignored Paraguayan nationalism and the potential ferocity of the Paraguayan people. If they failed to love López, they nevertheless thought him the symbol of their nationality. All the major players miscalculated, most significantly López, who thought that an Argentina at war would split apart. Like Mitre he failed to grasp that the citizens of his enemy's country were also patriots.

Francisco López conscripted so many young men that he weakened the economic fabric of the country, which would become crucial in a year or so. He transported many recruits to Cerro León, his military base to the west of Asunción. He based training methods of the Paraguayan army partly on those of the French army, whose manuals he had studied. One observer noted that nevertheless his army remained heavily influenced by its Spanish heritage, a natural condition after three centuries of Spanish rule. The young president himself decided which parts of French practice he would retain and which to disregard. Seemingly, he failed to ensure that his forces were trained in the art of orderly retreat,[58] which would discredit the marshal president, at least in his own eyes. He did not recognize that retreat is a maneuver essential to military success. Thus in the offensive phase of the war, troops under Major Pedro Duarte were inadequately schooled in minor tactics. Their inability to retreat ably or to maneuver effectively helped the enemy wipe them out at the Battle of Yatay, in August 1865.

The population totaled less than one-half million as López took his nation to war,[59] although the dictator thought it was closer to one million. His order of conscription of January 1864 had swelled the army. The figures are in dispute, but there might have been 30,000 troops on active duty at that time and another 14,000 in the ready reserve. By early 1865, the Paraguayan army, according to one British officer serving in it, numbered about 80,000,[60] a figure that is probably too high. The combined forces of Brazil and Argentina did not approach this number.[61] Owing to the dictator's impetuosity and careless logistics, the Paraguayan army had a motley assortment of weapons. The artillery was a mixture of styles and calibers. Shoulder weapons included outdated flintlock muskets— smooth bore weapons whose effective range was but a fraction of that of the rifle musket introduced in the U.S. Army in 1855. Some of his artillery dated from the 1600s. López had purchased a few modern rifles, but he had equipped only three of the forty Paraguayan battalions with them by the time he went to war. He rushed to find another ten thousand modern rifles in Europe. His impatience, which caused him to plunge into hostilities in 1864, overcame his knowledge that he needed better weapons.[62]

One can deduce López's lack of faith in his officers' fighting ability from the fact that he refused to let them take initiative. He opposed their creativity. He correctly assessed their mediocre quality. Because he refused to appoint able men, Paraguayan officers were as ill prepared for combat leadership as their leader was for devising strategy. The Argentines were little better, even though many had had battle experience. Some Brazilian officers were formally schooled in the art of war. Through war service, Paraguayan officers would eventually learn the essentials of their craft. López, however, remained strategically deficient.

Like other Latin American forces, the Paraguayan army was not yet a professionalized organization. Paraguay had no military school, and a half-century of peace had left the soldiers devoid of experience. Nevertheless, on their own soil, they were disciplined, as the whole nation was disciplined, and they became fanatically devoted to the cause. They sought to defend their homes and families and their nation and culture from alien invaders, especially the hated Afro-Brazilian troops of the imperial army. Their discipline was made effective by corporal punishment.[63] Flight or desertion would mean summary execution.

The personal nature of the Paraguayan state under López meant that military-professional standardization and growth were impossible. Modern armies separate military management[64] from political decision-making. López would never allow this. He gloried in his control of all aspects of life, especially his cherished army. Some Latin American militaries became modernized in the late 1800s, hiring advisers from abroad, especially from Prussia. Officers and men in Argentina and Brazil had some combat experience. Those in Paraguay did not, which contributed to the disasters of the first war year.

The navy, of which López was also proud, was even more poorly prepared for the conflict than the army. Its seventeen small steamships were mostly designed as merchant vessels.[65] They were obsolescent, many being wooden side-wheelers, inadequate even for close in-river combat against the Brazilian fleet. Technological progress in naval affairs meant that Brazilians' ironclads with underwater screw propellers would eventually be supreme.

The Paraguayan dictator had begun seriously to contemplate attacking Brazil in mid-1864. The empire's outstanding diplomat, José María da Silva Paranhos, viscount Rio Branco, who dealt personally with López, concluded that the Paraguayan dictator made war on Brazil primarily for military fame and secondarily for influence in the Plata region.[66] López himself gave several reasons for deciding on war, but he never stated his long-range military objectives and never outlined a military strategy. He withheld his objective even from his generals. His national strategy, as distinct from his military strategy, was the glorification of Francisco S. López. He evidently hoped that a short war could bring honor to him and his country on the field of battle. There was no other way. But because the ability to empathize was alien to his character, he was unable to find the judgment necessary to predict the Brazilian and Argentine outrage that his unprovoked attacks aroused.

After he seized the Brazilian *Marquês de Olinda* in mid-August 1864, López sent its passengers to the interior to their eventual deaths. Although López started the war, he told his people, "Peace has been the standard that always has guided us." He found it sad that he had to abandon that standard; but he believed "peace is incompatible with our honor, with our dignity, and with our interests." Under the present circumstances, peace could only come at the price of national degradation.[67]

Many scholars have been at a loss to explain López's attack on the Mato Grosso. One historian thinks that López concluded that war with Brazil was inevitable and that the best opportunity presented itself to him in 1864,[68] when his army was strong and Brazil's weak. Another says that the president backed himself into a corner by proclaiming Uruguay's inviolability as crucial to Paraguayan interests. He thus had to act when Brazil moved into Uruguay. Responding with violence, ignoring his father's advice to deal with Brazil by diplomacy, he signed a death warrant.[69]

The dictator's words yield insights into his attack on Brazil. He had planned a Mato Grosso attack for some time. He had gathered military intelligence about the region. He sent detailed questionnaires to his officers and agents in the north. Their responses told him of the few strengths and many weaknesses of the Brazilian force there.[70] *Why* he decided to attack the region remains unclear. The northward advance did not strike at the empire's force in Uruguay, which López labeled the cause of his war declaration. The Mato Grosso attack did, however, offer him the opportunity for a prestigious victory over his huge neighbor, or so he thought.

To lead the main invasion force of three thousand foot soldiers and artillery, he appointed his brother-in-law, Colonel Vicente Barrios. The dictator instructed Barrios first to take the Brazilian fort at Nova Coimbra. López ordered another contingent under Colonel Isidoro Resquín to support the main effort.

At the Brazilian fort, the attackers were hindered by logistical ineptitude, not having thought to bring ladders to scale the walls. Barrios's soldiers greatly outnumbered the Brazilian defenders. The four hundred

Brazilians evacuated the post under the cover of darkness after a two-day siege. The Paraguayans then sailed upriver to occupy the towns of Albuquerque and Corumbá, "sacking, looting, and raping the few women . . . in the town,"[71] shedding little blood of their own. Resquín was victorious over a small Brazilian force that made a token resistance and fled. The invaders seized weapons, ammunition, and livestock from the Brazilian government and despoiled the property of Brazilian citizens. They occupied the Mato Grosso; it was of so little strategic value that the Brazilian government did not bother to reclaim the province for years. Although his victories were strategically empty, they let the dictator proclaim his own greatness. In them, he found glory.

HISTORICAL RELFECTIONS

On December 24, 1864, López explained why he had attacked Brazil. In the first place, he said, his efforts at peacemaking had proved "sterile." The Brazilians brought the war on themselves. It was their fault. They failed to understand Paraguayan honor and enthusiasm, which López incarnated. Paraguayans, he said, now fought for their "honor (*honra*), dignity, and conservation of our dearest rights." His troops in the Mato Grosso collected the first "laurel" of the war, he said, by their "discipline and subordination," virtues the dictator held in high regard for all except himself. He wanted his soldiers to know that they were heading ". . . toward the field of honor and glory." He urged them ". . . to show the entire world how much the Paraguayan soldier is worth."[72] Their sacrifices would demonstrate their leader's merit. In the process, however, he ignored the principle of mass and that of the objective.

López further developed his argument a month later. Again he insisted that the taking of the Mato Grosso was his response to Brazilian aggression in Uruguay. In making war, he said, he was making peace. He claimed that a "profound and lasting peace" would result. His first attacks showed him that "opposing Brazilian plans with decision and valor" was his sacred duty. He had his official newspaper, *Semanario*, congratulate his soldiers for their "will and subordination"—subordination to López, it was understood.[73]

Over time, the empire mobilized. Brazil ultimately "deployed some 110,000 men" against Paraguay, less than 2 percent of the Brazilian population. But in late 1864 and early 1865, the empire had not begun to realize its superior potential. Its inability to mobilize rapidly contributed to a protracted war.[74]

All the while, López worried about Argentina. He denounced the "militant policy" of the Mitre government. Persuading himself that the governor of Entre Ríos would soon reveal pro-Paraguayan sympathies, he complimented Urquiza for remaining neutral in the conflict with Brazil. He told Urquiza that he would likely be forced to cross troops over Argentine soil. Again, his lack of empathy led to faulty assessment of adversaries. He thought that the Argentine government would ignore his violation of their territorial integrity. He hoped that Argentina would not think his troops on Argentine soil was an act of war, because he did not want them to think it so. But they would. He wanted Argentines to believe that he respected the Mitre government, he said, although in fact he resented Mitre. López misread earlier letters from Urquiza, which were vague. Urquiza was his "compadre" and that was important, although not important enough as it turned out. López chose to see the former president as a truer spokesman for his nation than the current president. Somehow López concluded that Argentines would know that he was upholding "the principles of equity and justice."[75]

In one of his final letters to Urquiza, written in February 1865, López accused the governor of breaking his word. Most men would find this charge insulting, but López disregarded this possibility, adding that he would not hold the turnabout against him. He reasoned that Argentina's earlier preferential treatment of Brazil had destroyed its right to deny Paraguayan passage over its territory. In the case of Argentine opposition to his war plan, he said, "there is no honorable explanation." As he prepared to march into Argentina, he proclaimed his friendship. Black was really white. He felt wounded when his compadre Urquiza refused to join with him against Mitre. If Argentina resisted, he said, "I will bring to the fight the satisfaction of not having provoked it."[76] His logic is puzzling.

Home Life during the Campaign

The personal was political in López's Paraguay. His family matters were of state importance. As the war began, López brought Madame Lynch from the shadows of ill repute to the sunlight of prominent social functions. He compelled national and foreign elites to pay court to her. Until Francisco's presidency, Lynch was scorned by self-appointed guardians of public morality such as Mme. Cochelet, wife of the French consul, and Sra. Bermejo, married to a Spanish intellectual hired by Carlos Antonio López to run his newspaper and his educational system. Their disdain was public disrespect for the hard-drinking Irish beauty. They must have been envious of her quick rise to great wealth. After Francisco took power, the rumors that she had been a prostitute in France went deep underground. Lynch was the closest person to the only power center in the nation. During the war, she retaliated against her tormenters. Resourceful, she rubbed her detractors' noses in the dirt.[77]

By now Lynch lived in an Asunción mansion, part of which today forms the dining room of the Gran Hotel del Paraguay. She conspicuously displayed sumptuous household furnishings imported from Paris, like her dressmaker and her hair stylist. Throughout the war, she remained loyal to López, although at times she feared him, as did his own mother.[78] Lynch now addressed him as "very esteemed Don Pancho,"[79] not the more affectionate "My Pancho" greeting she used a decade before. When he went to the front, she went with him. Although she grew stouter after six children and the passage of time, rich food, and fine champagne, she remained attractive to the marshal. During the terrible years of conflict, she pursued her own self-interests. She became a war profiteer.

Francisco López had spent much time at Camp Cerro León, the northern hub of his army and near to the summer home of Madame Lynch. There in fact he often lived, although not officially. Prodded by Lynch, Francisco's interest in Paraguayan expansion grew. Lynch deferred to López and then gingerly manipulated him. Apothecary George Masterman, a frequent guest at her social gatherings, thought her an able liar, although neither he nor anyone else was an objective observer. He charged that she was not Irish, as she usually claimed, or English, as she recorded on one legal document of the 1860s. Masterman believed instead that she had been born in France, although her English was as impeccable as her French. The pharmacist's assertion is as yet as unproven as her own claim to a privileged Irish schooling. What he could see firsthand was that she was a "clever, selfish, and . . . unscrupulous woman."[80] Most Paraguayan women agreed with this characterization in the 1870s.

MILITARY LOOSE ENDS STILL UNTIED

López had organized the construction of Cerro León. At the same time, he strengthened his personal relations with the army; the navy posed no threat to him. Mixing with the rank and file, his manner was casual and friendly. He had a special rapport with the men in uniform.[81] His visits flattered them, although there is no evidence that he had any real concern for their welfare beyond what they could do for him. The military, of course, was a hierarchy, and General López was its head. Thus, no ambiguity confused the relationship between López and his officers and men, who honored him, as subordinates ought. He chose officers who were ostentatiously subordinate and deferential.

Although López alone made every important political, economic, and military decision, he pretended otherwise. In March 1865, he promoted himself to the newly established rank of marshal of the armies of the republic, superior to a mere general. He had Natalicio Talavera, editor of *El*

Semanario, write the announcement of his promotion for Congress. Talavera was privately unenthusiastic about war with Argentina, and his war reporting came from the brain of López.[82] Although Talavera and other talented writers put out the newspaper, "every article was submitted to Lopez before printing. . . ."[83] The pretense that it was a real newspaper and not a government publicity relations tool fooled some observers of the war. Thomas J. Hutchinson, a British consul in Argentina, was taken in by López's propaganda. Many of his observations in *The Paraná, with incidents of the Paraguayan War, and South American Recollections from 1861 to 1868* are paraphrases of López's ideas that first appeared in *El Semanario*.

López wanted the world to say that Congress had spontaneously promoted him to his new rank, but no López Congress did anything spontaneously. With crocodile tears, Francisco declined the congressional offer of a fivefold salary increase, an offer that he had initiated. He said that he could afford to turn down so generous an offer because of his own resources. He thus declined, he thought, with dignity.[84] In fact the whole country was his financial playground. Because he lacked physical courage, he arranged for his puppet assembly to demand that he not leave the country. He also ordered them to request him not to expose himself to the dangers of enemy fire, one way to hide his timidity.

In January 1865, López asked the Argentine government for permission to send armies across its soil, the most direct way to confront the Brazilian army in Uruguay. Argentine President Mitre's hostility toward the Paraguayan was no secret. Newspapers under his influence and even those opposed to him described López as a barbarian, as someone who was maybe crazy. Mitre too cherished his own and his nation's honor, but the Paraguayan's inability to honor his opponents' honor blinded him. López hated the damnable Argentine rags that impugned his character, but he read them.[85]

As López tried to split Argentina apart by conspiring with Urquiza, he boasted of how he had helped build the Argentine nation. Although in 1859 he was a champion of Argentine unity, López in 1865 championed its dissolution. He told Urquiza that Brazilian intervention in Uruguay proved its hostility toward Paraguay and Argentina. López said that he was now obliged to fight the Brazilians in Uruguay. He assured Urquiza that his offensive moves were no threat to Entre Ríos. Angry at Mitre for his "moral support" of Brazil, López convinced himself that Mitre's domestic opponents would welcome the invasion.[86] When he launched a surprise attack on Argentina, the Uruguayan Blanco government, whose existence he had pledged to uphold, had already fallen.

If López had in fact read Antoine Henri Jomini, the French-Swiss military theoretician, as some attest, he overlooked Jomini's main point: Armies must be kept concentrated. López twice divided his forces, once in the Mato Grosso and then sending a two-pronged attack southward into Argentina and Brazil. He thus violated the principle of concentration or mass that Jomini and other military strategists prized. Some strategist-commanders violated this commandment successfully, but no good military reason can be found for López's so doing in 1864 and 1865.

When the Argentine government refused to permit Paraguayan forces to cross Argentine soil, López retorted that it had no right to do so. He rejected the reasoning of Argentine leaders. Mitre's refusal was hostile, an insult, an attack on his personal honor. Urquiza—who until now had no real animosity to either López or Paraguay—had previously conjectured that Paraguayan troops crossing Argentine soil without hostile intent might not offend the Argentine government. He was wrong. Mitre thought otherwise. Urquiza lacked official standing. He had no right to speak for his nation, and López knew it. Hearing only what he wanted to hear was central to Francisco's makeup.[87]

Thus, the marshal president invaded Argentina at Corrientes, an act of war. The Argentine province on Paraguay's southern border ethnically, linguistically, and culturally resembled Paraguay. To give his aggression veneer of legality, he convened his Congress. To a man, they feared López. They enthusiastically and unanimously endorsed the presidential request to declare war on Argentina. Congress approved the Paraguayan declaration of war—written by López—on March 19, 1865. It announced that Paraguay would fight Argentina to secure its legal rights and its *honor*, the honor of its government and more importantly Francisco S. López.

López insisted on shows of bravery by his officers and men. He observed, "My soldiers are accustomed to obeying me." He claimed that the outpouring of support for the war by the Paraguayan people was spontaneous, even as he ordered and subsidized these gatherings. He said the Paraguayan people ". . . have arisen as one man to give the cry of war." Argentina had besmirched the nation's (and his) honor, and through war Paraguay would be reborn.[88]

Paraguayan troops invaded Corrientes, Argentina, on April 13, 1865. The Argentine government only later received the Paraguayan war declaration. López also sent warships into Corrientes harbor. They surprised and captured two Argentine steamers, the *Gualeguay* and the *25 de Mayo*. The Paraguayan army occupied the city of Corrientes, where López created a puppet government. He imagined that it might gain popular support. It did not.

Before the war, President López charged that a Triple Alliance was forming against him. By attacking his neighbors, he pushed this fear into a reality. A Brazilian–Argentine alliance against Paraguayan aggression was the logical outcome of his attacks. He had worried about it for years. His invasions assured its formation.[89]

Scorn for López in Buenos Aires was rooted in several factors, not least in the porteño assumption of superiority over all things Paraguayan. Other reasons included the mutual ill will between López and Argentina because of the Canstatt affair, the López family's yerba monopoly, and liberal porteños' disgust with the governments of López and his father.

López accused Argentina of discriminating against Paraguay and favoring Brazil. It would make little sense, though, for Argentina to treat small, poor, landlocked Paraguay as it did a large nation like Brazil.

Argentina was unprepared for war. Although the dictator counted on Urquiza's goodwill, the old caudillo had retreated from his cordial overtures as early as January 1865. He exchanged correspondence with the Paraguayan leader, but Urquiza shared the contents of the letters with President Mitre.

López had now initiated wars of aggression with not just one but two larger neighbors. He sent his barefoot columns into Argentina and Brazil with ill-defined destinations and no specific military objectives. The marshal president blunted his striking force and divided his armies: He ordered one column under Lt. Col. Antonio de la Cruz Estigarribia to march southeast and then south along the Río Uruguay. López directed a distant parallel column under the directly alcoholic General Wenceslao Robles to march directly south to occupy Corrientes and then along the Río Paraná, a considerable distance from the other. The rationale for these directives remains elusive. As López moved his armies in the south, he spaced them so far apart that mutual support was impossible. López believed that his will—and their execution of his dreams—would overcome the obstacles. He told his troops that their mission was to erase the shame that Brazil and Argentina had cast upon their government and to avenge the insult to their "military honor." He promised a short campaign. Their triumph would be eternal. They would make the nation great.[90]

The dictator's commanders, Robles and Estigarribia, were military mediocrities. Their appointments and failures rested with the marshal president. López's military objectives beyond his quest for glory were unclear. He never assigned his generals specific and attainable military objectives that would contribute to victory. His most important motivation, according to his own words, was to win glory and honor. Far from the action, López ordered Estigarribia to march south and await further orders. Sending orders quickly enough to matter to Estigarribia, commanding between twelve and thirteen thousand men, was impossible because of the long intervening distances. Because Argentina and Brazil initially mustered only weak opposition, López praised his armies as victorious.[91] From his pronouncements, we see that he lusted after glory, honor, and influence. Although López was proud of the initial conquests in the north and the south, both efforts showed his military ineptitude.

The dictator's mismanagement of the army was complemented by his audacious and incompetent direction of his navy. He sent his fleet south to engage the Brazilian blocking squadron. Nine steamships towed six barges (chatas) that were transporting soldiers who were to board the enemy vessels, but they forgot grappling hooks. They attacked the Brazilian ironclads on the Paraná River. On June 11, 1865, at Riachuelo, the fleet executed López's plan. He hoped that bravery and determination would overcome Brazilian technology, weaponry, and leadership.

Captain Meza, the commander of the fleet, feared for his life if he did not follow the marshal's orders precisely. He would not innovate creatively, although a delay cost the Paraguayans the cover of darkness and thus the element of surprise. The Brazilians won, losing one ship to the Paraguayans' four. One act that heartened López occurred when Lieutenant Ezequiel Robles, seriously wounded and captured by the Brazilians, chose to bleed to death rather than be saved by enemy surgeons. "His gesture was taken by López to represent the height of Paraguayan self-sacrifice and courage."[92]

In early June 1865, López moved his headquarters from Asunción toward the front; there he could more closely control his forces. He lied to his countrymen, saying that his remaining in the capital and away from the fields of battle had been a sacrifice. He was now going to join "his companions in arms." Contradicting himself on the sacrifice issue, he said that circumstances forced him to endure personally the hardships of the war. His presence would now cleanse the stain on the nation's honor and confront the foreign threat to Paraguay's existence.[93]

At the front, López suffered no personal hardship. He brought with him Madame Lynch and their sons, vast quantities of fine wines, dress uniforms tailored in France, personal servants, and a large unit of personal guards. He remained beyond the range of enemy cannon. This was unusual in nineteenth-century battles, when risks to commanders and to those whom they commanded were normally about the same.[94] López was the exception. His life was unlike the privations and danger of his soldiers. He expected them to fight to the death, to carry out his orders absolutely and literally. At the front, he never ventured near enough to the battles to endanger himself. Avoiding peril, he also removed himself from effective communication with his subordinates. He could not revise orders quickly enough to provide tactical flexibility to Paraguayan armies. Normally, commanders must revise battle plans after the first shot is fired, at which point everything becomes fluid.

López attended his posterity before leaving for the front. In June 1865, he recognized eight of his illegitimate children, declaring them legitimate in the eyes of the state. He decreed that henceforth they would carry his name, not that of their mothers. He recognized first the children of his earliest and longtime mistress, Juana Pesoa, including Emiliano Victor, then 15, and in Europe for his education, Adelina Constanza, 14, and José Felix, 4, whose birth six years after he brought Lynch to Paraguay documents his lack of fidelity. All the surviving children that he had sired with Lynch, he now decreed, were legitimate: Juan Francisco, 10; Enrique Mariano (later Enrique Solano), 7; Francisco Morgan Lloyd, 6; Carlos Honorio, 4; and the baby, Leopoldo Antonio. A baby girl had died in infancy. He did not refer to Lynch as "doña."[95]

Arriving at the fort of Humaitá, he could more effectively direct the military. Proximity let him keep his hand on the pulse of the army, the only institution that could overthrow him. His refusal to allow subordinates any initiative revealed his distrust of them and his sense of their inferiority. He trusted only himself.[96] He worried about morale, especially the defections to the enemy. Some men deserted, although we will never know how many. López outlawed the exchanges of communiqués between his and enemy forces. He pretended that such exchanges would imperil the honor of the fighting men. As he directed the war effort up close, he also oversaw the nation's finances,[97] over which his control was absolute. He eventually brought the nation's gold and silver to his headquarters.

In the winter (northern hemisphere summer) months of 1865, the war turned sour. He had ensured the defeat of his armies—by failing to give them a strategic design, by his failure to identify any military objectives, by the incompetence of the senior officers whom he appointed, and by his own strategic ineptitude. He impugned the honor of Emperor Pedro II of Brazil by his aggression, the impertinence of his correspondence, and the arrogance of his public declarations. The Brazilian monarch ruled the country, but he was not an absolute monarch. He governed "with the cooperation and backing of national politicians" and represented Brazil's "dominant socioeconomic interests."[98] The emperor "was determined not to compromise on his determination to expunge the stain that the Paraguayan invasion had left on the nation's honor and his own honor."[99]

The absence of empathy, López's greatest character defect, led to his faulty judgment of other leaders, especially the Brazilian emperor. His lack of interest in the motivations and outlook of others caused his misreading of the emperor, who took López's words and deeds as attacks on *his* honor. The Paraguayan dictator was unable to understand how seriously he had damaged his presidency by arousing the personal hostility of Pedro II.[100]

NOTES

1. John Lynch, *Argentine Caudillo: Juan Manuel de Rosas* (Wilmington, DE: Scholarly Resources, 2001), 135; David Rock, *Argentina 1516–1987: From Colonization to Alfonsín* (Berkeley and Los Angeles: University of California Press, 1987), 79–117.

2. Arturo Bray, *Solano López: soldado de la gloria y del infortunio* (Asunción: Editorial Lector, 1996), 97, 106.

3. Bray, *Solano López*, 100–101.

4. Bray, *Solano López*, 101.

5. Bray, *Solano López*, 98.

6. John Hoyt Williams, *The Rise and Fall of the Paraguayan Republic, 1800–1870* (Austin: Institute of Latin American Studies, University of Texas, 1979), 182; Bray, *Solano López*, 112.

7. Thomas Whigham, *The Politics of River Trade: Tradition and Development in the Upper Plata* (Albuquerque: University of New Mexico Press, 1991), 193.

8. The concept is Russell Weigley's. See his *A Great Civil War: A Military and Political History, 1861–1865* (Bloomington: Indiana University Press, 2000), 218. In *The American Way of War* (New York: Macmillan, 1973), Weigley points out that at the outbreak of World War II, the War Plans Office estimated that inducting any more than 10 percent of the U.S. population would damage the economic capacity of the United States. A larger percentage threw into a tailspin underdeveloped and labor-starved Paraguay in the 1860s.

9. Charles A. Washburn, *The History of Paraguay, with Notes of Personal Observations and Reminiscences of Diplomacy under Difficulties*, 2 vols. (Boston: Lee and Shepard, 1871), II, 53.

10. Proclamation (*Bando*), Asunción, September 10, 1862, *Proclamas y cartas del Mariscal López* (Buenos Aires: Editorial Asunción, 1957).

11. FSL, Manifesto to the Nation, Asunción, Sept. 13, 1862, *Proclamas y cartas*.

12. Fidel Maíz, *Etapas de mi vida: contestación a las imposturas de Juan Silvano Godoy* (Asunción: Imprenta la Mundial, 1919), 10.

13. George Masterman, *Seven Eventful Years in Paraguay: A Narrative of Personal Experience Amongst the Paraguayans*, 2nd ed. (London: Samson Low, Son, and Marston, 1870), 35.

14. Benjamín Vargas Peña, *Espías del Dictador Francia (los Piragüés)*, (Asunción: n.p., 1982) locates the origins of the modern spy system in the independence period.

15. Maíz, *Etapas*, 10–14, 40.

16. Maíz, *Etapas*, 18.

17. Maíz, *Etapas*, 27–28.

18. John Lynch, *Caudillos in Spanish America, 1800–1850* (Oxford: Oxford University Press, 1992), 130.

19. FSL, Manifesto to the Nation, October 1862, *Proclamas y cartas*.

20. The American minister to Paraguay thought him poorly educated. "His knowledge of history was less than that of most New England schoolboys at the age of fifteen," Washburn, *History of Paraguay*, II, 46–47.

21. Thomas L. Whigham, *The Paraguayan War, Volume I: Causes and Early Conduct* (Lincoln: University of Nebraska Press, 2002), 177.

22. Bray, *Solano López*, 118–19.

23. Juan Crisóstomo Centurión, *Memorias o reminiscencias históricas sobre la guerra del Paraguay*, 4 vols. (Buenos Aires and Asunción: Imprenta de Obras de J. A. Berra/Imprenta Militar, 1894–1901), II, 337–38.

24. Thomas Lyle Whigham, "The Iron Works of Ybicui: Paraguayan Industrial Development in the Mid-Nineteenth Century," *TAM*, 35 (October 1976): 201–18.

25. Josefina Plá, *Los Británicos en el Paraguay, 1850–1870* (Asunción: Arte Nuevo, 1984), 113–20.

26. FSL to Carlos Calvo, Asunción, July 20, 1860; FSL to Gregorio Benítez, Asunción, Apr. 20, 1862, *Proclamas y cartas*.

27. FSL to Gregorio Benítez, Asunción, April 20, 1862, *Proclamas y cartas*.

28. Roderick J. Barman, *Citizen Emperor: Pedro II and the Making of Brazil, 1825–1891* (Stanford, CA: Stanford University Press, 1999), 197.

29. Pelham Horton Box, *The Origins of the Paraguayan War* (Urbana, IL: University Studies in the Social Sciences, 1930; repr. New York: Russell and Russell, 1967), 215.

30. FSL to Mitre, Asunción, July 5, 1863, *Proclamas y cartas*.

31. Important correspondence between Presidents Mitre and López appears in *Archivo del General Mitre: Guerra del Paraguay* (Buenos Aires: Imprenta de la Casa Editorial Sapena, 1911), II.

32. Bray, *Solano López*, 164.

33. FSL to Mitre, NP, June 16, 1853 [1863], *Proclamas y cartas*.

34. FSL to Mitre, Asunción, Sept. 19, 1863, *Proclamas y cartas*.

35. FSL to Mitre, Asunción, Feb. 4, 1864, *Proclamas y cartas*.

36. FSL to Gregorio Benítez, Asunción, Apr. 21, 1864, *Proclamas y cartas*.

37. FSL to Felix Egusquiza, Asunción, July 6, 1864, *Proclamas y cartas*.

38. Bray, *Solano López*, 131–34.

39. Box, *Origins*, 212.

40. FSL, Speech to the ladies of Asunción, September 3, 1864, *Proclamas y cartas*.

41. A few sources do exist: Barbara Potthast, "Protagonists, Victims, and Heroes: Paraguayan Women during the Great War," in *I Die with My Country: Perspectives on the Paraguayan War, 1864–1870*, ed. Hendrik Kraay and Thomas L. Whigham (Lincoln: University of Nebraska Press, 2004), 44–60.

42. FSL, Speech to the people of Paraguay about the conflict with Brazil, September 12, 1864, *Proclamas y cartas*.

43. FSL, Address to the people at a demonstration, Asunción, September 13, 1864, *Proclamas y cartas*.

44. FSL to Urquiza, October 22, 1864, *Proclamas y cartas*.

45. FSL to Berges, Cerro León, letters of Nov. 4 and 5, 1864, *Proclamas y cartas*.

46. FSL to Berges, Cerro León, Nov. 5, 1864, *Proclamas y cartas*.

47. When López's navy captured the *Gualeguay* and *25 de Mayo* in the harbor at Corrientes in April 1865, thirteen British citizens were serving on them. Only one accepted his invitation to enlist in the Paraguayan navy. He made the rest slave laborers.

48. Plá, *Británicos*, 129, 161. Since Francisco Solano López learned of every important development in Paraguay affecting him, it is difficult to believe claims of ignorance on his part.

49. Bray, *Solano López*, 134–41.

50. Williams, *Rise and Fall of the Paraguayan Republic*, 197.

51. Williams, *Rise and Fall of the Paraguayan Republic*, 198, says, "Neither Francia nor Carlos Antonio cared much what happened in Uruguay: certainly they never dreamed of intervening there in favor of one cause or another." The first two Paraguayan dictators knew that "neutrality and nonintervention were essential to national survival."

52. Bray, *Solano López*, 142–43.

53. Masterman, *Seven Eventful Years*, 95–96.

54. Bray, *Solano López*, 148.

55. Bray, *Solano López*, 150–51; Washburn, *History of Paraguay*, II, 544.

56. Barman, *Citizen Emperor*, 197.

57. Whigham, *Paraguayan War*, I, 174.

58. Loren Scott Patterson, "The War of the Triple Alliance: Paraguayan Offensive Phase—A Military History," Unpublished Ph.D. diss. (Georgetown University, 1974), 330, 341, 364.

59. John Hoyt Williams, "Observations on the Paraguayan Census of 1846," *HAHR*, 56, no. 3 (August 1976): 424–37; Vera Blinn Reber, "The Demographics of Paraguay," *HAHR*, 68, no. 2 (May 1988): 289–319; and Thomas L. Whigham and Barbara Potthast-Jukeit, "The Paraguayan Rosetta Stone," *LARR* 34, no. 1 (1999): 174–86. Whigham's and Potthast-Jukeit's "Rosetta Stone" is apparently not available to scholars; access to it—and thus the ability to analyze it—were impossible in 2002.

60. Loren Scott Patterson, "The War of the Triple Alliance," 18–19; George Thompson, *The War in Paraguay with a Historical Sketch of the Country, Its People, and Notes upon the Military Engineering of the War* (London: Longman, Green, and Co., 1869), 52.

61. Chris Luechars, *To the Bitter End: Paraguay and the War of the Triple Alliance* (Westport, CT: Greenwood Press, 2002).

62. Bray, *Solano López*, 155.

63. John Keegan, *The Face of Battle: A Study of Agincourt, Waterloo, and the Somme* (Harmondsworth, UK: Penguin Books Ltd., 1976), 188.

64. Allan R. Millett, *The General: Robert L. Bullard and Officership in the United States Army, 1881–1925* (Westport, CT: Greenwood Press, 1975), 7–10.

65. The largest steamships built in Asunción, up to 548 tons, "had a commercial capacity," but "their primary function was . . . to guard the river approaches to Asunción." Whigham, *Politics of River Trade*, 193.

66. Bray, *Solano López*, 156.

67. *El Semanario*, Nov. 26, 1864.

68. Leuchars, *To the Bitter End*, 34.

69. Williams, *Rise and Fall of the Paraguayan Republic*, 201–3.

70. FSL to Resquín, Asunción, October 1, 1864, ANA/CRB, 2539. López told Resquín to report on the size of the Brazilian garrison at Nova Coimbra, the name and rank of the commander, the number of cannons there, the garrison's vigilance,

the ships in the port, the distance from Nova Coimbra to Albuquerque, cavalry movements, the terrain, and thirty-four other issues.

71. Leuchars, *To the Bitter End*, 36.

72. FSL, Proclamation to the Expeditionary Division of the North, Asunción, December 24, 1864, *Proclamas y cartas*.

73. *El Semanario*, Jan. 14, 1865.

74. Peter Beattie, *Tribute of Blood: Army, Honor, Race, and Nation in Brazil, 1864–1925* (Durham, NC: Duke University Press, 2001), 38–39.

75. FSL to Urquiza, Asunción, Jan. 14, 1865, *Proclamas y cartas*.

76. FSL to Urquiza, Feb. 26, 1865, *Proclamas y cartas*.

77. Bray, *Solano López*, 157.

78. Washburn, *History of Paraguay*, II, 238–39, 255–57.

79. EAL to FSL, Paso Pucú, July 26, 1866, ANA/CRB, 4251.

80. Masterman, *Seven Eventful Years*, 58.

81. Bray, *Solano López*, 162.

82. Centurión, *Memorias*, I, 244–47; II, 30.

83. Masterman, *Seven Eventful Years*, 115–16.

84. FSL to the National Congress, March 7, 1865, *Proclamas y cartas*.

85. Bray, *Solano López*, 168.

86. FSL to Urquiza, Asunción, Dec. 23, 1864, *Proclamas y cartas*.

87. The issue of whether or not Paraguay had such rights in international law need not concern us here. The history of sovereignty and territorial claims over Misiones province and issues of international law can be found in Box, *Origins*, passim; and Whigham, *Paraguayan War*, I, 77–161.

88. FSL, Speech to Congress, March [u.d.], 1865, *Proclamas y cartas*.

89. Bray, *Solano López*, 184.

90. FSL, Proclamation to the Expeditionary Army of the South, Asunción, April 11, 1865, *Proclamas y cartas*.

91. Bray, *Solano López*, 186

92. Leuchars, *To the Bitter End*, 69.

93. FSL, Proclamation to the Nation, Asunción, June 2, 1865, *Proclamas y cartas*.

94. Keegan, *Face of Battle*, 366.

95. FSL, Testament, Asunción, June 4, 1865, *Proclamas y cartas*.

96. FSL to Luis Caminos, Humaitá, July 1865, *Proclamas y cartas*.

97. FSL to Caminos, letters of July [u.d.], 1865, and July 7, 1865, Humaitá, *Proclamas y cartas*.

98. Barman, *Citizen Emperor*, 161–62.

99. Barman, *Citizen Emperor*, 206.

100. Whigham thinks that seizing Corrientes rather than attacking "Brazil by way of Misiones" was "the marshal's major strategic blunder," *Paraguayan War*, I, 418. It was not. His major strategic blunder was one of national strategy, not military strategy. It was arousing the implacable hostility of the Brazilian emperor. This miscalculation—arising from his lack of empathy and failure to understand the motivations of an adversary—assured his eventual defeat.

5

López Invaded

THE WAR EFFORT AND LACK OF PLANNING

In early 1865, Francisco López addressed his people. "A new era has opened," he said. Coming battles would demonstrate "manly resolution." War was a new experience for the peace-loving young nation. Earlier leaders provided "a stable peace." Because of his neighbors' hostility, however, peace was no longer desirable. The war with Brazil was, to López, "a necessity for Paraguay." The nation's existence was endangered, he claimed, although he was not specific about what military threat Brazil had posed. He insisted that Brazilian policies offended Paraguay's "honor and dignity"—meaning *his* honor and dignity. Victories on northern battlefields brought the Mato Grosso, said López, and "proved the superiority of our soldiers over those of Brazil. . . ."

He urged his people to support the war effort, and he coerced them to do so. He had them all sign agreements "offering their lives and goods to sustain the cause. Even ladies and children were obliged to sign these documents . . . so that no one remained in the country who had not signed away his life, and his property. . . ." The dictator pretended to see a spontaneous "explosion of patriotism." Paraguayans in fact had a "very high opinion of the greatness of the country," and López convinced them of "its vast political importance."[1]

Persuading them to support war with Brazilians was not difficult. They had feared Brazilian invasion since the 1600s. According to López, Brazilians were racially degraded. Against them, he said, Paraguayans could "make heard the voice of the fatherland." López orchestrated demonstrations of popular support.[2] His people played as he conducted. To one foreign López employee, the celebrations showed a "fictitious gaiety and simulated devotion." Many among the elite regarded the marshal president "with equal dread and detestation."[3] Most of the popular classes respected him and feared him, but they were patriotic. They had known only authoritarian government, and most accepted Francisco Solano López's rule as legitimate. The models bequeathed by authoritarian Spain were modified by Supreme Dictator Francia and López's father, silencing elite voices. Such moderate dissent as in the Asunción cabildo in the 1770s was silenced.

Like his father and other Spanish American caudillos, Francisco Solano detested democracy. Because of the successful repression of Francia and los López, in Paraguay there existed no faction or party advocating representative government, such as those that resulted in the liberal constitutions of Mexico in 1824 and of Argentina in 1826. López father and son felt threatened by the openness in the Argentine government after 1852, dubbing it anarchy, and they saw no value in the press freedom there.

López convened a Congress on February 25, 1865. Its purpose was for show because he "always tried to make it appear that he ruled constitutionally."[4] Congress's purpose was to make Francisco's policies and passions appear to be the will of the people. He appointed only ardent supporters. They attended the sessions and cheered his pronouncements.

He called General Wenceslao Robles to Asunción in early 1865. He saluted "this brave soldier." The marshal president lauded Robles's patriotism and his soldierly skill, of which he in truth possessed little. He lauded Robles's goodwill.[5] He appointed the military mediocrity to a major command.

López meanwhile terrorized people into conformity. The confinements and deaths of the men whom he had imprisoned at the outset of his presidency were object lessons. Paraguayans knew what would befall them if they displeased the president. "People became afraid to breathe."[6]

In early March 1865, López was again infuriated by the criticism in Buenos Aires newspapers. Editorials in the port city[7] denounced his Mato Grosso aggression. Anti-López jokes in the porteño newspapers ". . . entered deeply into Lopez' soul, and he felt them more than he did any reverse he afterwards suffered in the war."[8] Lacking a sense of humor, he could not laugh at himself. Reading the Buenos Aires periodicals aroused his indignation over what he saw—correctly—as Argentine disrespect. One astute observer thought that newspaper ridicule was the major cause of his attacking Argentina.[9] This remark was overstated but contained more than a kernel of truth.

The dictator prepared his own defense. He argued that Brazil had intended to use the war materiel in the Mato Grosso for a war of aggression against Paraguay. López lied. Brazil was unprepared for war, and López knew it. López repeated his claim that Argentina and Brazil had already concluded an anti-Paraguay alliance and were "only waiting for the most frivolous pretext" to announce it. He misjudged the political maturity of the Argentine nation, thinking it more divided by factionalism and less unified than it was. While factionalism and regionalism still divided Argentina, both were beginning to wane. In his own musings, he returned to the porteños' low estimation of him and his nation. Their disrespect injured his pride, offended his honor, and jabbed at his ballooning ego. He saw the Argentine leaders as ingrates who had forgotten his noble effort of 1859. He complained, "The province of Buenos Aires was scarcely pacified [in 1859] by the interposition of Paraguay [that is, Francisco Solano López] when the *porteño* press began to attack us [him]. . . ." He contrasted their unjust attacks on his character with his own resignation and prudence,[10] but resignation and prudence were absent from his personal qualities. Impetuosity was not.

In his message to Congress, López predicted inaccurately on March 5, 1865, that the Brazilian government had no stomach for a lengthy war. It was pursuing "an insane policy" in Uruguay. Its leaders had lost their grip on reality, according to him, when they ignored Paraguay's (López's) advice and offer of mediation. Brazil had provoked the war, the president maintained, although neither his father nor Dr. Francia were disturbed by interventions in Uruguay. Brazil had continued "to interfere in that Republic's internal affairs"[11] after Uruguayan independence in 1828. It sent forces into the Oriental Republic in 1851 and again in 1854. On neither occasion did Carlos Antonio López issue a call to arms. He was not obsessed with personal honor, although he recognized the honor complex. The elder López controlled his ego. His son let his ego control him.

Also influenced by the honor complex were Francisco López's principal enemies. "Pedro II was extremely protective of his country's honor, which he equated with his own."[12] The Paraguayan dictator was unable to comprehend the royal honor or the emperor's motivations. The Paraguayan's inability to empathize thus warped his judgment and thus his grasp of international affairs. Soon Argentine President Mitre would also find his and his nation's honor at risk. After the Paraguayan invasion of the Mato Grosso, he "decided to maintain a strict neutrality."[13]

As López's attacks moved Brazil from adversary to enemy, he also grew more suspicious of Argentina. He disliked its leaders, especially Mitre. At the same time, he hungered for their respect. Argentine involvement in Uruguay, thought López, "today threatens to disrupt the equilibrium of the Río de la Plata." According to him, Brazil and Argentina, both guarantors of Uruguayan independence, were now undermining it. He was right, but they were merely continuing their policies of the past three decades. Their current intrusions were different only in that Brazil's intervention was open, and Argentina's support of the rebel Flores covert.

These actions were not new departures. Rosas had intervened in Uruguay in the 1840s to further the interests of his Buenos Aires. Brazil also had vital interests there. Provincial leaders in Brazilian Rio Grande do Sul, bordering on Uruguay, resented imperial policies. The Farroupilha Rebellion of 1838–1845 there had manifested local discontent. Brazil worried with good reason about the security of its southern border with the Oriental Republic. Cross-border conflict was endemic, partly because Brazilian settlers dominated the northern third of Uruguay. It was not the vital interests of Paraguay but its honor that moved López the more. He saw Brazilian intervention as ominous—and as a potential precedent for overawing his own nation. What disturbed him even more was Brazil's slighting him, especially his offer to mediate the Uruguayan problem.

Brazil rejected López's offer by ignoring it, the worst insult of all. The Brazilian government never bothered to reply to him. Pedro II thought civil war a natural state of affairs in Uruguay. Both he and Argentina's Mitre disliked its Blanco government. To López, Brazil's refusal to recognize his importance had stained his and Paraguay's honor and had obliged Paraguay to make war on the empire. In fact, the emperor did not desire war with either small nation. He hoped that independent Paraguay and Uruguay would remain barriers against Argentine expansion.

For López, the security of northern Paraguay demanded that the newly conquered territory, the Mato Grosso—which he contended, with partial if historically remote justification, Brazil had earlier stolen from Paraguay—must be retained. Military triumphs there had brought glory to the army—and to its supreme commander. His soldiers had shown their discipline and courage,[14] qualities he prized. Although Francisco failed to mention it, his soldiers also raped Brazilian women and pillaged private properties. General Barrios, López's brother-in-law, "took the lead" in forcing himself on the women of the conquered region.[15] To salute their contribution to national honor, soldiers brought to Asunción a trophy, a patent of nobility signed by the emperor, "which afterwards adorned Mrs. Lynch's bedroom," where López frequently reposed. That Brazilians retreated before the larger invading armies increased Paraguayan hatred of them. Brazilian soldiers were weak and fearful, López thought.[16] That many of the soldiers were black and mulatto increased his disdain.

To close with Brazil in Uruguay, López's army must cross the Argentine province of Corrientes. Paraguayan citizens harkened to the cry of the fatherland, López thought, which made him proud. They had no choice, however. The dictator forced their enthusiasm on them. He was angry when people were insufficiently fulsome in praising him and in supporting his war. He argued that his offensives were defensive. They protected the nation's vital interests. He said that the honor, dignity, and prosperity of Paraguay depended on the patriotism of Congress, on which he had his eyes,[17] a reminder that the deputies must do and say exactly what he and his functionaries instructed.

Members of Congress, of course, responded obediently. Arriving in Asunción from the interior, they stopped at executive offices to ask for "their cue as to what they were to say in congress. These cues were given on every subject."[18] The deputies gave President López rousing ovations as he entered the House of Congress, where he personally oversaw the proceedings.

He made Congress promote him to the rank of marshal. He insisted that they offer to raise his salary to 60,000 pesos, a gigantic sum in Paraguay in the 1860s, which gave him the opportunity to display his patriotism by refusing. This was a grand gesture and an empty one because the whole country was his for the taking. The deputy from the former *encomienda* town of Ypané probably spoke the truth when he said that "His Excellency the President of the Republic" was the embodiment of the nation. "This young general" was anointed "a sublime genius," the commendation originating in the mind of the sublime genius himself. He wanted his people to know that his martial abilities had been manifest throughout his long public career.[19] Deputy Urbieta, from the lovely town of Yaguarón, said that most Argentine people sympathized with the cause, the official line. As López ordered, Congress stipulated that it was declaring war against the present Argentine government, not the Argentine people.[20] Francisco López would not see turnabout as fair play.

Demonstrating not only cowardice but also a lack of martial values, he had the legislature beg him not to expose himself to danger, one of the first major public displays of his want of courage. For appearance's sake, he objected to this plea for his safety, but ". . . he promised to expose himself as little as possible." In the nineteenth century, of the attributes that officers needed to be effective, courage ". . . stood at the head of the list."[21] For López, his assertions that he was brave would be stand-ins for the acts of courage that most commanders routinely performed. For the next four years, he kept his promise. He exposed himself to no danger. Cocky when out of range of rifle and artillery fire, he cowered when it grew near. Meanwhile he subsidized fiestas in the plazas of every town in the country.

Although the people respected their young leader, they also feared him.[22] Like most of his people, his soldiers were "the most respectful and obedient men imaginable."[23] They were also motivated by fear of him and of the lash, the torture of the Uruguaiana, and the firing squad.

Because he had promoted himself to marshal, López now could order Congress to increase the number of brigadier generals to six and generals of divisions to three. When he was only a general he would not promote others to the rank. The new Field Marshal of the Armies of the Republic was entitled to all the honors, privileges, and salaries "that are inherent in the Supreme military rank." Because of his long military career, his organization of the armies of the republic, and especially his "aptitude, learning, and patriotism," Congress declared that the new marshal should be awarded a special sword of honor. On one side of the blade López wanted the inscription to read "To the founder and organizer of the forces of land and sea," and on the other, "To Marshal López, the country's thanks."

At the dictator's insistence, Congress created the National Order of Merit. Only the president would decide who deserved what gradations of this honor, modeled on the French institution, and he would personally select the recipients. He put himself first in line. He was the only candidate he deemed worthy of the highest grade. Decisions about who else to honor must be cosigned by the minister of war, then the dictator's brother Venancio. Now prepared, the new marshal said, Paraguayan forces would gain "triumphs crowned with laurels."[24]

Before January 14, 1865, when he requested that Argentine leaders permit his troops to cross their country, he sent a force into Misiones, a region claimed by both Paraguay and Argentina. On February 9, 1865, Argentine President Mitre refused López's request to tread on Argentine soil. He wished, he said, to maintain his nation's neutrality. A furious López thought the reply outrageous, a fable. Argentina had earlier permitted Brazilian warships to pass through its waters and its soldiers to camp on Argentine shores. To refuse Paraguay the same right would be unfair. That Argentina then lacked the power to resist Brazil was irrelevant. Presently, though, "When the Brazilians sought the right to move troops across his territory, he [Mitre] replied with a firm no."[25] He was sympathetic to Brazil, but widespread Argentine hostility to the empire tied his hands. Also galling to López was Mitre's covert assistance to Flores in Uruguay. López felt that "The Argentine government has been animated by a special antagonism against Paraguay since the defeat of the *porteño* army at Paraguarí. . . ."[26] Thus his war with Argentina was just. It would redress past grievances. For López, feelings mattered. He was "anxious to be looked upon by European powers as a civilized and enlightened ruler,"[27] and he insisted that his neighbors recognize his stature.

Paraguayans and their leader, the marshal thought, had suffered enough discrimination. With him as director they needed a larger stage on which to play. The Argentine cabinet had neglected its neighborly duties; its hostility was abundantly clear. The leaders of that nation had conspired against him and Paraguay.[28]

The marshal president should have devised a military strategy. If he ever devised one, he never said what it was, not even to the generals who must execute it. Even without a military strategy, he did have a national one—a politico-personal one, which he discussed repeatedly in his newspapers. Combats would advance his reputation and that of his nation. He assumed that he would be the chief of state, head of government, and commander of the army and navy for life. His views were developed in the articles and editorials in his newspapers. If the pieces in *El Semanario* and the other newspapers shed little light on the realities of politics, diplomacy, or military affairs in the region in the 1860s, they were nevertheless good guides to the López mind. The dictator employed talented writers to create exactly the language that he wanted. Yet he never trusted them, never allowed them autonomy. He himself always edited their copy. Thus, his voice speaks as clearly in *El Semanario* as in the later publications, *El Centinela*, and *Cabichuí*. Content analysis of them shows that José Maria de Silva Paranhos, Viscount Rio Branco, was correct when he said that López chose war to make himself and his country better known and more respected. That the dictator was a master strategist was no part of the truth, although he insisted that he was.

Having read French military literature, alone among Paraguayans in his estimation, he understood it only a little. López insisted that only he should plan strategy, a reasonable position. But he apparently never did any planning. Even worse, he would control tactics. He would micromanage the war. He was good at such things as the proper design of commanders' uniforms and medals and ensuring the loyalty of his followers. In some areas of logistics, especially the mustering of forces, his efforts rose above the level of mere competence. Unlike Napoleon, though, he would not allow subordinates to take initiative, a major mistake. Because his timidity kept him far from any action and he outright distrusted subordinates, he demanded a rigid obedience to his orders, retaining absolute control. He wrote these out in exhaustive detail prior to combat, sure that he could will the future course of action. Subordinates were thus hamstrung. On any battlefield after the opening shots, situations become dynamic. Too far from all battles save the last to revise his orders, López demanded obedience—as total and as literal an obedience in war as he did in politics. He never gave even his better generals the opportunity to initiate actions. In 1864 and 1865, "the marshal never let his right hand know what his left hand was doing." As the war progressed, he improved, though he never became a good commander. He did learn how to give useful orders on occasion.[29] He himself, though, never ventured near enough to combat actually to command his forces efficiently until the end of the war, when the bloodletting took place in a tiny arena.

On April 14, 1865, López commanded about forty thousand men with another one hundred thousand potential recruits and reserves.[30] He sent a vanguard of four thousand infantry and cavalry into Argentina's Corrientes province under the alcoholic General Robles. This force would swell to twenty-five thousand. Organized resistance was negligible. In the city of Corrientes, López created a puppet government because he believed that Correntinos would see him as a liberator. His ego allowed no other surmise. This supposition again revealed his lack of empathy, at personal and political levels. His inability to put himself imaginatively in another's place to assess the likely alternatives was damaging. Not as essential to leaders of great powers, this attribute is material to those of small nations, especially bellicose small nations taking risks.

Mitre "realized that war would put an end to Argentine internal development . . .,"[31] but "he could not allow any army to set a precedent by crossing Argentine territory." He was also concerned about national honor.[32] He told López to go by water, "since the rivers were open by treaty." Mitre "did not want war with López," but the conflict was now a "bitter necesssity."[33]

TOWN OF GOYA: ROBLES'S DOWNFALL

After occupying Corrientes, López sent his army south along the Paraná River toward the Argentine hamlet of Goya. There, the marshal halted them to await further orders. He sent a second column of some fifteen thousand men under Lt. Col. Antonio de la Cruz Estigarribia to the southeast through Misiones, which is the modern-day Argentine province of Misiones, a then-disputed territory. López ordered this unit to advance south along the Uruguay River. Because of López's lack of foresight, the Estigarribia command had no "means of even guarding its rear or keeping open its communications with headquarters and marched eight hundred miles through unfamiliar country."[34]

In April and May 1865, though, López's luck held. Argentina had no regular forces in the invaded regions, only irregular and militia units. Like Brazil, Argentina was unprepared for war, so both of López's columns advanced rapidly. What were the military objectives of the two Paraguayan armies? Historians are still unsure. The marshal kept his cards close to his vest. He gave neither Robles nor Estigarribia any clear idea of his or the other commander's objective. Robles and Estigarribia knew that they would suffer severe penalties if they disobeyed the marshal's directives. Neither of these men was able, but they were López's choices. Like all other senior officers in the army, they were well known to him. The peacetime army was small, and López had overseen it for a decade. He wanted no clever officer. Such a man could become a rival.[35]

As his expeditionary forces moved south, the dictator remained in Asunción. His forces ultimately ran out of luck. Defeats were inevitable, given extended supply lines and no clear objective. When they met misfortune, López blamed his commanders. He even executed one, Robles, for showing disrespect, and he wished to execute the other, Estigarribia. The latter wisely remained in Argentina after surrendering his hungry army. Estigarribia followed the marshal's example. He unwisely divided his own force as he traveled south along the Río Uruguay. He sent a part of his command under Major Pedro Duarte down the west side of the river, while he traveled down the east bank with the main force. Since Brazilian vessels controlled the river, these two units could not aid each other.

In the Argentine town of Goya, General Robles dithered. Lacking instructions from López, however, he had few real options. Making a bad situation worse, he misinterpreted one order from López and was dilatory in responding to another, a directive sent by the marshal on June 1, 1865, telling Robles to fall back on Corrientes. Ultimately, the dictator discovered that Robles, whom he had recently praised, was an abomination.

On June 7, 1865, Robles began his countermarch north. Before leaving, he received overtures from the enemy. Col. Fernando Iturburu commanded the anti-López Paraguayan Legion under Allied command. He was a liberal Paraguayan opponent of the López family. He had moved to Buenos Aires in the 1850s for business and political reasons. He and other Legionnaires urged Robles to defect.[36] There is no credible evidence that Robles betrayed his chief, but López so alleged, and many Paraguayans came to believe him a traitor. Fearful of betrayal and of losing control, López had prohibited parleys with the enemy, such as those Robles had entertained. López trusted no one.

The dictator turned on Robles because of the general's public demonstration of petulance, which the dictator saw as a sign of disrespect. In the field, the distraught General Robles, suffering from a hangover, had just learned that López had awarded him the National Order of Merit. He exclaimed before witnesses that he had done nothing to deserve the decoration. It should go to his brother, he said, who had fought valiantly and died in the naval battle of Riachuelo on June 11. When he heard about Robles's outburst, López found this refusal profoundly disrespectful; he believed that to be rude to Marshal López was treason.[37] Harried by Correntino guerrillas, Robles led his command back to Corrientes, where he found himself and his staff under arrest. With their commander, the staff members were eventually sentenced to death by López's kangaroo court. One author concludes, "it was evident that Robles was merely a scapegoat for López's tactical and strategic failures."[38] True enough, but it was even more than this. López was following the example of his father, who had interpreted one man's unthinking act of petulance as disrespect so serious as to be a capital crime.

In July 1865, López communicated the fate of Brigadier Robles to Robles's replacement, Francisco Isidoro Resquín. He ordered the stolid, unimaginative, but obedient Resquín to strip Robles of his command. The marshal now judged that the division of the man whom he had just singled out for meritorious conduct had been too inactive. His idleness let enemy patrols on the army's periphery become bothersome. He was executed the following January.

No detail was too small for the dictator's attention. Along with orders to arrest Robles, he sent his brother-in-law General Vicente Barrios to move the Robles-Resquín army to the right bank of a creek, the Arroyo San Lorenzo, again making tactical decisions at a distance. There, he concluded, potable water would be more plentiful. He instructed Majors Cabral and Díaz how to conduct scouting operations. Withholding the power to choose subordinates even from the unwaveringly loyal Resquín, López ordered one Major Nuñez to advance on the enemy vanguard. He gave detailed instructions about the disposition of infantry units. Although he pretended that Resquín was free to take the initiative if an opportunity presented itself, the detailed nature of his instructions belied this. As a warning, López sent his adjutant, Captain Corbalán, to spy on Resquín,[39] who was in any event disinclined to disobey or innovate. López further showed the totality of his control by promoting even subalterns and noncommissioned officers.[40]

For the dictator, Resquín's major mission was to gather evidence of Robles's public disrespect for the marshal president, that is, his rejection of his prized National Order of Merit. But, his talking with the enemy had aroused the dictator's suspicions. Unpunished, the general's behavior might encourage further subversion. López ordered Resquín to take detailed depositions from Robles's staff, especially Captain Juan Valiente and Lieutenant Manuel Gauna, who were remanded to Humaitá. Their crime was their loyalty to Robles—the "brave soldier," the patriot, and the man of "good will"[41]—and they were sentenced in February 1865. His good-hearted subordinates had failed to report his indiscreet and probably alcohol-induced outburst. López demanded that the trial and execution of Robles, whose guilt the president had already determined, take place at his headquarters. According to López, Robles's execution the next year was his own fault. He had strayed from the "straight path of patriotism and military honor."[42] The penalty for disrespect, even by a man under severe stress, was death. Most of Robles's staff was also executed. Loyalty to Marshal López meant loyalty to none other.

Several charges brought Robles death, including insubordination and disobedience; but the most serious, in the judgment of the dictator, was his public disrespect. Robles knew that he had done nothing to deserve the Order of Merit, that he was no hero, and that his late brother was. He was ashamed of the pretense. López had Robles shot in January 1866,[43] after a farcical trial.

BATTLES OF RIACHUELO AND URUGUAIANA

Earlier, the Battle of Riachuelo on the Paraná River at a tributary to the south of Corrientes took place on June 11, 1865. This is where General Wenceslao Robles's brother, Lt. Ezequiel Robles, had shown suicidal valor. This battle is also where López had tried to destroy the Brazilian fleet. He later characterized it as a "great combat" that "made the enemy know his ignorance" because "extraordinary was the bravery of our sailors."[44] Brazilian ships had blockaded the Paraguay–Paraná river system, blocking access to weapons' markets, and they threatened López's armies. On this occasion, "For once the marshal asked his subordinates' advice . . ." about how to proceed.[45] Nevertheless, López continued to demand unwavering obedience to a grandiose plan. If the Allied fleet could be captured or destroyed, the navy might then be able to blast through the blockade. To attack conventionally would be suicidal, López knew, because of the Brazilian vessels' superiority: bigger, faster, and better armed. Key to the plan was a surprise attack on the Brazilians on the night of June 10–11. The attacking fleet, however, was slowed by *chatas*, unpowered barges towed by steam vessels, carrying an artillery piece and combatants to board the enemy vessels. Unfortunately for López, his armada embarked too late to surprise the Brazilians. The imperial fleet won; the Paraguayans fought valiantly but in vain.[46]

Ezequiel Robles, captain of the former Brazilian merchantman *Marqués de Olinda*, was wounded and captured by the Brazilians, whose surgeons bound his wounds. Lt. Robles then ripped off his bandages and proclaimed that he would rather be dead than live a prisoner of Brazil. He got his wish, because he bled to death. "His gesture was taken by López to represent the height of Paraguayan self-sacrifice and courage."[47] López pretended that Riachuelo was a "great combat . . . of great significance . . ." that "made the enemy know his ignorance." It showed the Allies the extraordinary bravery of the Paraguayan fighting man. The battle also revealed, according to López, that Brazilians were inferior. The "negroes" of the empire did not know how to use their superior technology. They fought in a "cowardly" fashion by retreating inside their ships rendering Paraguayan boarders powerless, and, to him, this proved that Paraguay was winning. What was most important, said López in a later recollection of events, was that his forces taught the Allies a "fatal lesson."[48]

The Paraguayan navy in truth stood little chance of defeating the Brazilians. Making the struggle even more unequal, López again refused to allow naval commanders to depart from his orders, and he knew less about fighting on water than on land. "The lack of command flexibility"[49] imposed by López and his refusal to delegate authority helped doom the Paraguayan navy. At the opposite pole from López's roseate remembrances, the Brazilian emperor thought that the "battle of Riachuelo . . . has covered with glory the Brazilian navy,"[50] not that of Paraguay. "Pedro II called on Brazil's free citizenry to volunteer to defend their national honor."[51]

After Paraguay's southeastern forces succumbed in 1865, López, not having heard that the peso stopped at his office, blamed his subordinates. In truth, they were not blameless. He denounced Estigarribia the more. Since Duarte fought so fiercely that two-thirds of his command were killed or wounded, López softened his criticism of that officer. He praised his bravery. Still, he told the readers of his newspapers, he disapproved of Duarte's decisions. Apparently not realizing the difficulty of an opposed river crossing, he blamed Duarte's defeat at Yatay on Estigarribia's failure to come to the aid of his subordinate on the other side of the Uruguay River. He minimized the defeat by describing Major Duarte's force as "a little column of exploration." Since most of the men perished, López dubbed them "martyrs" who died to defend their country.[52] When he learned of Estigarribia's surrender at Uruguaiana, September 1, 1865, he was infuriated; but it was he who had "sent an army . . . far into enemy territory with no apparent plans and no effective means of resupply."[53] Defeat was preordained.

The dictator refused to accept blame. The national disgrace was twofold, López felt. First, the forces in the south had not done their duty. Additionally their commanders had disobeyed his orders. Major Pedro Duarte "effectively lost his entire army, with 2,000 killed" at the Battle of Yatay, August 17, 1865. He became an Argentine prisoner, but his troops had fought bravely against a vastly superior force under the Uruguayan Flores and the Brazilian Paunero. Their artillery gave them superiority. Duarte's men had none. López acknowledged that Duarte and his men had fought well. Most important, they upheld "the honor of the Paraguayan soldier." He wanted the rest of the army to know that the true objectives of the now defeated southeastern army had been to win honor and glory, "new laurels," and as far as he was concerned they had done so. The marshal correctly saw that Estigarribia's entrenching his army in the Brazilian town of Uruguaiana had been stupid. Worse, he claimed, it was the most "shameful act in Paraguayan history." Until now, the president proclaimed to his troops, the war had been merely "necessary and just." After Uruguaiana, it had been transformed. The conflict now, according to the dictator, was truly a "holy war." The Paraguayan objective, he told his men, was military honor. Bravery could save the day and the nation's honor. López urged soldiers to fight with renewed vigor to cleanse the stain of Uruguaiana. López promised his armies, now much reduced in size, that his Paraguay would henceforth make every effort to restore the honor lost at Uruguaiana.[54]

López learned few lessons from Uruguaiana. The reason for the defeat, he said, resulted from Estigarribia's direct disobedience to his orders. To bolster his own reputation, he then made Estigarribia's wife publicly denounce her husband. López feared that this setback might contribute to his enemies' morale. It did, because Allied leaders Mitre, Flores, and Pedro II were all present when Estigarribia surrendered his hungry soldiers on September 18, 1865. Pedro II saw them just as López feared he would, as "a rabble" that "was unworthy of even being beaten."[55]

LÓPEZ RECONSIDERS HIS ARGENTINE ADVENTURE

Retreat Begins

López withdrew from Argentina. He ordered his retreating soldiers to confiscate cattle and horses. To put a "civilized" face on their looting, López had them issue receipts. The marshal said that taking the livestock was necessary. It would deprive the enemy of their use,[56] a strategy of denial in a land teeming with livestock.

López was his own intelligence officer and a hapless one when considering non-Paraguayans. When his spies and scouts brought him negative reports, he chastised them. At the same time, his micromanagement style and inability to delegate compounded his poor judgment. In August 1865, for example, he worried over such details as the lack of pasturage for the livestock of the distant southeastern army, a search that would have been better conducted by an officer on the scene. He cautioned that it would be counterproductive to take furniture "from the enemy houses." His calculations about enemy movements were often wishful thinking, as in his hope that Urquiza would keep the Allies out of Entre Ríos. But attention to detail helped Francisco López maintain absolute control of his country and his military. His very existence depended on such control, as did his psychological composure. He dictated the form for officers' communiqués and told them how to send messengers and escorts. He decided

who should be promoted, even in the ranks.[57] The reason for the failure of
López, the intelligence officer, was not his overattention to detail and not
even his micromanagement. It was his lack of understanding.

One example was his failure to form a working government in Corrientes. At the outset of his Argentine adventure, in April 1865, the dictator-
president had created an interim government, a *junta* comprised of local
men with little following. He nevertheless wanted the people of Corrientes to back them. His puppets, whose reach never extended beyond the
city limits, were headed by the Paraguayan foreign minister, José Berges.
It existed only by force of arms. The people of the northern Argentine
province were unsympathetic. As proconsul, Berges was a failure because
Correntinos viewed the López-installed government as illegitimate. After
initially promising to behave well, the invaders plundered. One item that
they stole was "a new piano" presented to Madame Lynch,[58] who began
to profit from the war.

Because of heavy losses at Yatay in August and Uruguaiana in September 1865, López had thrown away the best part of his army—some four
thousand at Yatay and more than six thousand at Uruguaiana. The ruination of Paraguay was under way. He had gained honor, at least in his own
estimation. He had only a few avenues left to pursue. One option was to
surrender and depart Paraguay. Another was to go over to the defensive,
continue fighting, and remain in control.

López brought the army back from Argentina in late October and November 1865, signaling the failure of his offensives. In December 1865, the
dictator again told the people why they fought; they had been provoked.
The enemy's soldiers had showed their true colors by fleeing like os-
triches, although the Paraguayans had done the most recent retreating.
The southern offensive, he said, achieved "a day of glory for the Fatherland." His men had gained a major objective: they had caused the Triple
Alliance to respect Paraguay. (In fact, López's bumbling generalship
caused them to scorn him.) As Paraguayans disliked Brazilians, so did the
Brazilian leaders return the disrespect.

López pulled his forces back to carefully prepared positions of great
strength around Humaitá. He urged them to conduct themselves coura-
geously. He congratulated himself on being the author of his soldiers' discipline and morality.[59] These were the disciplined and moral men who
had looted the properties of the people of Corrientes and had delivered
the most valuable loot to the marshal and Lynch.

Family on the Front Lines

The day that López created the National Order of Merit in June 1865, he,
his retinue, Madame Lynch, and their children left Asunción for the front.

Announcing that he himself must participate in the privations of war, he nevertheless provided himself, Lynch, and their children a comfortable lifestyle at his headquarters at Paso Pucú, protected by the great fortress of Humaitá. They had spacious quarters, good food, plentiful wine and brandy, and servants—a stark contrast to the troops who were beginning to run out of almost everything. The López family was far enough from the fighting so that parents and children were in no immediate danger. López also brought with him "the whole of the gold coin left in the country."[60] He remained in daily contact with his subordinates in the capital by telegraph. At Paso Pucú, in his safe headquarters, he had soldiers dig him an underground bunker. He also had a brick house with a tile roof and a comfortable veranda. The telegraph office was adjacent to his quarters. He had a personal guard of 250 men with breach-loading rifles, better weapons than those of the frontline troops, because "Lopez was continually in fear of being assassinated. . . ." He had a guard officer escort him to Mass on Sundays. He ordered his musicians to play a special march when he left home and church. After Mass, he visited and bantered with enlisted men. Private soldiers appreciated these gestures. They deferred to him, and he was comfortable around them. The issue of who was superior was never in question. Mostly he talked and they listened. He told his men that they would "beat the blacks, as the Allies were indiscriminately called."[61]

Like their commander, many officers and soldiers brought their wives, consorts, or mothers to the front. They provided vital services; as cooks, laundresses, and nurses, they gave love and comfort to their men. When they traveled back and forth to central Paraguay, the women reported war news to the noncombatant population, often contradicting López's propaganda. To dispel rumors and obscure truths, the marshal president ordered Paraguayans "to consider every day a new triumph for López, and . . . they dared not show that they did not think so. . . ." Another precaution was the dictator's order that daily Masses for his safety and welfare be performed in the cathedral of Asunción.[62]

Retreat Continues

López's first stop in the south had been Paso de la Patria on the Alto Paraná River. He soon withdrew to Paso Pucú where he would spend the next two years. The imposing Humaitá, the great fortress on the east bank of the Paraguay River north of its confluence with the Paraná, would protect his army, home, and headquarters. Long a Paraguayan defensive site, it was manned by a few soldiers during the Francia dictatorship; but its origins were colonial. During the presidency of Carlos Antonio López, foreign engineers directed the construction of defenses there. It became known as "the Sebastopol of South America." The considerable contribution by Francisco had augmented the work of the technical experts whom he hired to design it and of those who did the heavy lifting. The purpose of the fortress, the ruins of which are seen today from ships traveling on the Río Paraguay, was to block hostile vessels sailing upriver. The fort's artillery and the massive chain across the river prevented enemy warships from ascending the Río Paraguay until early 1868. Since the fortress was "well protected on the south and east by marshes and lagoons," taking it by land seemed impossible. Facing the river, over banks that rose steeply to a height of 30 feet, the fort was more than a mile long, "450 feet across at the front and 21 feet high."[63]

Using Humaitá, the river, and the marshes, López stymied the Allies. After they invaded Paraguay on April 17, 1866, he held them off for twenty-two months. Almost ten thousand Allied soldiers crossed the Paraná River from Argentina at Itapirú in April 1866, and thousands more followed. López's armies remained on the strategic defensive for the rest of the war. The marshal ordered tactical offensives, and they furthered his claims to glory and honor.

The Alliance Moves Closer; Los López Grow Richer

A year after López's armies invaded the larger, wealthier, and more populous neighbors, the Allies finally mobilized enough men to fight their way into Paraguay. In the creation of armies, the Paraguayan leader had almost a decade's head start. Victory, which López left undefined in military terms, was now impossible, and he and his armies had failed as offensive warriors. If the war continued for years, he now hoped, and if Paraguayans fought bravely enough, maybe the enemy would suffer enough to agree to an armistice. Given the outrage of Pedro II and his need to restore his own and his nation's honor, however, this was unlikely. If López could survive, though, he would win.

He faced three opponents. On May 1, 1865, Brazil, Argentina, and Uruguay—now led by Venacio Flores—had signed the Triple Alliance Treaty. Their principal objective was to overthrow Francisco Solano López. From this goal, they would not waver. They guaranteed that Paraguay would continue to be an independent nation, although López convinced his followers to disbelieve this. He thought that independence without him, the natural leader of the nation, was no independence at all. Secret provisions of the treaty, which to the Allies' chagrin the British government made public in 1866, called for taking the maximum border claims of Brazil and Argentina at Paraguay's expense. The territories in dispute under Francia and Carlos Antonio, Francisco had now made available by war. He handed Argentina and Brazil the opportunity to seize the disputed lands. For Argentina, these included the Gran Chaco between the Bermejo and the Pilcomayo Rivers to the west of the Río Paraguay and a part of the Misiones province to the southeast of it. Brazil also wanted a piece of Misiones and sought title to the disputed lands between the Apa and Blanco (Branco) Rivers to the north of Paraguay.

López had miscalculated the nature of Argentine nationality. He thought that nation's consolidation in the 1860s more fragile than it was. In November 1865, López wrote to Argentina's President Mitre. He lectured him on the nature of war. It was necessary at times, he said, for a people to resort to force to decide questions of vital national interest. He explained that there were proper and improper ways of war, a statement that reflects a claim to justice by opposing sides in most wars.[64] A "civilized nation" like Paraguay, López insisted, would not practice a cruel barbarism. Such would dishonor the chief who gave the order, and above all, López wished to be seen as honorable. For example, López said—and in this, he was right about the form but not the substance—one of his first orders to his armies had been to treat prisoners according to their rank, respecting the honored status of officers. He protested that he had protected Argentine, Uruguayan, and Brazilian citizens, ignoring atrocities in Argentina and the Mato Grosso and overlooking his own persecution of the president-designate (governor) of Mato Grosso. A personal concern of the marshal was that Argentina had imprisoned Felix Egusquiza, his business agent in Buenos Aires, as well as José Caminos, his consul there. A parallel calamity was that Argentina had confiscated Paraguay's (that is, López's) funds. What offended him more than the monetary loss was how Argentines had dishonored him. One Argentine mob, he remonstrated, had publicly humiliated him. In the city of Rosario, a crowd had symbolically executed López, killing him in effigy. They also dumped the Paraguayan coat of arms into the Paraná River, further shame to his nation and to him. Despite these indignities, López said, he would not lower himself to the commission of "barbarous" acts. He lied.

Another serious affront, the fearful López maintained, was that Mitre had returned Paraguayan deserter Juan González through the lines to assassinate the marshal. The assassination order likely took place only in López's imagination. The poor González was likely just another soul lost in the fog of war. He was executed anyway. A more substantive complaint was that the Allies were now forcing prisoners to serve in their ranks, making them traitors. López maintained that the government, as he referred to himself, had done nothing to provoke such atrocious behavior, overlooking the fact that he had attacked two countries unprepared for war. He insisted that he always behaved honorably. He respected other heads of state, even at war, and he expected them to treat him chivalrously. The ritual shooting of his effigy was intolerable. Mitre must halt such offenses. López could not comprehend that Mitre did not control Argentina as López did Paraguay. Finally, the dictator was outraged that Argentina harbored anti-López Paraguayans. Their opposition to him was public and notorious. Some exiles had founded the Paraguayan Legion, which fought in Allied ranks under the Paraguayan flag. They considered themselves loyal to Paraguay but opposed to the dictator. López believed that anyone who defied him betrayed the nation. If Mitre allowed Legionnaires to fly the Paraguayan flag, López warned, he would take reprisals.[65]

Brazil took awhile to mobilize its army for war, partly because of the ruling classes' disdainful attitudes. "Neither Pedro II nor the Brazilians in general viewed the Paraguayans with any respect."[66] The emperor believed the Paraguayan forces were undertrained, although they were better trained than most of his own forces. Assuming a Paraguayan racial inferiority owing to the Guarani influence, Pedro II judged that their men would be poor soldiers, a grave miscalculation.

Brazil, Argentina, and the new Colorado government of Uruguay, a decidedly junior partner, agreed that the first objective of the Triple Alliance was to remove López from power. They specified that they targeted neither the people of Paraguay nor the independence of the nation. Few Paraguayans believed them. They disliked and distrusted outsiders anyway. López's propaganda pushed them further along in that direction. Potential opposition leaders were in exile or dead; he had sent the elites to their deaths by posting them to locations of certain death. The conflict for López and his people had now "become a war over the partition of Paraguay,"[67] although the disputed regions were not effectively tied politically or militarily to central Paraguay. When the British received a copy of the treaty including its secret provisions in 1866, they published it.[68] When Francisco learned of the secret clauses of the treaty, including Allied territorial claims, he used them to discredit his enemies. The knowledge that the enemy intended to split apart their nation encouraged Paraguayans to resist more fiercely, often suicidally. Within Argentina, the Mitre government had to contend with regional opposition to porteño hegemony and widespread resentment of Brazilians, hostility to whom dated from colonial times.

López had forced Argentina and Brazil, adversarial powers, into each other's arms by attacking them both. Their taking advantage of the war to press territorial claims was to be expected. When wartime, anti-Mitre risings occurred in Argentina, López concluded that a widespread Argentine sympathy for his cause existed.[69] But pro-Paraguayan sentiment was at best a pretext and lagged far behind provincial self-interest, especially hostility to Buenos Aires. The provinces opposed the increased taxation and loss of life that accompanied the war. Nevertheless, some in Argentina read Paraguayan propaganda. Thomas Hutchinson, the British consul in Santa Fe, was convinced by López's arguments. His assertion that Paraguayans were so self-sufficient that they could fight almost indefinitely is a virtual paraphrase of articles in *El Semanario*.[70] He was wrong.

In the southern campaign of 1865, Paraguay lost enough men at Uruguaiana and at Yatay that its ruination was now under way. By 1866, López faced a workforce shortage that would intensify in the coming months. In the late 1850s he and his father had made most adult men accountable for army service as ". . . the draft became nearly universal."[71] An American observer in the 1860s noted that after López pulled his army back into Paraguay, every able-bodied man in the country was in arms, as the dictator searched for new recruits. Later during the war, López's recruiters would to go after ". . . the very old and the very young, until all from eight to eighty, who were not in prison, were forced into the army."[72] Probably not many eight-year-olds were in the army, but boys of ten and eleven were. Young boys labored on his home-front projects. The loss of men was ruinous to the economy. Great sacrifices were imposed upon all. The civilian population, in turn, was mostly female.

Even in April 1866, López still commanded an army of forty thousand men, an effective force. He mobilized the nation for a war as close to a total war as was possible in the 1860s. Paraguayan women became war workers. They produced the food, clothing, and supplies for the front and for the domestic economy, too. They nursed the wounded. López mobilized Paraguay to a degree that the French authors of the *levée en masse* had only dreamed of in 1793. He had to do so to survive. He could not import war materiel or basic items like paper for the issuance of orders and for his newspapers, owing to the Allied closure of the Paraná River.

Of his three enemies, Brazil was the most formidable. Ultimately, the empire would mobilize "some 110,000 men . . . only 1.5 percent of Brazil's . . . nine million inhabitants."[73] The Brazilian warriors equaled about 25 percent of the entire Paraguayan population at the outset of the war.

At Paso Pucú, López worked diligently, as always. He wrote letters, dictated orders, planned strategy, made tactical decisions, operated his spy network, observed battles through his telescope, and read and edited or wrote all the copy in his newspapers. At the midday and evening meals, he interrupted his work. Surrounded by his mistress, senior officers, and sycophants, he consumed large meals. He began to imbibe more heavily. He continued to drink the fine wine while providing inferior brands to his retinue, who customarily dined with him. This group included military leaders, civilians visiting from Asunción, an occasional diplomat, Bishop Palacios, and Francisco's family, usually Madame Lynch and Panchito, their oldest son. Occasionally brother Benigno joined the repasts, as did his brothers-in-law. They ate the same fresh meat, poultry, and the fruits of the season that he ate, at a time when most of his soldiers hungered. To sit at his table was to be a flatterer of the marshal president. Mealtime guests avoided topics that offended him. After a glass or two of wine, López told jokes, at which everyone dutifully laughed. He discouraged joke-telling by others. Following dinner, López enjoyed cigars, coffee, and brandy.[74] The increased alcohol consumption was beginning to wear him down psychologically.

After meals, López usually returned to headquarters. There he analyzed reports, issued orders, and debriefed his spies, the dreaded *pyragüés*. Their mere existence enforced army loyalty and discouraged even mild dissents. Fear of the spies was universal. No civilian or military official enjoyed autonomy. To act independently courted the dictator's wrath, incarceration, or death. Nevertheless, López's relations with his immediate subordinates—chosen for loyalty instead of ability, intelligence, or creativity—was generally good in 1866 and 1867. He boosted army morale when he reviewed the troops and visited the wounded in hospitals. In dealing with his senior officers, his manner was usually reserved, except for the brave, illiterate General José Dìaz. The latter commanded Paraguayan forces at the battle of Curupaity in September 1866, when Paraguayans killed almost ten thousand Allied troops with a loss of fewer than one hundred of their own. When López engaged his barefoot soldiers, he dressed ostentatiously, believing that his elegance displayed his superiority.[75] As per usual, he spoke and they listened.

With war matters foremost in his mind, he continued to attend to personal interests, especially enriching himself and Lynch. Throughout the war, López enabled Lynch's plundering of Paraguayan citizens, as she amassed landed wealth. By July 1866, she still addressed him affectionately; but she was now more formal and respectful, indicating her realization of his potential danger even to her. One manifestation of her fears was her safeguarding of valuables at the American legation. By the mid-1860s, she wrote and spoke Spanish well. Her business sense remained sharp.

Writing to her lover when they were apart on his birthday, she enlisted his aid in adding to her properties. Her pose was that of a helpless female who needed his masculine support. She played to his vanity. She apologized for his not having yet received her birthday presents. With the country imperiled and impoverished by war, Lynch worried about her inability to find velvet. She fed Francisco's ego by praising the progress of his new palace in Asunción. She informed him of domestic developments. His boys Panchito and Leopoldo had been sick, but the family had enthusiastically celebrated Francisco's July 24 birthday. She had arranged great ceremonial toasts to him by headquarters personnel in the orange groves around their quarters. She sent him kisses from her and from his beloved children. She added a postscript. He needed to address financial matters, especially the account books[76] and the Lynch fortune.

Lynch wrote business letters to her factors without invoking her relationship to her "Don Pancho." Nobody was foolish enough to ignore their ties. Negotiating on her own, she paid 29,937 pesos for one property, although the total price was supposed to be 36,458 pesos.[77] In July and August 1866, she directed José M. Areco to present a valuable little box to López. The president would pay him for it. She fretted about the difficulty of obtaining a carriage for Leopoldo.[78] Like López, she negotiated through agents, especially Francisco Fernández, whom the marshal president had promoted from lieutenant to cavalry captain and eventually to colonel before his patron executed him. Despite his rank, Fernández's services to the nation were not military but rather advancing the fortunes of López and Lynch. She also used a front woman for her acquisitions. Lynch was active in many business ventures. She loaned 6,663 pesos to one Rafael Zavala at an annual interest rate of 8 percent. She paid only one-third of the total in specie, the rest in paper money, then almost worthless. She held a lien on Zavala's house on Calle Uruguay as surety for the loan.[79] Her lover also took advantage of wartime distress to add to his substantial prewar holdings. From Petrona Flecha, Josefa and Dolores Flecha, and Tomasa Pérez, López through Fernández bought one property on Calle León in 1865. The next year he purchased another on Calle Recoleta in San Roque from Rosa Isabel and María de la Cruz Ayala and others. He paid them 1,250 pesos in paper currency, which he printed as he wished. The agent with whom the sellers dealt was again Fernández, now elevated to captain because of his service to His Excellency the President.[80]

At the outset of the war, López was a military novice, despite his pretense of erudition. The marshal was no dullard, however, and he learned a little about tactics. He could plan a battle competently on occasion. He needed all of his talent, because by our spring, the Paraguayan otoño of 1866, he faced Allied armies on Paraguayan soil. On April 15–16, 1866, an Allied army of fifteen thousand had invaded Paraguay, first taking the fort of Itapirú. López did not resist effectively, and the crossing of the Alto Paraná to the Paraguayan side was virtually unopposed. López should have attacked then because an opposed river crossing is exceedingly difficult. The fearful dictator, though, fled north from Paso de la Patria alone, ahead of his guard, retinue, and family toward the safety of Humaitá. He then sent orders back south for the army to evacuate its riverine positions. He astutely positioned the bulk of his army above Estero Bellaco, a creek running through a swampy area and difficult for attackers to penetrate. At Estero Bellaco, the battle named for the creek, on May 2, 1866, López sent General José Díaz and four thousand infantry and cavalry to harass the invaders. Taking advantage of the terrain and of surprise, Díaz moved his men through the swamps. He startled an Uruguayan colonel, captured his artillery, and moved on to attack Brazilians and Argentines. Paraguayans suffered more than two thousand casualties, an astounding 50 percent casualty rate. López had conceived a plan for a reconnaissance in force, and Díaz's foolhardiness turned it into a too-costly engagement without a military objective. As after other contests, López proclaimed it "a splendid victory," although careful observers thought otherwise. A year later, he recalled May 2, 1866, as "a day of national pride and glory for the victors of that memorable journey." Besides demonstrating a willingness to die for their devotion to him, another reason that he thought the effort splendid was, "The plan of attack was drawn up by the Excellent Marshal López."[81]

The battle of Tuyuty, on May 24, 1866, was "the greatest battle in South American history"[82]—that is how he wanted it remembered, and it certainly was one of the bloodiest. López left the execution of his orders to his handcuffed subordinates. He pursued a tactical offensive while remaining on the strategic defensive. Lacking formal military training or command experience, López had little chance of a positive outcome. The López of López's imagination was Napoleonic, but the Napoleonic way of war had little relevance for a small nation like Paraguay.

Tuyuty lay between the Paraguayan bastion of Humaitá and the Allied base of Paso de la Patria on the Río Paraná. The Allied army numbered possibly thirty-five thousand, with a Brazilian majority. López at that time commanded about twenty-five thousand Paraguayans. In the modern world, commanders seek to outnumber defenders at the point of attack by 3–1 or 4–1 to ensure success, a partial explanation of his holding out so long. On the tactical offensive, López ignored the conventional wisdom. He concluded that the bravery of the Paraguayan soldier, which was considerable, could overcome Allied numbers. He ignored military reality. He planned a three-pronged attack against the enemy. He appointed his brother-in-law, General Vicente Barrios, to command five thousand men. Barrios's force and a similar number under General Francisco Isidoro Resquín would attack simultaneously, a reasonable plan. Surely surprise would overcome his enemy's superior numbers.

López, however, had drawn up the plan without adequate knowledge of the terrain over which his men must advance. He also incorrectly gauged Allied intentions. He conducted no prior reconnaissance, thus depriving his army of tactical intelligence. Owing to the difficult terrain, Barrios's force arrived at the battle too late. There was no surprise. Since López was far from the action, he could not revise his orders when his plan went awry. Obeying Marshal López's orders even after he realized that he was in trouble, Barrios attacked. López's subordinates had learned not to prepare for contingencies. Deviation from his orders would require innovation, which the commander could not tolerate. Barrios understood that his brother-in-law would ignore marriage ties if he disobeyed. The marshal was out of contact. He had retreated even farther from harm's way, far behind his headquarters. The general officers of the Paraguayan army were slaves to the rigidity of López's commands. They and their men fell victim to the marshal's failure to scout the terrain. Just as significant was López's fear of able, intelligent senior officers.[83]

López himself must bear responsibility for the Paraguayan defeat at Tuyuty in May 1866. That Paraguayans lacked detailed knowledge of the terrain and that several units failed to coordinate their movements removed the element of surprise. That these were López's fault, he, for once, recognized. The unimaginative Resquín was a typical López officer. He wasted precious Paraguayan manpower in frontal assaults. The Paraguayan fighting man in 1866 and after was often close to starvation. Still he fought tenaciously, often fanatically. Given the absence of true flanks and of the inflexibility of the supreme commander, frontal assaults were the only possibility open to López's army. The marshal insisted on conducting tactical offensives, which gained glory in his mind. Paraguayan casualties totaled an astonishing eleven to twelve thousand killed and wounded, contrasted to about four thousand for the Allies. It is also possible that there were eight thousand Allied and six thousand Paraguayan deaths, as the figures throughout the war were imprecise at best. What was not in doubt was that Paraguayan manpower was finite. López's best remaining soldiers died at Tuyuty, extending the nation's ruination. The war settled into a stalemate. López continued to sacrifice his soldiers, staving off defeat. He wanted people to remember Tuyuty as a "glorious and splendid battle," a version that later became gospel in Paraguay.

THE TRIPLE ALLIANCE PUSHES HARDER

The Paraguayan soldier had earned new laurels, López boasted. What was noteworthy was that the "plan of attack was drawn up by the able warrior, the Most Excellent Marshal Lopez," producing "that great victory." Tuyuty was, the Marshal exulted, "an event that history will tell in pages of gold . . . a memorable epoch in the annals of Paraguayan valor."[04] Tuyuty, however, was a defeat for Paraguayans. As usual, the marshal awarded numerous decorations for valor, announcing the promotions himself. He had no other inducements to proffer.

After a year and a half of war, López held his armies behind strong defensive positions. His willingness to sacrifice his nation's people, his soldiers' preference for death at the hands of the enemy over dishonor, their fear of corporal and capital punishment, and Paraguayans' fear and hatred of the Brazilian enemy allowed the dictator to check the Allies. At that point, some women "became increasingly critical of the . . . regime."[85] They were punished harshly.

López had chosen where to take his stand sagaciously. Allied armies lacked accessible flanks to attack. On their left, ran the Río Paraguay, and Paraguayan canon and river obstructions blocked their warships from sailing upriver. To the west of the river lay the supposedly impenetrable Gran Chaco, although both Paraguayan and Allied armies would ultimately move north through it. On the Allied right (the Paraguayan left) lay a series of impenetrable swamps. Between the river and the swamps stretched the entrenched Paraguayan army. Its men were incredibly brave, or foolhardy, or more fearful of López than they were of the enemy, or a combination of all of the above. They had cannons of many calibers and arsenals that could supply the guns with ordinance.

For two years, the Allied way of war would be bloody, unimaginative frontal assaults. The casualties on both sides were shocking. Those of López's forces were the more ruinous, given the small population base. Waging a war of attrition that eventually reduced the Paraguayan population by half, the Allies kept up the pressure. Bartolomé Mitre, the first Allied commander as well as the president of Argentina, was cautious. He opposed a flanking attack through the Chaco. Most others agreed that it was impenetrable. In fact, the Chaco terrain was merely difficult, not impassable.

The problems of coalition warfare and national rivalries slowed the Allies.[86] Mitre attributed the length of the war to Argentine disunity, although the majority of Allied forces were increasingly Brazilian. Mitre had "the slows," which compounded the problems inherent in a coalition command.[87] The Brazilian navy was less helpful than it should have been.

Marshal López also dallied throughout 1866, having no objectives other than to continue to rule Paraguay and seek glory, which meant repelling Allied advances. His efforts had caused a shocking loss of life at Tuyuty in May 1866[88] and astounding Allied casualties at the Battle of Curupaity in 1866. Although he called these conflicts victories, with such "victories" as Tuyuty López would eventually run out of men. Before both Tuyuty and Curupaity, the marshal prepared detailed battle plans. Unfortunately for the officers and men who had to do the fighting, the intervening distance meant that the marshal was again too far away to revise his orders as the initial ones became obsolete. He liked to position himself just close enough to the action, possibly on the reverse slope of a hill, so that he could observe the fighting through his powerful telescope and yet stay out of harm's way.[89]

At the Battle of Corrales in May 1866, López's men had showed fighting spirit and tenacity, which pleased him. He had sent them across the Río Paraná to the Allied southern bank of the Alto Paraná River under General José E. Díaz, a commander courageous to a fault, a charismatic leader devoted to López. That he came from a humble background, was virtually illiterate and uncomfortable in Spanish, meant that he posed no threat to the dictator, who sent raiding parties across the river to rattle the Allies and boost morale. Corrales was merely a large raid. In this inconclusive contest, the Paraguayans suffered a casualty rate of greater than 40 percent, a shocking number. Corrales was militarily a useless battle. If Paraguayans had won, the battle would still have been a waste. The marshal had no clear military objective when he ordered it, as his goals were propaganda and personal glory. He crowed that his men displayed to the world their bravery, the exhibition of which was his objective. Their apparently suicidal devotion to the cause and their hatred of the enemy were what López sustained through his propaganda and also by capital punishment for the disobedient. He bragged that the boldness of his orders and their bravery would cause other nations to honor and respect Paraguay.

A FRUITLESS PEACE TALK

In mid-1866, Francisco López decided that he had had enough of the war. He wished to end the conflict. He had never defined what victory meant. He wished glory and honor for himself and his nation and little more, although he occasionally mentioned territorial gains, boasting about taking the Mato Grosso and settling disputed boundaries. Proposing to return to the antebellum status quo, he sought a peace. He requested a talk with the Alliance leaders. Earlier, however, the Brazilian emperor and his council of state (or council of ministers) had forbidden their military and civilian officials even to meet with the Paraguayan dictator. This sprang partly from Pedro II's "undying hatred of López."[90] It also resulted from the situation. As Brazil understood it, a large state cannot tolerate a small state springing an unprovoked attack. The Uruguayans, the insignificant partner in the alliance, also refused to negotiate with López because of his insults to Flores, the current Uruguayan president. Only the Argentine leader agreed to talk with him.

Thus at Yataity-Corá, located between Humaitá and the Allied lines, on September 12, 1866, the Paraguayan marshal met alone with President Mitre. Outfitted in the uniform of a French general, López wore the Order of Merit that he had awarded himself. He set out with a large party that included his son Panchito and numerous subordinates. Before reaching his destination, he had to stop for a drink of brandy. One of his subordinates later conjectured that he needed spirits to overcome his anxiety before meeting with the Argentine leader. He was truly anxious, but it is also probable that he was by now physically dependent on alcohol.

López's Argentine adversary, Mitre, had only limited strategic command of Allied forces, with incomplete control of Uruguayan and Brazilian units. He could not order Brazilian or Uruguayan officers to attend the conference. In contrast to López's ostentatious garb, Mitre dressed humbly for the meeting, in a frock coat and old black hat. To one observer, he appeared "Quixotic."[91] Because Pedro II and his government were determined to remove López from power, they refused to discuss any terms that did not begin with the marshal president's resignation. Marshal Polidoro, head of the Brazilian army, boycotted the meeting. Because López insisted on retaining control over Paraguay, the talks were doomed. The Brazilians demanded López's unconditional surrender. He would not budge. He loved power. Mitre honored the conditions of the Triple Alliance treaty. The two men talked for several hours, but they talked alone. Their conversation must be inferred from each man's later recollections and behavior. Given the intransigence of Brazil and of López, what was said at the Mitre–López chat made little difference anyway. A peaceful settlement was impossible.

After the Allies rejected López's overture, the contestants fought the Battle of Curupaity, a terrible, bloody affair, on September 22, 1866, that resulted in many Allied and few Paraguayan casualties. What mattered to López was that the engagement brought Paraguay another "brilliant laurel." He wanted the world to recognize that it brought "illustrious renown" to Paraguay and its leader, according to its leader.[92]

Thus, López's account of what transpired at Yataity-Corá must be seen through the mind of a man who could take pride in so many deaths. Not even a scribe was present to take notes. Still there is no reason to disbelieve López's claim that he sought "an honorable settlement." His concept of honor, however, was one in which honor was for him alone. His quest for honor was a zero-sum game. To gain honor, one must take it from another. López could conceive of no honorable settlement that would force him to relinquish control of Paraguay. He argued, though, that the bloodshed by both sides had been worth the sacrifice. Paraguay had demonstrated its honor on the field of battle. His men had proved the nation's worth, at least in his estimation. The blood of the young men of all four nations, he thought, was sufficient to drown the issues that had led to the rupture. He hoped that he and his nation could resume peaceful relations with its neighbors. Unable to fathom any other point of view but his own, López had vainly hoped that the Allies would agree. He failed utterly to comprehend how gravely his attacks had offended the Brazilian emperor and the Argentine president. Pedro II and his government believed that allowing López to remain in office after attacking their country would dishonor them. Even the marginally more conciliatory Argentines wanted the marshal gone as a condition of peace. After five hours of talks, Mitre and López could not even agree on the wording of a memorandum about what they had discussed.

López was unhappy with the outcome. He blamed his enemies. He later had one of his newspapers dub Flores, Mitre, and Pedro II "the three bandits." He told his people that the Paraguayan soldier "has inspired terror in the negroes of D. Pedro."[93]

No effective opposition to the dictator developed because the López family had chased away men with leadership ability. Francisco eliminated most remaining men of the Paraguayan upper class, who might have had political aspirations, early in the war. He drafted them and assigned them to units where the fighting was fiercest and the casualties heaviest. At the front, Allied armies finished the job for him. Most Paraguayan men, unlettered and fiercely patriotic, obeyed López's orders, having been conditioned by three centuries of authoritarian government. They fought tenaciously and most died. They believed "that the Brazilians," supposedly the last remaining slave power in the hemisphere, "wished to enslave them,"[94] knowing that a large number of Brazilians were in fact chattel slaves. A host of factors—the Paraguayan tenacity, the Allies' delay, Allied military incompetence, the difficulty of coalition war, and a disunified Allied command—allowed the marshal to claim numerous victories for himself and his forces. Tamandaré, the Brazilian naval commander, for example, refused to take orders from an Argentine army general, Mitre. Most engagements that are still called triumphs in Paraguay today were only Pyrrhic victories.[95]

The Battle of Curupaity, named for a town along the Paraguay River below Humaitá, occurred on September 22, 1866. López's forces won a stunning tactical victory that in fact had little impact on the outcome of the war. In Paraguay today, this contest is characterized as a glorious episode in patriotic tracts, schoolbooks, and the daily press. One recent textbook writer tells schoolchildren that it was "the greatest of the victories recorded in our military annals," and it "was achieved by the heroism of our Paraguayan race."[96] Another account correctly calls it an "Allied disaster." The Allies suffered ten thousand casualties and Paraguayans just 92,[97] figures that are probably close to the truth. General Mitre ordered the attack, ignorant of the unforgiving terrain over which his forces would march. A large measure of credit for repelling the attack must go to the foreign specialists who prepared the defenses, although López took full credit. These fortifications included a trench, six feet deep and eleven feet wide, an earthwork barrier topping twelve feet, and numerous cannons.

López appointed as battlefield commander the illiterate General José Díaz, an inspiring leader. His soldiers are credited with nearly superhuman feats of heroism. At Curupaity, they held a good defensive position, with the Río Paraguay on their right and the virtually impassable Laguna Mendoza on the left. Allied forces attacked over a narrow front against concentrated fire. Although the Argentine and Brazilian soldiers fought well, the obstacles were too great to overcome. British observers then and now agree that the Allied forces endured a loss of nine thousand men killed and wounded, while Paraguayan losses were "incredibly small."[98] The Paraguayans failed to follow up their victory with a vigorous pursuit, because like most other nineteenth-century armies they were too exhausted to do so, although the Paraguayans were not bloodied by Curupaity. During the battle itself, as on all other occasions until the last days of the war, López remained a safe distance from the battlefield. He followed it by telegraph as the conflict unfolded. Because Allied losses were so great, the three nations were forced into relative inactivity for the next ten months.

López was joyous. For him Curupaity was another "brilliant laurel." He immodestly spread the word that "its hero is the most Excellent Marshal López," who was "the pride of Paraguay."[99] For the marshal president it was a suitable triumph. He honored General Díaz with a banquet. He invited Mrs. Lynch, Bishop Palacios, and Díaz's brother officers. One hopes that they enjoyed the party, because Díaz and the bishop would soon be dead. In February 1867, Díaz exposed himself to enemy fire and was killed. Marshal López executed the lickspittle Bishop Palacios the following year.

López was so pleased by Curupaity, a successful defensive engagement extending his rule by as much as a year, that he extended his magnanimity to Father Fidel Maíz. The gifted cleric had suffered torment under the terrible conditions imposed by the dictator for four years. Agony had broken his spirit. The learned priest was now a tool of the dictator, whom he feared, with good reason. Maíz publicly confessed that he had erred four years earlier, but he added that he had done so in a spirit of patriotism. López ordered Maíz to praise Díaz, prolonging his humiliation and emphasizing how tenuous was his freedom. Díaz was the arresting officer who had confined Maíz in physical restraints. As he freed the priest, López warned Maíz to be carefully obedient, obedience being one of the dictator's favorite virtues. Maíz did as he was told and even praised his former jailor. He was erudite and an expressive writer. Having suffered, he now zealously supported the dictator. He helped to publicize Marshal López's battlefield success and his generalship through his periodicals.[100]

The Paraguayan president had a practical motive for releasing Maíz. It was not an act of goodwill, of which he had precious little. Recently Pope

Pius IX had made the bishop of Paraguay subordinate to the archbishop of Buenos Aires, an administrative inferiority that López found unacceptable. He had heard of the reform of clerical jurisdictions from *La Tribuna*, an Argentine newspaper, and by way of telegraph. He then ordered his military and clergy, headed by Bishop Palacios, to respond. The bishop kept Maíz, unquestionably the brightest cleric in Paraguay, away from the meeting. When the assembly produced its report, López rejected it on the grounds that Maíz had not participated. Maíz's theological training and mastery of canon law outshone that of all other priests, especially the intellectually challenged Bishop Palacios. Rather than revising the original document, Maíz wrote a new one. López published it in *El Semanario*. Father Fidel argued that the papacy's policy needed revision.[101] He wrote effectively and impressed the dictator with the power of his argument, although he did not impress the pope. López, however, was the man on whom Maíz's life depended, not Pius XI. As Maíz's star rose in the eyes of the only man in Paraguay whose opinion counted, Bishop Palacios's fell. The bishop's servility was soon rivaled by that of the ex-convict priest. Father Maíz would commit atrocities in the dictator's name that would dwarf the sickening adulation of the buffoonish bishop.

NOTES

1. George Masterman, *Seven Eventful Years in Paraguay: A Narrative of Personal Experience Amongst the Paraguayans*, 2nd ed. (London: Samson Low, Son, and Marston, 1870), 63.

2. George Thompson, C.E., *The War in Paraguay with a Historical Sketch of the Country, Its People, and Notes upon the Military Engineering of the War* (London: Longman, Green, and Co., 1869), 21.

3. Masterman, *Seven Eventful Years*, 73.

4. Masterman, *Seven Eventful Years*, 57.

5. *Semanario*, Feb. 25, 1865.

6. Thompson, *War in Paraguay*, 44.

7. Since the newspapers were completely partisan, entire issues should be considered editorials. All citations are from the first page unless otherwise noted. López made sure that pieces about himself began on the front page.

8. Thompson, *War in Paraguay*, 23.

9. Thompson, *War in Paraguay*, 23.

10. *Semanario*, Mar. 4, 1865.

11. Roderick J. Barman, *Citizen Emperor: Pedro II and the Making of Modern Brazil, 1825–91* (Stanford, CA: Stanford University Press, 1999), 196.

12. Barman, *Citizen Emperor*, 197.

13. William H. Jeffrey, *Mitre and Argentina* (New York: Library Publishers, 1952), 202.

14. FSL, Message to Congress, Asunción, March 5, 1865, appearing in *Semanario*, March 14, 1865.

15. Thompson, *War in Paraguay*, 36.

16. Thompson, *War in Paraguay*, 39. The Brazilian commander's order to retreat was militarily correct. López thought it pusillanimous.

17. Thompson, *War in Paraguay*, 42–43.

18. Thompson, *War in Paraguay*, 42.

19. *Semanario*, March 11, 1865.

20. *Semanario*, March 18, 1865.

21. John Keegan, *The Face of Battle: A Study of Agincourt, Waterloo, and the Somme* (Harmonsworth, UK: Penguin Books, Ltd., 1976), 190.

22. Thompson, *War in Paraguay*, 43–44.

23. Thompson, *War in Paraguay*, 56.

24. *Semanario*, March 25, 1865.

25. Jeffrey, *Mitre and Argentina*, 202.

26. *Semanario*, April 1, 1865.

27. Thompson, *War in Paraguay*, 29.

28. *Semanario*, April 22, 1865.

29. Thompson, *War in Paraguay*, 82.

30. Thomas L. Whigham, *The Paraguayan War, Volume I: Causes and Early Conduct* (Lincoln: University of Nebraska Press, 2002), 187.

31. Jeffrey, *Mitre and Argentiina*, 202.

32. Jeffrey, *Mitre and Argentina*, 203.

33. Jeffrey, *Mitre and Argentina*, 204–205.

34. Masterman, *Seven Eventful Years*, 110.

35. Arturo Bray, *Solano López: soldado de la gloria y del infortunio* (Asunción: Editorial Lector, 1996; orig. publ. Buenos Aires, 1945), 204.

36. Whigham, *Paraguayan War*, I, 339.

37. Fidel Maíz, *Etapas de mi vida: Contestación a las imposturas de Juan Silvano Godoy* (Asunción: Imprenta la Mundial, 1919), 12.

38. Chris Leuchars, *To the Bitter End: Paraguay and the War of the Triple Alliance* (Westport, CT: Greenwood Press, 2002), 64.

39. FSL to Resquín, Humaitá, July 21, 1865, *Proclamas y cartas del Mariscal López* (Buenos Aires: Editorial Asunción, 1957).

40. FSL to Resquín, Humaitá, July 27, 1865, *Proclamas y cartas*.

41. *Semanario*, February 25, 1865.

42. FSL to Resquín, Humaitá, July 28, 1865, *Proclamas y cartas*.

43. Francisco Barriero al general Vicente Barrios, Asunción, Feb. 8, 1866, ANA, SH, vol. 347; The manuscript copy of the "trial" is in ANA, SH, vol. 447, no. 6, especially "Notificación de la sentencia a los sentenciados a pena capital," Paso de la Patria, Jan. 8, 1866. Also executed were Valiente, Gauna, and private soldier José Villalva.

44. *El Centinela*, June 13, 1867.

45. Whigham, *Paraguayan War*, I, 308.

46. For accounts of the Battle of the Riacheulo, see Loren Scott Patterson, "The War of the Triple Alliance: Paraguayan Offensive Phase—A Military History," Unpublished Ph.D. diss. (Georgetown University, 1974); Whigham, *Paraguayan War*, I, 308–27, *passim*; and Leuchars, *To the Bitter End*, 65–70.

47. Leuchars, *To the Bitter End*, 69.

48. *Centinela*, June 13, 1867.

49. Patterson, "War of the Triple Alliance," 240.

50. Barman, *Citizen Emperor*, 202.

51. Peter M. Beattie, *Tribute of Blood: Army, Honor, Race, and Nation in Brazil, 1864–1945* (Durham, NC: Duke University Press, 2001), 39.

52. FSL to V.P. Sánchez, GHQ, Humaitá, Sept. 7, 1865, ANA/CRB 2539. "Victory or Death" was not just a slogan with Marshal López. If a commander did not emerge victorious, he had better return from battle either wounded or with casualty rates high enough to prove the bravery of Paraguayan soldiers and thus their devotion to President López.

53. Leuchars, *To the Bitter End*, 84.

54. FSL, Proclamation to the Paraguayan Army, G.H.Q., Humaitá, Oct. 6, 1865, *Proclamas y cartas*.

55. Pedro II to countess of Barral, Sept. 19, 1865, in Barman, *Citizen Emperor*, 205, 465.

56. FSL to Resquín, Humaitá, Oct. 30, 1865, *Proclamas y cartas*.

57. FSL to Resquín, Humaitá, Aug. 16, 1865, *Proclamas y cartas*.

58. Thompson, *War in Paraguay*, 84.

59. FSL, Proclamation to the Division of the South, G.H.Q., Paso de la Patria, Dec. 1, 1865, *Proclamas y cartas*.

60. Masterman, *Seven Eventful Years*, 102.

61. Thompson, *War in Paraguay*, 52, 114–16.

62. Thompson, *War in Paraguay*, 140.

63. Whigham, *Paraguayan War*, I, 185.

64. Michael Walzer, *Just and Unjust Wars: A Moral Argument with Historical Illustrations* (New York: Basic Books, 1977).

65. FSL to Mitre, Humaitá, Nov. 20, 1865, *Proclamas y cartas*.

66. Barman, *Citizen Emperor*, 199.

67. Leuchars, *To the Bitter End*, 45.

68. See Whigham, *Paraguayan War*, I, 276–81, for a view of the treaty sympathetic to a patriotic Paraguayan point of view.

69. Bray, *Solano López*, 191.

70. Thomas J. Hutchinson, *The Paraná, with Incidents of the Paraguayan War and South American Recollections from 1861 to 1868* (London: Edward Stanford, 1868).

71. Whigham, *Paraguayan War*, I, 183.

72. Charles A. Washburn, *The History of Paraguay, with Notes of Personal Observations and Reminiscences of Diplomacy under Difficulties*, 2 vols. (Boston: Lee and Shepard, 1871), II, 167.

73. Beattie, *Tribute of Blood*, 38.

74. Bray, *Solano López*, 214–16.

75. Bray, *Solano López*, 214–16.

76. EAL to FSL, Paso Pucú, July 26, 1866, ANA/CRB 4251.

77. "Gastos hechos en la compra deel terreno . . ." (Expenditures made in the purchase of lands . . ."), ANA/CRB 4251.

78. EAL to José M. Areco, n.p. [Paso Pucú], letters of July 30 and August 23, 1866, ANA/CRB 4251.

79. "Elisa A. Lynch, natural de Inglaterra y residente en la Repulica desde ha muchos años c/ hijos ciudadanos del pais digo . . . ," ("Elisa A. Lynch, native of England and resident in the Republic for many years w/ children citizens of the country says . . .") Paso Pucú, July 20, 1866, ANA/CRB 4251.

80. Sale, Asunción, July 20, 1865, ANA/CRB 4125; and "Documentos a la finca que compro el ciudadano Francisco S. López, Presidente de la República ubicada en el 2.o distrito de San Roque," ("Documents relating to the property that Citizen Francisco S. López, President of the Republic, purchased, located in the 2d district of San Roque") ANA/CRB 4297; this transaction finally closed Nov. 12, 1866. This document lists Fernández as a captain of cavalry, infantry, and artillery.

81. *El Centinela*, May 2, 1867.

82. Leuchars, *To the Bitter End*, 117.

83. Bray, *Solano López*, 224.

84. *El Centinela*, May 23, 1867.

85. Barbara Potthast, "Protagonists, Victims, and Heroes: Paraguayan Women during the Great War," in *I Die with My Country*, ed. Hendrik Kraay and Thomas L. Whigham (Lincoln: University of Nebraska Press), 53–54. According to records of the justices of the peace, throughout the nation, ". . . Paraguayan women (and men) never followed their president so unconditionally as certain foreign observers and some later historians have argued," 53–54.

86. Bray, *Solano López*, 217.

87. Bray, *Solano López*, 217–18.

88. There were two battles of this name. One occurred in May 1866 and the other in November 1867. The first resulted in 11,000—or maybe only 8,000—Paraguayan casualties although the number was possibly only 6,000. Either way, it was an incredibly bloody battle. The figures of dead and wounded for the second battle were lower but with more Paraguayan than Allied casualties. Like the Allies, López called them both victories, and this has been parroted for many decades by his glorifiers; see Leuchars, *To the Bitter End*, 117–28, 173–76; and John Hoyt Williams, *The Rise and Fall of the Paraguayan Republic, 1800–1870* (Austin: Institute of Latin American Studies, University of Texas), 212–14, 222.

89. Bray, *Solano López*, 220.

90. Leuchars, *To the Bitter End*, 147.

91. Thompson, *War in Paraguay*, 174.

92. *El Centinela*, Sept. 19, 1867.

93. *El Centinela*, Aug. 8, 1867.

94. Masterman, *Seven Eventful Years*, x.

95. Miguel Rigual, *Lo mejor de la Historia Paraguaya* (Asunción: Editorial Gráfica Mercurio, 2002), 85.

96. Rigual, *Lo mejor de la Historia Paraguaya*, 85.

97. Luis G. Benítez, *Manual de historia del Paraguay* (Asunción: n.p., 2002), 113.

98. Thompson, who was there, says that the Paraguayans lost 54 men killed and wounded; *War in Paraguay*, 178; Leuchars, writing in 2002, essentially concurs, saying that Paraguayan losses were "fewer than 100," *To the Bitter End*, 153.

99. *El Centinela*, Sept. 19, 1867.

100. Maíz, *Etapas de mi vida: contestación a las imposturas de Juan Silvano Godoy* (Asunción: Imprenta La Mundial, 1919), 16–17.

101. Maíz, *Etapas*, 24–26.

6

The Final Agonies

HONOR, ABSOLUTE POWER, AND THE FAMILY TIES THAT BIND

From September 1866 to August 1867, López oversaw a partial recovery of his nation and armies. He had sent so many men to their deaths, possibly forty thousand in 1865, however, that a major revival of striking power was impossible. The Allies' war of attrition was bleeding Paraguay to death. López nevertheless shored up his southern defenses. He still held major celebrations for the two greatest days in the nation's history—his birthday, July 24, and the day he became president, October 16. On both occasions, López gathered his senior officers in full dress uniforms and went to Mass. There they listened to Bishop Palacios, who "would address him a most complimentary speech, to which López, who was a very good speaker, would reply at length."[1] He was an effective speaker to a captive audience. He was a vigorous conversationalist because of his "good command of the language"[2] and because none dared to interrupt him. After Mass, the dictator hosted a banquet, serving champagne, beer, and tasty food. His guests enjoyed themselves in the shade of the orange grove at his headquarters. He was close enough to the front lines so that he could boast of his martial ability and so that the fiction was not seen as incredible by people at a distance. But "at the very time that he was . . . hid away from danger, he had his correspondents for the *Semanario* around him, writing the most extravagant articles, in praise of his valor, his sacrifices, and his generalship."[3] There he maintained surveillance over disloyalty and defeatism. His retinue toasted him, and lubricated with alcohol López exhibited good humor. He did not permit them to honor any one else. Of course, they were drinking his wine and eating his food. Nevertheless, López distrusted "those around him, even those . . . most strongly bound to him by ties of blood and self-interest. . . ."[4] By now, five years of absolute power had combined with his other faults to corrupt him absolutely.

He nevertheless supervised his family in Asunción. He communicated by telegraph with his brother, the ailing Venancio, suffering from "chucho," sometimes referred to as a recurring fever but reported by others to be syphilis. Francisco had appointed Venancio a colonel, though he was without interest in or aptitude for military matters. Francisco reported war developments to his brother. Once, he referred to the search for a traitor. Another time he was pleased by the discovery of saltpeter (potassium nitrate), necessary for gunpowder. Routinely he asked about Venancio's health and that of their mother, whose good spirits came and went. At times, he asked about Rafaela and Inocencia. He told Venancio to monitor their mother's activities. He showed his concern about whether or not she passed the night comfortably, but, in this, he displayed his need for control. He also asked Venancio to keep tabs on Fernández, overseer of the finances and properties of López and Lynch. In 1866 and 1867, he instructed Venancio to carry out minor tasks, including payments to wounded soldiers: 100 paper pesos to married private soldiers, 25 to single men, and 100 pesos for wounded sergeants. He thought about building a park next to the railroad at Cerro León. López expressed interest in his children with Lynch, who traveled by boat from the front to Asunción, while neglecting his other offspring. In the capital, Lynch's boys visited their grandmother. Francisco was sometimes on cordial terms with his brother Benigno and sometimes not.[5]

In this correspondence the lack of empathy, even for his siblings and his mother, is striking. The letters confirm impressions gleaned from his behavior, especially after 1868, and other correspondence. Although he professed sympathy and concern, Francisco made no effort to understand—nor is it likely that he was psychologically or emotionally equipped to understand—how his mother, siblings, or children felt. A typical example was his earlier absence from Inocencia's wedding. They were his family, and to be seen as honorable he must look after their welfare, when it did not interfere with his own. His sense of honor propelled him to inquire about their welfare. Any insult to them would blemish his own honor, unless he himself was the one who gave the insult, in which case it was acceptable.

When Venancio replied to his older brother, he never addressed him familiarly or affectionately, always formally. He saluted Francisco as "Most Excellent Señor Marshal President of the Republic," a measure of deference that even in that more formal age was seen as extraordinary. Venancio felt it necessary to report how honored he was by the previous communiqué. He described his mother's health and he asked after that of his president. In the body of one letter he called him "Your Excellency," not "Pancho" or even "Francisco." He reported on Francisco's son, Enrique, who in the heat of December 1867, had gone with Benigno to visit his grandmother, as did Leopoldo later. Venancio also discussed the doings of Rafaela and her husband, Bedoya. Venancio passed on useful gossip, especially about the conduct of army officers, the state of public order, and the course of the cholera epidemic.[6] At the time, the disease was killing forty to sixty men of the Paraguayan army daily, although López insisted that they died because the Brazilians were poisoning the water.[7] The formality of these letters and the honorific terms by which Venancio addressed his brother shows him debasing himself and flattering the marshal, just like everyone else who wanted to see the next sunrise. Francisco used fear to increase his power. It was rumored that he ordered Brazilian spies "thrown alive to" his jaguars, "immense brutes in a cage," and that his men were to cut the throats of wounded Paraguayans to keep them from falling into enemy hands.[8]

In September 1867, López honored the women of Paraguay, as he had done on previous occasions. He did this by allowing them to honor him. He praised "the fair sex" for their civic virtue. He was especially gratified when the women offered their jewels to honor the nation. López decided that women had become eligible for a new category of the National Order of Merit. As was his custom, he decreed the design, the color, and how to wear the medal, similar to his control of the medals of the males who were grand officers of the group.[9] He seems not to have noticed that the profusion of such awards devalued them. He did not have to mention that any woman who refused to donate her jewelry would cause trouble for herself and her family, although many quietly gave only their less valuable jewels.[10] Neither did he call attention to the fact that his sisters, Rafaela and Inocencia, led the supposedly spontaneous feminine support for their brother.

Even during the busiest periods of the tragic war, which astute contemporary observers still maintained López waged "for the purpose of acquiring fame and power,"[11] no detail escaped his concern. In October 1867, he ordered Major Francisco Fernández to remove the symbol of the nation's arms that the officer had placed in front of López's house in Asunción. It was improper. The escutcheon was to be fixed only on *public* buildings, not private ones.[12] López knew the forms of honor displays, but the substance of the code often gave him trouble. One of his worries was the behavior of the few Paraguayan diplomats in Europe. He could not completely control them, owing to the Allied blockade. Official correspondence got through occasionally, as the Allies allowed neutral ships to pass if they carried no contraband. At the legation in Paris, López ordered Gregorio Benítez to rotate officers between the London and Paris legations, although he refused his son Emiliano's request for a job. He ordered Paraguayan diplomats Benítez, Barrero, and Pérez to represent Paraguay with honor (*honra*). They must refrain from vain ostentation, an order that his own vain ostentation would make hilarious if the war were not so devastating the Paraguayan nation. He refused to allow diplomats leeway, stifling his civilian subordinates as he did his military ones. He ordered them not even to debate important matters. Policy was reserved for López alone. Maintaining the legations was important, he thought, to uphold Paraguay's image in Europe. He made his diplomats attend to López family matters. He had sent his son Emiliano—formerly Pesoa, and now legitimized as Emiliano López—to study in Paris. López ordered Benítez to correct the young man's deficiencies in English and French. He must make the wastrel Emiliano, whom the dictator scarcely knew, into a master of Italian and German.[13]

Deeper into Ruin

López addressed the people again. He praised them for doing what he had ordered them to do. He spun out the fiction that their war service and donations were voluntary. He was proud that they had found the resources for the famous sword, "the sword that you offer me in the name of the virtuous children of the Fatherland." He assured them that with the support of God—and God *was* on his side—the people, through the courage of his army, would conquer a peace. Many troops apparently believed him. Once they were fighting on Paraguayan soil, they fought to the death with the same kind of *esprit* that Japanese soldiers would exhibit at Tarawa and Saipan in 1943 and 1944. The lives lost so far, he said, were a "glorious sacrifice for the Fatherland." He lauded their efforts, but he never trusted the people. He continued to provide subventions of alcohol and food for their demonstrations of support for him and the war. Like other caudillos, Francisco was convinced that he could intuit the national will. He counted on the people, he said, to obey his orders. Together they would save the nation.[14]

Now, however, his armies were withering. Losses from combat were surpassed by those from disease.[15] "From a population base of perhaps four hundred thousand in 1864, at least sixty thousand men were dead, captured, or hopelessly mutilated within two years. . . ."[16] Cholera and other diseases ravaged the increasingly youthful army. They hit the Allies as well, but Brazil and Argentina had deep reservoirs of manpower from which to renew their ranks. López drafted boys younger than thirteen years old. He removed wounded men from the hospitals and returned them to service. He emptied the nation's jails and sent convicts to the front. Using whatever came to hand to promote the cause, he ordered his soldiers to gather spent ordinance from the Allies. His technicians fashioned them into musket balls and projectiles for cannon. His British technical experts were essential to this work.

In addition to their jewelry, President López encouraged women to volunteer their services to the nation. He declined to use them as combatants. But he and Lynch retained much of their jewelry for themselves. He enabled Madame Lynch, that "ambitious and unscrupulous woman" and "his chief confidant,"[17] to provide for her own future. She exchanged worthless paper money for hard currency that the troops had taken from Allied prisoners. There was no immediate use for specie.

López encouraged the fabrication of war materiel from local animals, vegetables, and minerals, since importation was impossible. One innovation was the manufacture of paper for his propaganda sheets, *El Semanario*, *Cabichuí*, and *Centinela*, from a local fibrous plant so that he could proclaim his glories. The papers trumpeted Paraguayan self-sufficiency, and they circulated downriver. On some readers, their arguments had an impact, convincing British Consul Thomas J. Hutchinson, for example, that the nation was managing the challenges and that its people suffered but little, although the suffering was immense. López's foreign, especially British, technical experts were essential to the war effort. Hired before the war, they included Dr. William Stewart and apothecary George Masterman. Civil engineer George Thompson had helped construct the railroad and then designed the bulwarks and the trenches protecting Humaitá and Curupaity, becoming a self-taught military engineer and finally a commander of troops. The British served López well, although none liked him and all feared him.

U.S. Minister to Paraguay Charles Ames Washburn tried to mediate between the warring camps; he arrived to Paraguay in 1861. As the years went by, he became increasingly hostile to López, especially after his returning from home leave in 1865–1866. Cantankerous, querulous, and hard to like,[18] his relations with López grew steadily worse. Moreover, his mandatory stay behind Allied lines on his return gave López further reason to distrust him.

Nevertheless, the relationship had not so deteriorated as to prevent him from trying to bring an end to the war, with modest cooperation from the dictator. In early March 1867, Washburn traveled from Asunción to Humaitá. He got López to allow him to contact the Allies, who were holding official communications from Washington, D.C. On the ship that sailed to the marshal's headquarters, Washburn chatted with Benigno López, then in a precarious position. Francisco had awarded Benigno the National Order of Merit but had also placed him under house arrest and condemned him to internal exile. When Francisco said, "Jump," Benigno asked, "How high?" Benigno "at the public meetings and festivals . . . made several speeches very eulogistic of his brother . . . ,"[19] which allayed Francisco's suspicions of him for a time.

Brazilian General Luis Alves de Lima e Silva, then Marquess (later Duke of) Caxias, ordered a cease-fire to let the North American diplomat pass from one army to the other. The marshal, still unable to comprehend another point of view, took the developments as a personal insult, charging that it was a ruse. Nevertheless, on March 1, 1867, Washburn left the marshal's headquarters in Paso Pucú for Allied lines with an escort of thirty men, including Colonel Thompson and Panchito López, formerly Panchito Lynch. The American tried to negotiate with Caxias, now interim chief of the Allied army. The young López spoke to Brazilians arrogantly, apparently having taken to heart his father's propaganda and imitating his behavior.

Washburn learned that Alexander Asboth, U.S. Minister to Argentina, had been instructed to offer mediation. He came to the full realization that the Allies meant to continue the war until López left. The Brazilian position was that "the unlawful and barbarous acts of López" had caused the war.[20] Washburn believed the Brazilians meant what they said, that if López left Paraguay and headed for Europe, the Allies would allow him to go and would find sufficient funds for him to live comfortably.

When he returned to López, he said, in reply to the marshal's question, that Caxias lived comfortably and ate well. López took this as an insult. Washburn informed the marshal that the Allies had rejected mediation. López did not want to hear the details. Until this failure, Marshal López's relations with Minister Washburn were proper but strained. Afterward, the dictator manifested an increasing aversion to the American,[21] who outspokenly and unwisely returned the antipathy. López felt aggrieved that no foreign government was prepared to rescue him from his current predicament, as he believed that they should. He thought that the United States owed it to him to do so. Why he thought this is unclear. He adamantly rejected the offer of a comfortable European exile. "He would fight to the last, and fall with his last guard . . . all would fight until they were killed. . . . Unless he should succeed and come off a conqueror, there was no future for him, nor did he want to live."[22] He believed that his legend would transcend those of other South American heroes, including Bolívar and San Martín, and that he had already won enough glory to secure his place in history. Indeed he had, but only in Paraguay and only after a fifty-year lapse. López the coward still proclaimed himself a hero, the greatest hero ever in South America. He blamed the suffering of his people on the United States and other countries that refused to come to his aid. Minister Washburn "could hardly believe that he could really be such a dolt and a fool."[23] Although most of the rest of the world who had heard of him would see him as a lunatic and certainly a bad man, it was the case that, in Paraguay, López's prediction of his historical legacy would prevail in the early twenty-first century, not Washburn's. Then, however, López began to entertain the possibility of defeat.

In April 1867, he founded another newspaper, *El Centinela*, which was to appear every Thursday. He wrote the first issue personally, and he oversaw its every thought.[24] Unlike the sober *El Semanario*, the new paper was illustrated by talented young artists. He established another periodical *Cabichuí*, whose gifted draftsmen, Saturio Ríos, Francisco Velasco, and others, created original woodcuts. No image contradicted the written words of the dictator. Drawings and prose all lavished praise on the marshal, and they pictured the enemy in unflattering, usually racist, ways. López dedicated the first issue of *Centinela* to himself, "the most Excellent Sr. Marshal President." He told readers to think of the new paper as "one of those young soldiers whom you have made famous on the field of battle." It had been "baptized by the great priest of the Fatherland. . . ."[25]

The war demanded everyone's sacrifice and suffering; but López wanted his readers to understand

> How much the Fatherland owes to its First Magistrate. To its most ardent defender! The very excellent Marshal López has set the example for his fellow citizens, blazing for them, with his own trail, the scabrous path of sacrifice.[26]

In truth, though, the marshal still did not want for comfort at the front. He and his family continued to live luxuriously. López nevertheless informed readers that "he has been placed at the head of his armies, leaving the comfort of his Palace to fulfill the holy duty."[27] As yet, he had never, ever, placed himself at the head of his armies or even ventured within a cannon shot of a battle, in violation of the practices of good nineteenth-century commanders.

He also praised his family, including "Treasurer General Saturnino Bedoya, to whose tireless efforts we owe such an important acquisition" as the new paper that was made from Caraguatá, a local plant.[28] López maintained that "bravery, obedience, and union" distinguished his soldiers from the enemy's, because "the sweet name of their magnanimous Marshal" inspired his people. According to López, he knew "how to incarnate in a virtuous people VALOR, OBEDIENCE, and UNION."[29] López's country was "resolved only to obey the dazzling sword of its adored Marshal, who leads it to glory and to greatness (*engradecimiento*)."[30] His newspapers reminded his people how essential loyalty was. Without it, there could be no honor. Paraguay owed its present greatness to the virtue of loyalty, according to López, as his people sank deeper into misery and the nation into ruination.

Another Attempt at Mediation

In August 1867, G. Z. Gould, secretary of the British legation in Buenos
Aires, made another stab at a settlement, disproving a later canard that
the United Kingdom promoted the war. According to one of López's subordinates who survived the conflict, the terms were generous. The proposed solution was for Marshal López to go to Europe, leaving the government in the hands of his vice president. Gould's main objective was
to rescue the marshal's British employees, vital to the war effort, and his
suggestion that "Paraguay's independence and territorial integrity be
recognized by the Allies," was something of an afterthought.[31] The Allies
expressed interest in the proposal, but López refused to budge. He loved
power and privilege even more than his life. Thus, "the caprice and
whim of an absolute ruler" was the "cause of the destruction of a nation."
The unofficial British proposal would have produced an honorable
peace,[32] as that concept was understood at the time by most men other
than López.

López boasted that he controlled everything in the country with "mod-
eration, circumspection, and insight."[33] Because he could convince himself of almost anything, he believed that he possessed these qualities,
even though they were antitheses of his true personality. He had his day-
dreams. Napoleon had achieved greatness, and so would he. Ignoring
the objective conditions that allowed Bonaparte to win such stunning
victories, until his equally stunning defeats in Spain and Russia, López
imagined that he could win similar triumphs. In August 1867, he moved
to inspire the boy soldiers of his dwindling army. He informed them,
"Bravery and nothing more than bravery made Bonaparte great . . . ,"[34]
overlooking the facts that Napoleon led the largest nation in Western Europe, had studied the military arts, and allowed his able subordinates lat-
itude. In *El Centinela*, the dictator announced that "the unconquered
sword of Marshal López has been raised to signal the attack, and to announce to us the glorious moment of victory."[35] But Francisco López's
luck was running out.

López loved the glory of Napoleon, his victories and his fame. He
dreamed of exemplifying Napoleonic principles; but as war leader he ignored them, especially concentration (or mass) and trust in subordinate
commanders. When López wrote detailed battle plans, he set them in
stone. He demanded that military reality conform to them, an impossibil-
ity. López's claims to be Napoleonic were balderdash. Those assertions of
later authors that he was—and comparisons of him to Napoleon—stem
from either ignorance or mendacity.

CHANGES IN ARGENTINA AND
PARAGUAYAN PROPAGANDA PERSISTS

Bartolomé Mitre, Allied commander until 1868, had usually run the Argentine government from the front through his vice president. His modest military ability was further limited by his lack of command authority over the Brazilians. Joâo Marques Lisboa, Baron Tamandaré, heading Brazil's naval arm, was unhelpful and at times insubordinate. Neither did Mitre make especially good decisions on the field of battle. He was not a good intelligence officer, and he "lacked the aggressive mentality needed in an invading commander. . . ." He blundered ". . . into events without proper awareness."[36] He returned to Buenos Aires for good in 1868, the year of a presidential election in which he was ineligible to succeed himself. He had left temporarily in 1867 to deal with internal disturbances, because Marcos Paz, the vice president, died, and Mitre was needed in the capital. Internal discord vexed Argentina. Regional uprisings expressed war weariness. They were also a continuation of long-standing regional grievances. Unlike López, Mitre had had military experience prior to the war. His major contribution to the Allied effort was to keep the coalition together, no small feat. His shortsighted or wrongheaded military decisions were compounded by the limitations on his authority. Mitre turned over command to Brazilian General Luis Alves de Lima e Silva, the Marquess of Caxias, in early 1868.

López imagined that Mitre's departure signaled the beginning of a revolution in Argentina. He concluded that Argentine public opinion would force an end to the war. What had happened was merely the election of a new president, Domingo Faustino Sarmiento, who "saw the necessity for winning the war. . . ."[37] He would continue to support the aims of the Triple Alliance, but the Argentine effort declined. General Juan Gelly y Obes commanded the Argentine contingent, but Argentine troop strength was now only a fraction of Brazil's.

As he ran short of men, López sent Afro-Paraguayan slaves to the front. Their numbers were not large, and virtually all of them would die. On the state estancias, López continued to employ female slaves until the end of the war. With his army of boy draftees, he still hoped to survive the war and dominate his country. The cholera that first struck the Brazilian army left it unable to move. The disease crossed the lines in May 1867. Countless Paraguayans died, "and López himself was laid up for some days in fear of it, thinking that he was ill."[38] Once he recovered from his fright, he grew angry. That he lacked control over the epidemic enraged him.

In May 1867, López founded *Cabichuí*, a more fully illustrated periodical than *Centinela*. Its purpose was to rally the morale of the troops, to
laud the greatness of Marshal López, and to demonize the enemy. Its
graphics were its most original and persuasive feature.

To demonstrate how much the people esteemed their leader, López
had Paraguayans donate what remained of their liquid wealth for three
projects. One was an equestrian statue of himself. Another was more
bizarre. It came from a forced collection of "thousands of pesos to prepare a golden sword" to be presented to López on his birthday in 1867.[39]
Also approved by the dictator for himself was the fabrication of "a
crown of laurel leaves in gold."[40] For decades, even centuries, most families had hoarded jewelry and silver plate. The people were poor, but
many families had kept precious metal over generations. Now López
obliged them to "volunteer" their savings to honor him. In the town of
Caacupé, for example—today an attractive hamlet where tourists and
pilgrims travel to a basilica commemorating the appearance of the Virgin Mary—152 women of the humble pueblo contributed six gold
rosaries, 150 grams of gold, fifteen golden earrings (*sarcillos*), one golden
cross, a gold ring, a gold chain, and jewels for the fabulous sword,
whose creation was a national cause. In Itaguá, now known for the pro-
duction of Ñandutí lace, the women of the village gave many of the
same items: eight gold necklaces, twelve gold rings, and several gold
buttons joined the list.[41] The pattern was the same in other villages.
Many women privately bristled; they thought that this was the doing of
Lynch. "The pressure on them to give up their jewelry was not well received."[42]

The sword was one of Francisco's own. He had it refitted with "Saint
George and the dragon, all in gold."[43] Craftsmen set diamonds and
other gem stones into the hilt. The sheath was of gold. A delegation of
notables and longtime, loyal servants of the López family, headed by
the dictator's brother-in-law, Saturnino Bedoya, sailed from Asunción
in late 1867 to present it to the dictator. López thereafter kept Bedoya
close. When he later became distraught over the movement of the
Brazilian ironclads, the marshal put him in irons. He finally died in torment from torture administered by the president's soldiers. When
López learned of Bedoya's premature death, he was irate; "had he
known that he was dying, he would have had him shot, for the sake of
appearances."[44] Some of the members of the sword-of-honor committee
eventually died of cholera. López pushed others into the army, in effect
a death sentence. He gave the commissioners no reward. Gratitude was
foreign to his nature.

BATTLE OF TUYUTY AND FAMILIAL CONSEQUENCES

Before major fighting resumed in late October 1867, López sent raiding parties into Allied lines. He gained nothing militarily by these forays, although they boosted his own morale and demonstrated his control. They also provided anecdotes of heroic deeds to fill his periodicals. When his scouts infiltrated enemy lines, López seldom worried about their possible desertion. He likely knew that they feared him but hated the enemy even more, especially the now abundant Brazilians. Additionally, he continued to insist that officers and men spy on each other and to report disloyal, disrespectful, or disobedient behavior. The execution of Robles and his staff in 1866 stood as an object lesson to any who pondered what loyalty meant. They spied on the enemy and each other. Spying on comrades was more rewarding than reports about the enemy. When they returned from Allied lines, they shied away from accuracy. It could be fatal to report the truth because López disbelieved accounts that he disliked. When soldiers brought realistic intelligence about the Allies to the marshal, he raged. That he threatened his subordinates was common knowledge. López's scouts "soon learned to tell a tale which would please him."[45]

The most important battle of 1867 was the second Battle of Tuyuty,[46] in late October and early November. López's initial orders show that two years of fighting had taught him a little about the art of war. Allied armies began a flanking movement in July, as López worried about Brazilian naval operations. He ordered new trenches dug to halt their advance. The Allies threatened to encircle his army, making an amphibious landing a dozen or so miles above Humaitá. The Brazilian cavalry, however, avoided the Paraguayan cavalry, even though their mounts were virtual "skeletons,"[47] starving for lack of food. López then attacked in force and beat the main Allied party to the punch. He ordered an assault on Tuyuty, a storehouse. He hoped to slow the enemy and to capture artillery, the best way to obtain it. The fighting went well until discipline broke down, owing to the men being too long deprived of all but the barest necessities. Soldiers plundered Allied stores, ate the food, and drank the drinks. López's attack inflicted heavy initial casualties. The Allies lost focus. They retreated. They rallied, however, and routed the disorganized but sated Paraguayan infantry, whose losses outnumbered those of the Allies. In terms of the ratio of casualties to available manpower, the Paraguayan losses were even greater. This attack was outrageously expensive, although López gained valuable artillery. His misplaced sense of honor prompted him to create two new separate medals to honor the combatants. He also promoted Bernardino Caballero to lieutenant colonel.

López decided that the second Tuyuty was a victory. Whether or not he actually believed it, he said, "The alliance is defeated." He had *El Centinela*—ostensibly edited by the sycophantic Bolivian Tristán Roca but absolutely controlled by López—proclaim "Glory . . . to our heroic marshal." He singled out for acclaim his brother-in-law, "the brave General Barrios."[48] Because of the plans of "THE GREAT LOPEZ," Paraguay was on the road to "glory and immortality,"[49] according to the great López. In his telling of the story of the war, his soldiers had, on one hundred occasions, humiliated Allied armies. Because enemy armies were larger, Paraguayans won the field of honor. They would triumph, López wanted all to know. Tuyuty, "that valorous and heroic assault, has been a mortal blow to the Alliance."[50] It was such a mortal blow, ironically, that López had to retreat. His dwindling armies pulled back to the line at Humaitá, the Sebastapol of South America.

In February 1868, new Brazilian ironclads cracked the river defenses. Their artillery fire depressed the half-foot chain that blocked their way upriver. The river rose. They sailed their ships past the obstructions. Shelling inflicted little damage on the Brazilian warships. The Allies now had a foothold above Humaitá. This rendered the defenses of the Cuadrilateral, including trenches, obstructions, and artillery, redundant. On March 2, 1868, López, not yet having led his army into battle, led it in retreat. He directed the men of his army and women who followed across the Río Paraguay in canoes and rafts. When they reached the Chaco, on the river's west bank, they turned north. It was a difficult journey. López then recrossed his army to the east bank and established new headquarters at San Fernando on the Tebicuary River. San Fernando would become synonymous with sadism. The approach of Allied warships would have serious consequences.

López left behind enough men at Humaitá under Colonels Paulino Alen and then Francisco Martínez to hold the fort for four months. They held out until they reached the brink of starvation. In July 1868, after Alen's attempted suicide, Martínez pulled out to save his men, intending to rejoin the main force. When he came under Allied attack, he and his men fought valiantly. After crippling casualties, Martínez surrendered his famished force on August 5. López was livid. He ordered Martínez's wife, Doña Juliana Insfran de Martínez, to denounce her husband publicly as a traitor, not a new practice. Earlier he had forced Doña Carmelita Cordal, whose husband, Fernando, was wounded and captured in Corrientes, to denounce her spouse as a traitor and deserter. In that case, he had threatened Doña Carmelita, whose father had served his father, with internal exile and the confiscation of all her possessions.[51]

López now demanded that Juliana Insfran sign a letter written according to the dictator's specifications, stating that she was disgusted by her husband's surrender. The denunciation was scheduled for publication. Doña Juliana, however, refused. She knew that her husband had bravely defended the Fatherland. Thus, López had her apprehended and confined. He had her tortured to betray her husband. She would not. She remained a loyal wife to a man who had served the marshal well. The dictator subjected her to daily beatings, but she refused to denounce her husband. She six times underwent the bone-crushing ordeal of the Uruguaiana, a regional practice. Her body was covered with wounds and "her face blackened and distorted."[52] Formerly a friend of Madame Lynch, Sra. Martínez found herself abandoned by the dictator's mistress. López finally directed the impenitent Sra. Martínez to be shot, although he stayed the order and allowed her to remain alive for several months in order to torture her some more.

The dictator terrorized his own family. His brother Venancio was so afraid that he refused to speak even in private about any public issue on which *El Semanario* had not first given him the official word. "He appeared to be in a chronic fright."[53] The other brother, the unlovable Benigno, who before 1862 had preyed upon his fellow Paraguayans to enrich himself and sate his lust, feared his brother with good reason.

Following the Allied passage of Humaitá in January 1868, Francisco López ordered the evacuation of Asunción. Government functionaries must depart the capital. Civilian residents and diplomats were also to evacuate their homes. The new capital was to be Luque, a town about ten miles east of Asunción, now so integrated into the life of the capital that numerous buses daily commute from there to Asunción's city center. The dictator removed all from Asunción who could collaborate with an Allied invasion force, meaning almost everyone. The move caused great suffering. The citizens of the capital took only what they could carry. Behind they left homes and furnishings open to thieves. Stubbornly Minister Charles A. Washburn refused to leave. He harbored refugees from López's persecution in the American legation. These included Portuguese Consul Leite Pereira, English apothecary George Masterman, and Porter Cornelius Bliss (whose first two names are reversed in some accounts), an American who worked as secretary to Washburn.

When the Allies approached López's positions on the Tebicuary, Caxias discarded the wasteful frontal assaults. He ordered flanking movements, which the Tebicuary terrain allowed. He conducted a war of maneuver, impossible in the swampy area to the south. López watched his army being enveloped. More things were now beyond his control than ever before. He lashed out. He raged. His anxiety levels rose. His agitation was intensified by years of heavy drinking, an addiction that now took hold of him. He imagined a conspiracy afoot; its objective was to kill him. Like

Yossarian, he was partly right. There *were* people who wanted to kill him: the Allies and his countrymen in the Paraguayan Legion. He had, however, no control over them, but he did have control over those who were within reach. He accused hundreds of people, most his supporters, and tortured and executed them. He sent many to the Cepo Uruguaiana, a technique of doubling over a person and tying him or her to a musket barrel stuck under the knees, often crushing bones. Officials had always used corporal punishment, in and out of the army. Its intensification now made the difference one not of degree but of kind. Torture was a locally grown plant. What was new was the status and gender of its victims.

Francisco López, Conspiracy Theorist

López established his headquarters at the old state estancia of San Fernando near the confluence of the Paraguay and Tebicuary rivers to the south of Asunción. He increased his alcohol consumption. Daily drunk, the dictator was "seized with a sudden fit of devotion." He had his men build a chapel in front of his partly underground headquarters. He attended noon Mass at his private chapel. He often spent two or three hours a day kneeling and praying. His religiosity and his drunkenness grew in tandem. López passed much of "his time in alternate fits of intoxication and devotion."[54] At San Fernando, López committed his most infamous atrocities. The most shocking he directed against his family. He had imagined that a conspiracy originated in Asunción upon the appearance of Brazilian vessels. A number of notables, in fact, *had* gathered to discuss how to meet the threat. What the dictator found intolerable was that they had made decisions on their own.

López brought his brother Benigno to San Fernando. He now stood accused. He denied disloyalty. Their brother-in-law Saturnino Bedoya had earlier exclaimed under torture that Benigno was subversive. Francisco's treatment of Benigno had until now been erratic. He had subjected his brother to minor punishments, like his house arrest. Yet sometimes he honored him, at one point awarding him the nation's highest decoration. But Benigno proved his disloyalty by suggesting a surrender to the Allies in order to save the López family's lives and their property. This insufficient devotion to Francisco doomed him. The outraged marshal branded Benigno as more of a *negro* that the *negros* of Brazil, words as strong in Paraguay in the 1860s as in the southern United States, given Paraguayan contempt for "the negro," in Guarani, the *cambá*. Francisco placed his youngest brother under arrest, this time in a hovel, not a house. He prohibited Benigno's communicating with anyone. At the same time, Francisco jailed one of his most loyal officers, General Brugués. Another victim was his other brother-in-law, General Vicente Barrios, husband of his sister Inocencia, whose bravery and martial gifts he had earlier lauded. He sentenced Barrios to fifty lashes (*lazazos*). Worse treatment was yet to come.

Increasingly fearful of plots, the marshal doubled the size of his personal guard surrounding his residence. When a friend tried to comfort Benigno, the dictator sent him to prison. The marshal now imagined that a gigantic conspiracy against him was unfolding. It had to be centered around and concocted by U.S. Minister Washburn, who had frequently defied López. Because of diplomatic immunity enforced by nearby U.S. warships, Washburn was beyond López's reach. The dictator charged that the conspirators were in communication with the enemy. He might even have believed that they were. After the war, the Allied commander denied knowledge of or participation in any such plot. The American minister then, and to the end of his life, also denied being part of a plot. It is unlikely that the voluble Washburn could have kept such a secret.

López created military "courts," punitive bodies whose objective was to placate the marshal. The tribunals sought no justice; rather they were inquisitorial facades. One was headed by Captains Adolfo Saguier and Matías Goyburu. Another was staffed by priests, including Father Fidel Maíz.

San Fernando became a hell on earth. Everyone was terrorized. If one showed compassion for the accused, he or she was also liable to be judged guilty of treason, guilt by association. The number of people accused of treason and condemned to prison, torture, and death swelled. The condemned included most of the remaining elite men and some of the leading women in the country. Barrios was doomed by a marital spat. Inocencia, in a snit, denounced her husband. Realizing that he was finished, Barrios tried suicide. He cut his own throat, poorly. He lived for a time, because British physicians saved him—for execution.

In the "trials" of San Fernando, López allowed the accused no lawyers, no defenders; nor were they allowed to defend themselves. Even at the time, few believed in the existence of a conspiracy, because ". . . all the declarations [confessions] had been extracted by . . . barbarous and cruel torture." Innocent people incapable of rebellion were sacrificed. After López had seized the British apothecary Masterman, Masterman falsely accused U.S. Minister Washburn of treason. Washburn had given the druggist-turned-doctor permission to say whatever he wished in order to save his life. His "confession" did so. He put into Washburn's mouth his own belief that López was "a cruel and avaricious tyrant and an incompetent general." Masterman did feel that Washburn had talked "imprudently" about the dictator. And he had. The American had called the dictator cruel and selfish, as, of course, he was, although wise diplomats keep their own counsel about such matters. But the dictator's spies were everywhere, often serving as domestics in the homes of his enemies, as Washburn knew. Yet Masterman never believed Washburn guilty of conspiring against López and never thought that a conspiracy existed.[55] Since López absolutely controlled the army and police, obvious to everyone, no plot could succeed.

López would ultimately take out his frustrations by killing or imprisoning hundreds of people, including every adult member of his family. The reprisals would continue into the next year. The most tragic torture and death he saved for Pancha Garmendia, the beautiful virgin who had once refused his advances and caused him public humiliation. Her death in 1869 would become a symbol for anti-López Paraguayans who ruled after the dictator's death. They named a school for her, the Escuela Pancha Garmendia.[56]

LOSS OF CONTROL

In 1868, López, his government, and his army retreated from San Fernando. They headed for Pykysyry some twenty-odd miles south of Asunción and arrived in early September. Now, the presidential lodgings were humble, more like the Spartan surroundings about which he had falsely bragged since leaving for the front in 1865. Even there he did not suffer. He had his men build a house for him and his family at Itá-Ibaté. The army, then mostly boys in their early teens and pre-teens, and wounded men turned out of hospitals on the marshal's orders, numbered about twelve thousand.[57]

The persecutions and executions ordered by López in September 1868, yield telling insights into his character. López became obsessed by the supposed conspiracy organized by Washburn, a calumny spread in Paraguay to this day. His public defiance of the dictator and his open contempt made him the central plotter—in the dictator's mind. The diplomat Washburn *did* make intemperate and undiplomatic remarks, especially after the failure of his mediation efforts and his and López's growing mutual hostility. He refused to be bullied by López. To defy Francisco Solano López was intolerable to the marshal. The dictator insisted, even with a lack of evidence, that the American diplomat had conspired with Brazilian General Marquess of Caxias, Luis Alves de Lima e Silva. López accused Washburn of plotting with others, including the younger López brothers, to overthrow the dictator. After the war, Caxias denied promoting a coup in Asunción.[58] Had he been able to generate discord in enemy ranks, he surely would have boasted of it. Under torture, most of the accused confessed to a host of crimes; they said mostly whatever the dictator wanted them to say. His functionaries, including General Resquín and

Father Maíz, handed out sentences of torture and death by the score. They persecuted people to force them to authenticate a conspiracy against the president; their confessions are not credible. Most who died in agony were not López opponents but supporters.

The alleged conspiracy originated in the frustrated and enraged López's mind. He seethed after learning that Paraguayan officials met in Asunción in early 1868, and he had not called such a meeting, a grave offense. An elite group convened hastily as Brazilian warships approached. The assemblage included the aged Vice President Domingo F. Sánchez; Venancio López, titular commander of the Asunción garrison; and others. They naively caucused to decide how to meet the Brazilian peril. The supreme commander was at the front, although usually reachable by telegraph. They should have realized that he would not countenance anyone except himself discussing policy—even in a crisis, or even for the good of the country, for the security of the capital, or for the López family fortune. The elderly Sánchez talked his way out of trouble. He confessed his own shortcomings and saved his ancient skin by lying about the perfidy of others.

López's judgment, never good when he had to assess the thought process and attitudes of other men, was now truly warped. By 1868, his officers could not report to him honestly even about the size and strength of Allied forces. They tailored the facts to suit their commander. They feared that he would kill them if they reported depressing developments, and all the news was bad. He especially hated hearing how large the armies of "*los negros*" of Brazil were.

The available evidence and the absence of any trustworthy facts about a conspiracy leads to the conclusion that no anti-López conspiracy existed, even though logically there should have been one. The accused conspirators, including family members and López's officers, were average at best, like most of the dictator's family and subordinates, but they were not suicidally stupid. No conspiracy aimed at López would have been successful because the marshal firmly controlled the army, now quite small but still loyal to him. Its force was overwhelming when compared to anything that the alleged conspirators' could create. The successive armies raised by López remained faithful to him to the end. To soldiers, he symbolized the nation.

López's family members, including his mother, Juana Pabla Carillo, were alarmed by the likelihood of impoverishment if the nation lost the war. By 1868, all assumed that the war was lost, although most kept defeatist opinions to themselves. One who did not was his brother Benigno. Doña Juana Pabla also advised Francisco to make peace on Allied terms to safeguard the family's holdings, which of course implied her son's removal from office. Her contention indicated that she was not a diehard supporter of her son's lifetime presidency. Francisco had his mother confined, and he discussed executing her with his senior officers. He merely had her beaten. Francisco Solano ordered two of his former foreign ministers, both loyal supporters, José Berges and Gumesindo Benítez, Berges's former assistant, to be degraded, disgraced, tortured, and put to death. Benítez had praised the marshal fulsomely in *El Semanario*:

> he seemed to have been convinced by his own words that Lopez [*sic*] was a being of a superior order. He was one of the very few who in praising Lopez seemed to believe what he said. His faith and fidelity, however, availed him no more at the last than did the hypocrisy and submission of the others, [all of whom died] as traitors or conspirators.[59]

The atmosphere of bloodlust corrupted everyone. Father Maíz, the ex-convict, ex-rector, and ex-opponent of López, now did the dictator's bidding. He tortured one Dr. Carreras for three days. With a mallet the learned priest smashed the doctor's fingers. Carreras, of course, confessed to whatever he was accused of—a confession that he recanted as soon as the torturing stopped, although he was soon executed. Colonel Alén, López's former secretary and his traveling companion in Europe, also stood accused of treason. The dictator's men so maimed him that he could not stand. It made little difference, though, because López had him shot.[60]

The Uruguaiana was López's favorite instrument of torture. López tortured promiscuously, probably to relieve himself of imagined challenges to his authority by prominent men whom he suspected of being only tepidly loyal. Others he sent to the front instead of having them shot. He ordered wounded Paraguayan soldiers' throats cut to prevent their falling into Allied hands. López's own cruelty encouraged that of his hirelings.[61] These actions returned to him the appearance of control.

The list of Paraguayans accused of conspiracy and sentenced to die should rightly begin with the dictator's family. López spared none of his siblings, although he made his brothers suffer the ultimate penalty. He confined his sickly brother Venancio in a straw structure as low as a dog kennel. Similarly, brother Benigno had to crawl from his confinement on all fours. Both brothers expired in a torment of their older brother's making. López imprisoned his sisters Rafaela and Inocencia in small enclosed carts about four feet long and five feet wide for months after he had them beaten. He had already killed both of their husbands; they died in front of their wives. Earlier having lauded General Vicente Barrios's bravery under fire, the marshal had Inocencia's husband tortured and shot. Bedoya, the other brother-in-law, had, a few months earlier, died in chains. He had been charged with embezzlement of government funds. His spine was dislocated under torture, and "he died in intense agony."[62] Even Madame Lynch feared her Pancho. She had no trouble imagining that "a man who had imprisoned his brothers, flogged his sisters, shot their husbands and threatened his mother" might turn on her as well.[63]

At the center of the opposition, López saw U.S. Minister Charles A. Washburn, and he made him his favorite scapegoat. Washburn was many things, including cranky, irritating, undiplomatic, and intemperate, but stupid he was not. He despised the dictator behind the screen of diplomatic immunity. Even this privilege was not a certain guarantee that the president would recognize international law and spare him. But in Washburn's case it did, probably because of nearby American warships. Washburn had no force to command. Neither did he have trusted contacts within the Paraguayan military. The alleged plot, supposedly aimed at overthrowing Francisco in favor of one of his brothers, was certainly a fantasy, a figment of the imagination of a man who had controlled his environment and whose world was now spinning out of control. Thus, President López sent hundreds of people to military tribunals at San Fernando and other stops on his long retreat. Until December 1868, according to George Masterman, 107 foreigners were executed and 113 died in prison. López executed 107 Paraguayans and allowed 88 to die in prison. There were 85 people of unknown nationality who were also executed and another 27 who were bayoneted on the retreat from San Fernando to Pykysyry. Of the 700 to 800 people whom López and his torturers and hangmen arrested as conspirators, most died.[64]

One of the most unjust sentences was that of former Foreign Minister José Berges, who had served López faithfully. López accused him of treason and of communicating with the enemy. The accusation was a fiction and a death sentence. It would have been virtually impossible in 1868 for Berges to have contacted the enemy, but he was spoken of as a possible successor.[65] López discharged him as foreign minister[66] before he tortured and killed him.[67]

The wife of the truly brave Colonel Francisco Martínez, the equally brave Juliana Insfran de Martínez, and her mother, Dolores Recalde, refused to denounce the humane commander and valiant defender of Humaitá. On López's orders they both died painfully, as did the bruised and emaciated Pancha Garmendia. Another 76 women, including Argentines from Córdoba, Entre Ríos, Corrientes, and Mendoza, as well as Brazilian women, languished in the concentration camp at Cerro León.[68]

Lynch remained untouched by Francisco's wrath, although she did fear him. How she did so must remain a matter of speculation, although he clearly needed her physically and emotionally and as a symbol of his stature. She knew better than others how to manage his moods.

Sickly brother Venancio, whose "miserable state of health . . . had been caused by his early excesses,"[69] was one of Francisco's most pathetic victims, first humiliated and condemned to ten years' imprisonment and stripped of citizenship. After President López imagined a new plot against him, which surely existed only in his disheveled mind, Venancio expired from physical privation during imprisonment, including pain of the shackles that bound him, malnourishment, and forced marches. López ordered his fearful, obedient inquisitors to apprehend his sisters, Rafaela and Inocencia, who "were imprisoned each on a bullock cart . . . about seven feet long, four wide, and five high."[70] Through frontmen, he condemned them to a decade of internal exile and painful confinement. López allowed Father Fidel Maíz to revenge himself on his rival, the ignorant Bishop Palacios. The sycophantic cleric's fawning over the dictator failed to save him in the end. Judge Maíz sent him to a firing squad, and López approved. Maíz exacted his revenge for Palacios's role in his own unjust imprisonment.[71]

Postwar Wealth

Now as before, Elisa Lynch exerted indirect influence on Francisco's policy decisions. Her encouraging her lover to inflate his image and her feeding his ego had political implications. Throughout the war she had persuaded him to enable her enrichment; she did so until the last days of the war. The Brazilian diplomat José María da Silva Paranhos, the Viscount do Rio Branco, who first visited Paraguay in the late 1850s, inventoried her possessions after the Brazilians apprehended her. He reported that Lynch did not leave Paraguay with great wealth. In truth, most of her capital was invested in real estate. She carried only a modest fortune in transportable riches. But before and even during the war she sent money abroad. She took jewels and currency with her when she left. Her savings were enough to provide her a comfortable postwar life, living and traveling in comfort. Rumors of her fabulous treasure, hidden during the long retreat and never found, still surface in Paraguay. No treasure hunter has reported finding the cache. Her true wealth, aside from the astounding gifts of public property that Francisco made to her at the very end, was the complex of urban and rural properties that he helped her to acquire.

Although Francisco used frontmen to purchase properties for himself, for Madame Lynch, and for his siblings before and during the war to coat the transactions with a veneer of legality, he had no real understanding of private property, at least as most of the Atlantic world understood the concept. If he wanted a material good, he got it, even if, as in the last year or so of his life, it was only on paper. Although all of Paraguay was his for the taking, he had previously set limits. In 1868 and 1869, however, his enormous land grants to Lynch demonstrated that his recognition of those limits had crumbled.

Like most other caudillos of the Plata region in the fifty years after independence, except Dr. Francia, Francisco López and his father had made themselves fabulously rich, mostly in land, the most valuable commodity in Paraguay. During the war years, the de facto López family monopolies of the yerba trade and timber exports brought no income. Paraguay still conducted commerce with Bolivia, whose merchants did business in the occupied Mato Grosso. Transportation costs across the northern Chaco and the Pantanal were so high that this commerce ended up small in volume and value.

As Francisco disposed of Paraguayans suspected of disloyalty, as previously stated, foreigners also succumbed to his wrath. Their offenses were rarely those of active political opposition to the dictator. They were personal. Some had not expressed enthusiastic devotion to him. Even worse, they were outsiders and so became victims of Paraguayan xenophobia. Often they were "guilty" of only talking with someone charged with complicity in the imaginary plot, true guilt by association. Some were disrespectful to López, which he could never tolerate. Merely a bad man when he became president, Francisco López in 1868 was now an evil one, evidenced by his torture and execution of his family and of such ardent supporters as Berges and Benítez and especially his selfish ruination of the country.

THE WAR WINDS DOWN AND LÓPEZ
PAINTS HIS HISTORICAL PICTURE

At the end of 1868, the Brazilians encircled the small Paraguayan army. Marshal López rounded up 3,500 men, most actually young boys. He assigned them to now General Bernardino Caballero and ordered them to slow the enemy advance. They did so, but his boy army was nearly wiped out. General Caballero escaped to safety. An even more reduced force rejoined the marshal president at Lomas Valentinas, some twenty miles south of Asunción, also referred to as Itá-Ibaté. At the end of 1868, the Paraguayan garrison holding the river fort of Angostura under Colonel George Thompson surrendered to the Allies. Thompson survived to write an invaluable book about the war and life under López. Thompson's surrender infuriated the dictator. Dr. William Stewart, a Scot and chief army surgeon, also defected. He was a conduit through which López and Lynch sent money to Europe, allegedly as much as 200,000 gold pesos, which finally disappeared into a black hole of Stewart's bankruptcy.

López now had no use for treasure. He had apparently decided that if he could not command his army and rule the country, he would rather be dead. He did, though, wish to prolong his rule as long as possible. He clutched at straws. He had dreamed of dividing the Allied coalition. Risings in Argentina gave him hope that Argentina would withdraw from the war. He rejoiced when he thought that Mitre had died in 1867. To himself, López was "the Paraguayan David," who had rendered the giant Triple Alliance prostrate.[72] Mitre, Pedro II, and Flores were "the three bandits."[73] He renewed the hope that intervention by the United States might save him. That nation had sent a new minister, Martin T. McMahon, who met López at his temporary headquarters, Itá-Ibaté, in December 1868. The former Union general became friendly to the cause. That the North Americans had sent such an important man could be a forecast of help. When aid was not forthcoming, López must have felt aggrieved.

At Lomas Valentinas, Marshal López confronted his certain defeat. To prolong his power a little longer was his goal, and he sent his army of beardless youths into battle, many boys of twelve years old and even younger. They went off to be slaughtered alongside the wounded and crippled men whom López had expelled from hospitals. Here for the first time, López took real command of his youthful army. His determination to remain marshal president, with total control over everyone within reach, was for a moment stronger than fears for his personal safety. Until now, he had stayed far from battle. When he earlier had fled his headquarters and raced to the rear in an unseemly fashion as an enemy shell fell a half mile away, his cowardice was widely noticed. Now he would face up to his obligation, but only briefly.

The Brazilian "Caxias took the surprising step of sending an ultimatum to López, calling on him to surrender."[74] López refused. He insisted that he would only end the hostilities in an honorable fashion, by which he meant his own honor. Honor to him meant retaining control of the government. He knew from the Triple Alliance Treaty that the Allies sought to remove him. He finally realized that they were serious.

By the end of 1868, most of his army was gone. Those who remained "were no older than ten or eleven and . . . many were wearing false beards . . . to convince their enemies that they were up against men." Their action has been celebrated as heroic devotion to the Fatherland for the past half century in Paraguay. Despite his precombat decision to lead from the front before hostilities began, López's fear again overcame his will to dominate. He fled again during battle.[75] For a man untrained in the art of war, fear of combat is normal. Soldiers need months, often years, of drill to acquire the steadying habits demanded in battle. Thus, it was not López's timidity in such situations that provokes interest. It is that he had boasted for two decades of his bravery.

López now obsessed about his place in history. The desperate fighting of December 21, 1868, at Itá-Ibaté (or Ivaté), "the first in which he had been in real danger,"[76] constituted for him an opportunity for a "splendid victory." When the setbacks came, he admitted that his forces had been defeated. But, egotistical to the end, he blamed it on bad luck and the immobility of the Paraguayan artillery, rather than superior Allied arms. López was not to blame. God was. The dictator concluded that the outcome was divinely ordained. "Our God," he said, "wants to test our faith and constancy in order to give us afterwards a greater and more glorious country." Paraguay had suffered, he wanted people to know, but the cause had not. Paraguayans, he said, were responding to his call to arms. They would fight until the enemy was exterminated.[77] In fact, they would fight until most of *them* were exterminated. Most of the men were already dead.

López carried on his war, and his nation continued suffering. As the Allies entered Asunción in early January 1869, the marshal established a headquarters at Piribebuy. Although the war should have been over then, López would survive another fourteen months, because the Brazilians foolishly failed to follow up their victory.

Francisco López stayed in character. He protested that the Allies had tarnished his and his country's honor. Their demand for his surrender was insulting. He reminded them that he had sought peace, an "honorable" peace, in 1866. Unable to conceive of a Paraguay without him, López said that with God's help he would prevail. Like Hitler in his bunker seventy-five years later, López insisted that Allied resources versus his country's scarcity were less crucial than honor and valor. He embodied these virtues. Yet he remained blind to the Brazilians' and Argentines' quests for honor. Honor was vital in Buenos Aires in nineteenth century,[78] as it was throughout Latin America. The ruination of his country, López claimed, was a legitimate and necessary defense of honor. Should any further blood be shed, he argued, it would be the Allies' fault, not his. Only on "honorable" terms would he lay down his arms. Honor still meant his power.[79]

As his policies imposed an ever-greater agony on Paraguayans, Lopez still had to assert that his succession to office was legitimate. It was the Paraguayan National Congress and not his control of the military that made him president in 1862. His 1869 story was that he and his forces were fighting to preserve independence, although the Allies insisted that the extinction of the nation was not a war aim.[80] López's aggression had imperiled the nation's independence. He had attacked larger, richer, and better-located neighbors, he insisted, because Argentina and Brazil had besmirched his honor. He had gone to war because a "unified cry" that arose from the Paraguayan people had compelled him to fight. This prewar cry for war was a cry only he had heard.

Although the whole of Paraguay must have known otherwise, López said, "in more than three years, I have not been absent from the head of our legions."[81] Unlike decent and skilled nineteenth-century command-ers, López led from the rear of his legions, not at the head of them, except in retreat, and his efficient propaganda let him get away with it. That he remained safe from enemy fire was widely known. His superb propa-ganda machine allowed him to prevaricate that he delighted in the fatigue and danger of war, though he lived luxuriously until its final months. He praised his soldiers for their bravery and congratulated their families for abandoning their homes and joining their menfolk, although by now his soldiers were now mostly boyfolk. He continued to rage at the Paraguayan Legion. At the end of his life, López still believed he embodied the nation. If men opposed him personally, they were disloyal to Paraguay. An Allied victory, he preached, would mean enslavement.[82]

In 1868, López prepared to die. He made ready to take the remnants of his nation down with him. He had earlier written his will, leaving all property to Elisa Lynch. Since Martin McMahon had replaced the irritat-ing Washburn in December 1868, relations between the United States and López improved, or at least relations between López and McMahon did, which López took as a sign of friendship between the two countries. He courted his favor. A war veteran himself, McMahon was impressed by the sacrifice and heroism of Paraguayans.[83] Insofar as he trusted anyone, López trusted McMahon, whose sympathy for the cause probably devel-oped in part from "the obsequiousness of the president and his mistress." One historian notes that from ignorance or denial, "The American minis-ter appeared unaware that a few hundred yards from his quarters lay the prison camp, filled with scores of wretched beings who languished in conditions of misery and torment while they awaited . . . torture and prob-able execution."[84] The dictator entrusted his will to the American minis-ter, and he also asked McMahon to protect Panchito and his other children under his protection. Facing defeat, he worried about the continuation of his line.[85]

Unable to grasp the meaning of Argentine politics, López had hoped that the electoral victory in 1868 of Domingo F. Sarmiento over the candi-date favored by the detested Mitre would take Argentina from the war. It did not. Since Brazil had long been his most formidable enemy, this hope was a fantasy. Brazil was now unstoppable.

Still, López retained his hauteur. In late 1868, as Allied generals called on him to cease his futile resistance, he chastised them for ignoring proper military honors. He would continue his fight because it promoted "reli-gion, civilization, and humanity." These ideals continued to guide him, he convinced himself, since his unsuccessful peace effort of 1866. When his instructions elicited Allied scorn, he concluded that they aimed to destroy the Republic of Paraguay. He was the nation. He would fight until God decided the outcome. Bravery could still defeat Allied resources. Denouncing the Allies' lack of chivalry, he stood ready to make peace, he said, "on bases equally honorable for all belligerents."[86] He meant the honor of Francisco López. That of the Allied leaders was unimportant, and he was unable to empathize with their position in the matter anyway.

Although just about out of resources, López was still an effective recruiter of men for his armies, his best military talent. He was assisted by the "quiet competence of Vice President Domingo Francisco Sánchez, who worked diligently to keep the armies supplied. . . ."[87] In 1869, López enlisted the willing and the reluctant into a new army of 2,500, mostly boys of 12 and under and men over 60. The author of the best one-volume history of the war says, "López's concern for his reputation and his belief in his destiny . . . best explain why he could not surrender. . . ."[88] This observation is correct, as far as it goes, but a fuller explanation of the dictator's motivation must add that he simply was unable to surrender personal control. It meant everything to him.

The presence of Paraguayans in Allied ranks continued to outrage López. Protocol remained important. In May and June 1869, he demanded that the Count D'Eu, who replaced Caxias as the Brazilian commander and head of Allied armies earlier that year, prevent the disloyal Paraguayan Legion from serving Paraguay's enemies while flying the nation's flag. He demanded that D'Eu, a prince of the French House of Orleans and Pedro II's son-in-law, halt this wickedness.[89] Legionnaires were "denaturalized Paraguayans . . . and collaborators." According to López, they must leave.[90]

Letter to Emiliano

In June 1869, the end was near and López knew it. Yet he would not relinquish control to save his life. He was Paraguay, although by August a rival government sat in Asunción. He desired control over what he now could not control. Frustrated, he wrote a long letter dictating the future life course of a long-estranged son, Emiliano Victor, son of Juana Pesoa, then in Paris on a government grant. López's instructions for the young man give a concluding insight into the dictator.

López decided that Emiliano must move to the United States, although he knew no English. There General McMahon would see to his welfare. Toward the former American minister, Emiliano should be "docile" and "obedient," as López was to his own father. One difference was that Francisco had enjoyed his father's esteem. Emilio had not. He was the son of a woman whom Francisco had doubly insulted, both failing to marry her and rejecting her for his fair foreign treasure: Lynch.

If President López should die, Emiliano must support his little brothers, the dictator counseled. Actually, they were only his half brothers, the children of Lynch. The dictator mandated that Emiliano avoid the Parisian pleasures, which he liked too much. He should shun low companions and seek the company of industrious ones. The dictator had previously refused Emiliano's request to become attaché of the Paris legation because he had not yet proved that he deserved the honor. Young Francisco had had no such compunctions about his own lack of worthiness in taking an important job for which he was unprepared—army chief—without any qualifications except his blood tie to the president. Francisco was dismayed by Emiliano's lack of seriousness. At Emiliano's age, Francisco López could combine heavy drinking, active womanizing, and hard work. He expected a son whom he never mentored and had seldom even seen to do the same.[91]

He failed utterly to empathize with his son. He never tried. He gave no thought to his son's wishes. The dictator insisted on commanding the son despite having been an absent father who had dishonored Emiliano's mother. Through the stewardship of McMahon, he would provide for his son's financial support, if he moved to the United States. He had allocated a considerable sum of money.

In the United States, Francisco directed, Emiliano should devote himself to legal studies, apprenticing himself to the ablest lawyer whom he could find. McMahon had agreed to help with the search. Once settled in a prestigious practice, he should work diligently so that the senior partners would appreciate his talents. He must learn the principles of the law, ironic coming from a man who ignored the rule of law and ruled by force. Owing to the subvention, earning a handsome salary should be less important to Emiliano than legal training. The young man must reside in New York rather than Washington, his father advised, having seen neither city. In New York, McMahon would teach him honor and respect. Emiliano should advance himself socially, which would have been difficult in the racially intolerant American circles of the post–Civil War era. Francisco instructed Emiliano to take a room in a boarding house and eat his meals in a hotel. His living would cost, Francisco estimated, about US$1,500 a year. He had given MacMahon 100 ounces of gold[92] for Emiliano's support, about $2,000 at the time and probably between $30,000 and $40,000 today. McMahon would provide a little more when Emiliano got to the United States. This sum was as much as he could hope for, the father said, because the López family fortune had been ruined by war, although at the time Francisco was in possession of all the gold and silver in Paraguay.

Francisco said that when Congress was in session, Emiliano should move to Washington to observe it. Living would be cheaper. During the summer, Emiliano should move to the countryside with the gentle folk of New York and with them ingratiate himself. He should also take music lessons. That Francisco wanted Emiliano to impress the firm's senior partners with his industriousness and work ethic and also be flitting between New York and Washington and the countryside shows how out of touch the dictator was.

Francisco told Emiliano that if Paraguay fell, he would fall with it. Finally, he assured Emiliano that he loved him, although he had seldom seen him. The dictator nevertheless closed the letter posing as "your loving father." He then signed himself Francisco S. López,[93] not Papá. It is unlikely that Emiliano ever received the missive, but its importance lies in its clues to Francisco's state of mind. López admitted that he did not know Emiliano well. But he had reports from Gregorio Benítez, the Paraguayan chargé d'affaires in Paris and London, about his offspring and could direct him at a distance.[94]

END OF THE ROAD

On June 30, 1869, Francisco Solano López bid farewell to McMahon, who had been recalled from Paraguay by the new secretary of state, former Minister Washburn's brother. López described their relationship as short but amicable. The dictator instructed the North American to explain Paraguay's heroism to the world,[95] which he did.

Only a fraction of those Paraguayans remaining alive, mostly women, followed him now. Most of the men were dead or missing. Hoping to increase his mobility and save food for his family and retinue, the marshal president advised the women and children to leave and await the Brazilians. Expecting them to do so after having taught them that Brazilians were demonic is symptomatic of his desperation. He focused on personal survival. If all the noncombatants left, they would no longer burden him. He could subsist with his tiny command. He would still command men who called him the marshal. He could also flee more rapidly. Nevertheless, the women continued to follow. Most had nowhere else to go.

Meanwhile a puppet Paraguayan government was functioning. In August 1869, the Allies created and directed it. Because they had an overwhelming force and the new government had none, officials in Asunción did what the Allies, especially the Brazilians, ordered. Two of its three members had served in the Paraguayan Legion that López reviled. They ruled for fifteen months, until after López was dead.

As López reached the old Jesuit mission town of San Estanislao in the Taruma region, he conjured up another conspiracy. He created new tribunals to dispatch his putative enemies. The fearful, obedient judges included the priests Maíz and Román and the sinister Silvestre Aveiro, a former clerk. Among those whom López executed in this bloody charade was Colonel Mongelós. The dictator knew that the colonel was not an anti-López plotter, but he condemned him for his ignorance of the nonexistent plot. López's mother and sisters now detested him. It was assumed that women were adept at using poison, and López was a fearful man. López had Aveiro beat his mother. Without evidence, he executed a lieutenant and sixty-nine soldiers for conspiracy. He executed still more supposedly disloyal followers in Igatimí and more again in Panaderos. Because bullets were in short supply, he dispatched them with lances. His ailing brother Venancio had surprisingly survived the nearly daily beatings and forced marches until very late in the march. He was nearly naked and covered with sores. He finally expired from his afflictions while begging for water.

It was rumored that López hid forty cartloads of public treasure by throwing them over a precipice. Then he killed the drivers and porters to prevent their informing others of the treasure's whereabouts. Treasure hunters from that era until the modern day have searched for the loot. If any succeeded, he wisely kept the news to himself.

In February of 1870, López, his family, and his retinue reached Cerro Corá, a site that is known at least by name to every Paraguayan. Except for the dictator, Lynch, and their children, who continued to eat and drink well, most others were on the verge of starvation, diseased, and covered with sores. Weapons were sabers and lances, because powder and shot for firearms were exhausted. Paraguayans ate animal bones ground into powder. They cooked belts and shoes instead of meat in stews. When oxen expired, the López party ate them. Lynch and her children traveled in a coach, and López's mother and his sisters, though confined, rode in a leather-covered cart, which kept up appearances of *honra*. López needed his tiny army, now a mere handful. Without them, no one would call him Marshal President. Honor must be acknowledged by others, and López saw himself as forever honorable. In late February 1870, he ordered one last medal created for veterans of the last campaign. Still supervising the details, for he had little else to supervise, he ordered it to be oval shaped. It should bear the nation's star in the middle. On one side, the legend would read "Vanquished Penuries and Fatigue." On the other side, Marshal López ordered that the inscription be simply "MARSHAL LOPEZ."[96]

On March 1, 1870, the Brazilian army under General José Antonio Correa closed in on López's pathetic party. They quickly brushed aside the feeble Paraguayan defenders. Lynch pushed three of her sons into her coach for protection. The oldest, Panchito, was then fifteen years old and a colonel. He brandished a saber at the enemy. They killed him, but they spared Madame Lynch because of her sex, her station, and her nationality.

López himself mounted his horse and fled. As the Brazilians closed the gap, the legend goes, he turned to face them, saber in hand and bravely died from lance thrusts and rifle bullets. Faced with the Brazilian demand to surrender, López was now without his aides. Aveiro and Ibarra had slipped away. He allegedly said, "I die with my country," and then expired. According to other accounts, including Centurión, who was there though badly wounded, he said, "I die *for* (por) my country." He fell with a bullet in his heart, his body penetrated with lance wounds. The hero, the legend continues, had refused to surrender his sword or his position. How Portuguese-speaking soldiers in the heat of battle could quote exactly what the dying dictator said most likely in Guarani, his first language, with the sound of musket fire creating confusion must remain forever unclear. Nevertheless, as George Thompson would write to Richard Friedrick von Truenfeld, it was thought at the time that López had died well. A careful student of nineteenth-century Paraguayan history concludes that he died from "a bullet in the back from a Brazilian army carbine. . . ."[97] Few die heroically from a bullet in the back. Lynch said that she saw him fall to Brazilian bullets.[98]

López was buried at Cerro Corá by Lynch and Brazilian Major (and later President) Floriano Peixoto. Panchito was buried there too. López's mother, doña Juana, had been unable to protect her younger sons from the murderous Francisco, who had executed Benigno, her favorite child, and tortured to death another, Venancio. When Francisco died, she alleged that he was not the child of Carlos Antonio. His sisters thought him a monster. Their husbands had been persecuted and executed by their brother. They responded by joining his enemies. Rafaela married Milciades Acevedo Pedra, a Brazilian, demonstrating her abhorrence of her brother.

Nevertheless, Francisco Solano López would return to Paraguay in legend. In the twentieth century, he became the hero in memory that he never was in life. A carefully crafted and mendacious rewriting of a glorious life took root. This outcome would have pleased him.

NOTES

1. George Thompson, C.E., *The War in Paraguay with a Historical Sketch of the Country, Its People, and Notes upon the Military Engineering of the War* (London: Longman, Green, and Co.), 198.

2. Charles A. Washburn, *The History of Paraguay, with Notes of Personal Observations and Reminiscences of Diplomacy under Difficulties*, 2 vols. (Boston: Lee and Shepard, 1871), II, 48.

3. Washburn, *History of Paraguay*, II, 50.

4. George Masterman, *Seven Eventful Years in Paraguay: A Narrative of Personal Experience amongst the Paraguayans*, 2nd ed. (London: Samson Low, Son, and Marston, 1870) 138.

5. See FSL to Venancio López, 20 telegrams in ANA/CRB 4385 and 92 missives in CRB 4545. Another letter from the dictator to this brother rests in ANA/CRB 4687. These include a friendly message from May 1, 1868, shortly before the marshal turned on his brother. He sent Venancio orders about recruiting, about education of the new recruits for the army, about desertions, and about the harvest of saltpeter.

6. Venancio López to FSL, Asunción, letters of Dec. 15 and Dec. 17, 1866; Dec. 21, 25, 28, and 29, 1867; and Jan. 10, 1868, ANA/CRB 4923.

7. Masterman, *Seven Eventful Years*, 164.

8. Masterman, *Seven Eventful Years*, 26, 187.

9. Decree of FSL, H.Q., Paso Pucú, Sept. 12, 1867, *Proclamas y cartas del Mariscal López* (Buenos Aires: Editorial Asunción, 1957).

10. Barbara Potthast, "Protagonists, Victims, and Heroes: Paraguayan Women during the Great War," in *I Die with My Country: Perspectives on the Paraguayan War*, ed. Hendrik Kraay and Thomas L. Whigham (Lincoln: University of Nebraska Press, 2004), 49.

11. Masterman, *Seven Eventful Years*, 90.

12. FSL to Major Francisco Fernández, Paso Pucú, Oct. 15, 1867, ANA/CRB 4475.

13. FSL to Gregorio Benítez [Paso Pucú], Oct. 24, 1867, *Proclamas y cartas*.

14. FSL, Speech of Thanks for the Sword of Honor, H.Q., Paso Pucú, 1867 [*sic*], *Proclamas y cartas*.

15. The figures are imprecise, but there is no reason to think that Paraguayan exceptionalism overcame epidemiological realities. In all wars before 1900, disease killed far more men than combat did.

16. John Hoyt Williams, *The Rise and Fall of the Paraguayan Republic, 1800–1870* (Austin: Institute of Latin American Studies, University of Texas, 1979), 215.

17. Masterman, *Seven Eventful Years*, 91.

18. Readers of Washburn's two-volume *History of Paraguay* usually grow irritated at his whining even at the distance of 135 years. But, he was a sponge for local gossip, often the only means of communication in a dictatorship and certainly more reliable than the "news" in López's periodicals.

19. Washburn, *History of Paraguay*, II, 180.

20. Washburn, *History of Paraguay*, II, 185.

21. Juan Crisóstomo Centurión, *Memorias o reminiscencias históricas sobre la Guerra del Paraguay*, 4 vols. (Buenos Aires and Asunción: Imprenta de J. A. Berra/Imprenta Militar, 1894–1901), II, 346–47.

22. Washburn, *History of Paraguay*, II, 191.

23. Washburn, *History of Paraguay*, II, 191.

24. Masterman, *Seven Eventful Years*, 61.

25. *El Centinela*, April 25, 1867.

26. *El Centinela*, May 9, 1867.

27. *El Centinela*, May 9, 1867.

28. *El Centinela*, May 16, 1867.

29. *El Centinela*, May 30, 1867.

30. *El Centinela*, June 6, 1867.

31. Chris Leuchars, *To the Bitter End: Paraguay and the War of the Triple Alliance* (Westport, CT: Greenwood Press, 2002), 166–67; Washburn, *History of Paraguay*, II, 203-05.

32. Centurión, *Memorias*, II, 350, 352.

33. *El Centinela*, July 11, 1867.

34. *El Centinela*, Aug. 8, 1867.

35. *El Centinela*, Aug. 8, 1867.

36. Leuchars, *To the Bitter End*, 129–30, 154.

37. William H. Jeffrey, *Mitre and Argentina* (New York: Library Publishers, 1952), 221.

38. Thompson, *War in Paraguay*, 202.

39. Williams, *Rise and Fall of the Paraguayan Republic*, 221.

40. Thompson, *War in Paraguay*, 199.

41. Joyas y alajas de Caacupé; Joyas y alajas de Itaguá, March–April 1867, ANA/NE, 2853.

42. Potthast, "Protagonists, Victims, and Heroes," 51.

43. Potthast, "Protagonists, Victims, and Heroes," 51.

44. Thompson, *War in Paraguay*, 200.

45. Thompson, *War in Paraguay*, 206.

46. The first Battle of Tuyuty, May 1866, was the "greatest battle in South American history," Leuchars, *To the Bitter End*, 116.

47. Centurión, *Memorias*, III, 24–35.

48. *El Centinela*, Nov. 7, 1867.

49. *El Centinela*, Nov. 21, 1867.

50. *El Centinela*, Nov. 28, 1867.

51. Washburn, *History*, II, 168–69.

52. Masterman, *Seven Eventful Years*, 272.

53. Washburn, *History of Paraguay*, II, 212.

54. Masterman, *Seven Eventful Years*, 208–9.

55. Masterman, *Seven Eventful Years*, 207, 90, 248; Centurión, *Memorias*, IV, 190–214, 248.

56. The Escuela Pancha Garmendia fell victim to the pro-López authoritarians who took power in the 1930s following the Chaco War. See this book's chapter 7.

57. Centurión, *Memorias*, III, 224–30.

58. Centurión, *Memorias*, III, 214–15.

59. Washburn, *History*, II, 230–31.

60. Masterman, *Seven Eventful Years*, 223–30, 250.

61. Masterman, *Seven Eventful Years*, 216–17.

62. Masterman, *Seven Eventful Years*, 245.

63. Masterman, *Seven Eventful Years*, 234.

64. Masterman, *Seven Eventful Years*, Appendix, 308.

65. Masterman, *Seven Eventful Years*, 242–43.

66. Decreto del Mariscal Presidente de la República y General en Gefe de sus Ejércitos, San Fernando, July 14, 1868, ANA/CRB, 4755.

67. Recognizing the injustice of Berges's sentence, twentieth-century Paraguayan officials rehabilitated him by stealth. They named a street for him in Asunción. Ironically, Berges's short street runs parallel to the grand avenue named for the marshal.

68. Lista de los reos traidores y asesinos paraguayos; Lista de de los reos de diferentes nacionalidades que quedan en la Carcelería pública de este campo; Reos políticos; and Mugeres prisioneros (List of criminal traitors and Paraguayan assassins; List of criminals of different nationalities who remain in the public jail in this camp; Political prisoners; and Women prisoners), all Campamento (Camp) de Cerro León, June 3, 1868, ANA/CRB 4712.

69. Washburn, *History of Paraguay*, II, 212.

70. Masterman, *Seven Eventful Years*, 244.

71. Juan Silvano Godoi, *Documentos Históricos: El fusilimiento del Obispo Palacios y los Tribunales de Sangre de San Fernando* (Asunción: Imprenta Cromos, 1996 [1916]).

72. *El Centinela*, Dec. 5, 1867. In 1867, López fantasized that "the brave General Barrios," whom he would execute in 1868, had dealt the Allies a mortal blow, while acting under the brilliant strategic eye of López, whose plan he carried out; *Centinela*, Nov. 14, 1867.

73. *El Centinela*, Aug. 8, 1867.

74. Leuchars, *To the Bitter End*, 209.

75. Leuchars, *To the Bitter End*, 209.

76. Leuchars, *To the Bitter End*, 207.

77. FSL, Proclamation, Cerro León, Dec. 20, 1868, *Proclamas y cartas*.

78. Sandra Gaydol, "*Honor moderno*: The significance of Honor in Fin-de-Siècle Argentina," *HAHR* 84, no. 3 (August 2004): 475–501.

79. FSL to Allied Generals, Pykysyry, Dec. 24, 1868, *Proclamas y cartas*.

80. Since they left Paraguay an independent nation after the war, the claim was and is credible. The Argentine–Brazilian rivalry that prevented either power from annexing Paraguay after the war could have been foreseen in the 1860s.

81. FSL, Manifesto to the Nation, H.Q., Pykysyry, Oct. 16, 1868, *Proclamas y cartas*.

82. FSL, Manifesto to the Nation, H.Q., Pykysyry, Oct. 16, 1868, *Proclamas y cartas*.

83. FSL to Martin McMahon, H.Q., Pykysyry, December 1868, *Proclamas y cartas*.

84. Leuchars, *To the Bitter End*, 204.

85. FSL to McMahon, H.Q., Pykysyry, December 1868, *Proclamas y cartas*.

86. FSL to Allied generals, H.Q., Pykysyry, Dec. 24, 1868, *Proclamas y cartas*.

87. Jerry W. Cooney, "Economy and Manpower: Paraguay at War," in *I Die with My Country*, ed. Hendrik Kraay and Thomas L. Whigham (Lincoln: University of Nebraska Press, 2004), 43.

88. Leuchars, *To the Bitter End*, 215.

89. FSL to Conde d'Eu, H.Q., May 29, 1869, *Proclamas y cartas*.

90. FSL to Count d'Eu, H.Q., June 3, 1869, *Proclamas y cartas*.

91. FSL to Emiliano López, Ascurra, June 28, 1869, *Proclamas y cartas*.

92. In 1869, an ounce of gold was worth US$20.67.

93. FSL to Emiliano López, Ascurra, June 28, 1869, *Proclamas y cartas*.

94. FSL to Gregorio Benítez, Cordillera, June 30, 1869, *Proclamas y cartas*.

95. FSL, Farewell Address to McMahon, Piribebuy, June 30, 1869, *Proclamas y cartas*.

96. FSL, Decree, Aquidabán-ñiguì, Feb. 25, 1870, *Proclamas y cartas*.

97. Cooney, "Economy and Manpower," 22. López had numerous wounds, the autopsy reports. It is available to readers of Portuguese and Spanish in the Paraguayan national archive.

98. López's body had four major wounds, including a musket ball that remained in the thorax and lacerations of his intestines and bladder produced by a sharp instrument, likely a lance. The cutting weapons and bullets entered from both his front and rear. Certificado de la heridas causantes de la muerte del Mariscal Francisco Solano López expedido por los cirujuanos del ejercito Brasilero Dr. Manuel Cardoso de la Costa Lobo y Dr. Militâo Barbosa (Certificate of the wounds causing the death of Marshal Francisco Solano López issued by the surgeons of the Brazilian Army Dr. Manuel Cardoso de la Costa Lobo and Dr. Militâo Barbosa), Concepción, March 25, 1870; ANA/SH 356, no. 18.

7

⊙━✦━⊙

The López Legacy

In the 1870s, most surviving Paraguayans reviled the late dictator. The country was a wasteland, with its population reduced by more than half. There were twice as many females as males. Thousands of men had perished in battle. More died from disease, a universal characteristic of all wars before the twentieth century. One scholar says that the population was reduced to 116,000, or about a quarter of the 1864 figure.[1] Others think the number somewhat larger.[2] In any event, the loss of life was staggering. The economy was in shambles. The nation was to lose the disputed territories to Argentina and Brazil.

Looking backward, many remembered the tyrant's ". . . cruelty, his cowardice, his monstrous egotism, [and] his contempt for human dignity."[3] Others, however, were cowed by decades of repression. They had never enjoyed freedom of speech. Men remained so fearful of reprisals that they refused to speak of the departed despot. López's sisters remembered him as "a monster."[4] Rafaela López showed her scorn for her brother and his ghastly enterprise by marrying a Brazilian. López's mother recalled that he had Silvestre Aveiro beat her. Most articulate survivors of the war were anti-López. Those who had profited from their service to the dictator and wished to recapture their prior influence defended him. More numerous were those like one veteran who had fought bravely in the war—Procurador Izquierdo said of the dead marshal, "I spit on his shadow."[5] Until 1876, the Allies, especially the Brazilians, whose troops were the principal occupiers, controlled the country, and they discouraged tributes to their fallen enemy.

ELISA LYNCH'S LAST CHAPTER

When the Allies took Asunción in January 1869, they created a provisional government from former exiles. If not totally controlled by the Allies, the new government made no moves to offend them. It declared López an outlaw on August 16, 1869, his official status for fifty years. It also proclaimed Lynch a criminal. Over the next few months, the new authority expropriated López real estate, now property of the republic. The new rulers also nationalized holdings of Lynch and the late Venancio and Benigno López and the lands of their sisters and mother. Eventually, though, the government returned Doña Juana Pabla Carillo de López's lands to her, and those of sisters Rafaela and Inocencia were restored as well. Their detestation of the departed marshal was no pose. Abroad, Lynch resolved to regain her Paraguayan wealth.[6]

When captured in 1870, she had about $25,000 in jewels, $8,000 in gold, and £25,000 in the Bank of England.[7] The victors allowed her to keep the gold and jewels. She entertained the hope of possessing the vast land holdings, title to which the father of her children, now the "criminal traitor,"[8] had bestowed on her. She also desired the other properties that López had helped her acquire at fire-sale prices. Elite women had always hated her. Now they acted. Lynch narrowly escaped death at the hands of an angry mob of Paraguayan women. One postwar visitor guessed that the female horde was led by the late marshal's mother and sisters. The Brazilians saved her.[9]

Having sent unknown sums to Britain during the war, Lynch had fled immediately after Francisco's death. The British government refused to offer her its protection because she was still married to a French citizen. She took her sons nevertheless to the United Kingdom. There she brought lawsuits against British subjects, including the Stewart brothers, who had assisted her wartime money transfers. She won the suit but no money. She moved to Paris and purchased a house on the Rue de Rivoli, although she returned to England during the Paris Commune in 1871. One man in London, in 1873 or 1874, observed that although she had put on weight, she still dressed fashionably and was "handsome and distinguished looking."[10]

She went back to Paris in 1875, then sailed with her son, Enrique, to the Río de la Plata to claim the 3,000 square leagues of state land deeded her by her former lover.[11] She argued that the properties were rightfully and legally hers, showing how far out of touch she was. She said that she was also a victim of the recent war, having lost Francisco and Panchito to Brazilian bullets. She cited her wartime suffering. What people remembered were not her losses but her war profiteering. She said that she had witnessed President López fall to Brazilian musket balls.[12] If true, of course, it would have been difficult for anyone to hear Francisco say the immortal words, "I die with my country," essential to the López legend. Given the confusion and the noise of gunfire and the fact that his deepest feelings were expressed in Guarani, what Francisco said at the end must remain problematic.

In any event, Lynch demanded the return of thirty properties. She had acquired most of them from distressed owners suffering from the privations of war, which she had not. Lynch, like all the López women, had made a show of paying for purchases. We may be sure, however, that she paid for her acquisitions in worthless paper currency. Her argument was that she only bought properties from people forced to sell them; she was altruistic. She denied that coercion played any role in the transactions, a falsehood, because business deals of the López clan were accompanied by an implied threat of force.

She attempted to reclaim her properties worth more than 100,000 pesos. One holding that she demanded was in San Lorenzo. She had purchased it from the Bedoya family in February 1868, as Brazilian warships were advancing on Asunción. Another asset was "purchased" from Hilario Marcó, then in the army under her lover's command. Had Marcó refused to sell, he would have signed his own death sentence. In late 1869 and early 1870, as the Allied armies were cornering López, Lynch, their children, and their few followers, she purchased from the state, or so she claimed, lands in the district of Victoria del Salvador, for which she paid 30,000 pesos. Since "the state" meant the father of her children, it was later impossible to determine that any money had changed hands. She also "purchased" a gigantic tract of undeveloped land in the wilderness between the Ilanara-Guazú and Aguaray-Guazú Rivers in December 1869; she paid another 50,000 imaginary pesos. These two acquisitions of state property made conspicuous her exploitative and coercive purchase of more modest properties earlier in the war. In 1867, for example, she had bought a house on Calle Palma in center city Asunción for 2,500 pesos from the widow of Bernardino Ferreyra.

In October 1867, she had acquired a prime lot at the corner of Palma and Encarnación in downtown Asunción. She insisted that she had paid only 600 pesos, a low price, because the house was in ruins. In October 1868, as her lover's blood lust brought the torture and execution of hundreds, she bought a lot from Bartola Morrilla near Lambaré. The marshal had helped Lynch buy seventeen other properties when it was clear that the war was lost. Ten of these she purchased through front woman Dolores de Pereira. Lynch also tried without success to regain her luxurious residence, an entire city block, now a part of the Gran Hotel del Paraguay. As the Allied-backed provisional government declared López an outlaw, the fugitive president turned state lands over to his eldest son, Juan

Francisco, Panchito. Lynch demanded these as well, as heir to her son's estate.[13] By the time of her death to stomach cancer in Paris in 1886, the money had mostly run out. She was supposedly broke and alone.

Most Paraguayans in recent decades have learned that she was destitute and that the "municipality of Paris paid for her funeral."[14] Actually, she was not destitute, although she never again lived a luxurious life. In Paris she posed as "a respectable widow of moderate income." When she died, her and Francisco's son, Frederico, arranged for her funeral Mass and bought a plot for her in the Père Lachaise cemetery.[15] Significantly, reliable accounts of Lynch's early and later life do not appear in Paraguay or anywhere else. Several historians have tried to authenticate her claims about the date of her birth, her schooling, and her family and its connections. They have been unsuccessful, and her claims have not been authenticated.

THE POSTWAR LÓPEZ LEGEND IN REGIONAL CONTEXT

To understand the vicissitudes of the postwar López legend requires a survey of post-1870 politics, alternating periods of instability and authoritarianism.[16] In the 1870s, Brazil and Argentina seized the prewar disputed territories. These had not been of enough strategic or economic value to take by force. The Argentines made good their claim to the Chaco south of the Pilcomayo River, and Brazil took the lands between the Apa and Blanco Rivers. (See map on page ii.) Argentine soldiers camped in Villa Occidental in the Chaco. The larger Brazilian army dominated eastern Paraguay. López's defeat gave them the territory until then also claimed by Paraguay. Under pressure, the Asunción government renounced any claim to these regions.

The postwar López legend is tied closely to post-1870 political developments. Despite the current belief, created by Colorado Party propagandists like Juan E. O'Leary and Enrique Solano López, the anti-López exiles of the Paraguayan Legion played only a minor military and political role. It was never cohesive, because "hatred of the López clan was the principal bond that held the Legion together. . . ."[17] After 1870, Legionnaires forged alliances with supporters of the late dictator. One result was the foundation of the Colorado Party in 1887, which included former Legionnaires and *Lopistas*, López followers. Colorados would eventually ally themselves with several dictators. One distinguished historian says, "Coloradism was political and economic opportunism. . . ."[18] The party claimed descent from the heroic marshal. Colorado publicists lionized authoritarian rulers and arbitrary rule.

In the late 1800s, the leading political figure was Bernardino Caballero. With little formal education, he had risen from enlisted ranks to general by currying favor with López and escaping unscathed from battles. The cofounder of the Colorado Party was a man of limited ability, and "he owed much of his success to the fact that he looked like a president." President of Paraguay from 1880 to 1886, he was the foremost Colorado politician until the Liberal Revolution of 1904. He led uprisings against some governments and served in others. A park named for him in Asunción near the Paraguay River would have pleased him as a proper tribute, at least in the 1970s and early 1980s. It was a lovely place for family gatherings, with a playground for soccer and basketball and a road on which the comfortable classes jogged. By 2002, however, surrounding squatter settlements made the Parque Bernardino Caballero a dangerous place. Symbolically, it is a twin of the neglected park at Cerro Corá dedicated to Caballero's patron, Francisco Solano López.

Brazil and Argentina departed in 1876; occupation was expensive and unrewarding. For seven years, they had made crucial decisions for the anti-López puppet government in Asunción. While the dictator fled into increasingly remote areas to his death, the triumvirs played off Brazil and Argentina—López's demise at Cerro Corá made the former allies rivals again. The new government declared López an outlaw, his official status for the next half century. Ex-Legionnaires initially represented Argentina. Brazilians backed Cirilio Rivarola, a war veteran. Thus began a factionalism that plagued all political groupings—except during the dictatorship of Alfredo Stroessner—into the twenty-first century. The liberal Constitution of 1870 created a paper democracy with a separation of powers among executive, legislative, and judicial branches. It was often ignored, owing to a political culture unprepared for democracy.

A SHORT POSTWAR PARAGUAYAN HISTORY: THE POLITICAL

After 1876, admirers of the fallen marshal, the Lopistas, defended him. Their economic policies, however, were generally liberal. They never reasserted a López-style control over the nation's economy, preferring the dominant laissez-faire ideals of the Atlantic world. Factions formed and soon would call themselves political parties. Legionnaires were never a cohesive political group.

The first domination of Paraguay by the grouping that became the Colorados—one of the two important groups—began in 1880, seven years before the party's official founding. It grew from the so-called Bareiro Faction.[19] Its most important leader, General Caballero, was president from

1880 to 1886. Colorado control lasted until 1904. Most people welcomed this period of stability, except out-of-power members of the political class. The Colorado Party, formally the National Republican Association, was founded in 1887, two months after the creation of the Liberal Party, known as the Centro Democrático until 1894.

Colorado presidents financed postwar reconstruction by sales of public lands. The purchasers, often foreign firms, bought large tracts, *latifundia*, at bargain prices. Twentieth-century Colorado propagandists damned early Liberals and their heirs as *vendepatrias*, sellouts, springing from the loins of Legionnaires. In fact, however, prominent Legionnaires were Colorado cofounders, including José Segundo Decoud and Juan G. González. One former Legionnaire, Juan Bautista Egusquiza, was both a Colorado and president of the nation from 1894 to 1898. But Caballero remained the maker and breaker of presidents for a quarter century. As before, no true democracy functioned. Corruption was normal. Both Colorados and Liberals broke into competing factions. Patronage and personal loyalties overshadowed institutional ones.

In 1904, the Liberals took power. They directed policy into the 1930s, when war with Bolivia heightened old tensions and created new ones. The group split into the Radical Liberals and the Civic Liberals. Like the Argentine Radicals before 1916, the Colorados in the Liberal Era refused to participate in elections, protesting that they were rigged and that their participation would legitimize an illegitimate polity. Liberals, rhetorically committed to democracy, seldom followed democratic procedures. Most leaders advocated laissez-faire economics. This changed under President Eduardo Schaerer, who ruled from 1912 to 1916. A Radical Liberal with strong military ties, Schaerer's government intervened in the economy, opposing liberal orthodoxies. The economy grew to feed the Allies in World War I, who needed primary products like cattle and cotton. Internal strife plagued the Liberal party, and Schaerer's attempt to enforce a military-like discipline within its ranks failed. His endeavors, though, were a preview of Alfredo Stroessner's reform of the Colorado Party after 1954.

After the Colorado Era, periodic revolts made politics risky. Some uprisings were lengthy and bloody, others bloodless coups. In 1928 "a real contest was held for the presidency,"[20] but any semblance of democracy would have to wait until the 1990s. Various Liberals ruled into the 1930s. The Chaco War with Bolivia testified that they had paid insufficient attention to national security.

A harsh authoritarianism returned to Paraguay in 1936. It remained the dominant political posture into the 1990s, although its practitioners and parties would change. During ascendancies of both Colorados and Liberals, party names identified large groups only loosely connected. Under their umbrellas, rival factions cherished personal loyalties. Thus, factional struggles were "a confusing series of brief alliances" with constantly changing compositions.[21]

The decade of the 1930s was one of transition. Liberal inattention to national security hastened their fall. Paraguayans won the war so convincingly as to embarrass Bolivians. On the eve of the conflict, the Andeans seemed to have all the advantages. Despite the odds, however, the Paraguayans won. Their soldiers possessed superior initial, sustaining, and combat motivations and a national cause. They believed that the Chaco was theirs and worth fighting for. They dominated the ineffective, mountain-dwelling Bolivians in the hot Chaco lowlands. They also enjoyed the brilliant generalship of José Félix Estigarribia. They kept the Chaco Boreal.[22]

But the wartime president, Liberal Eusebio Ayala, and his government fell on February 16, 1936, to a group later known as the Febrerista Party, whose influence steadily waned. Still liberalism was discredited. The new government had a corporatist orientation, although it drew supporters from the far right and left.

In Latin America, many *authentic* heroes were reviled at their death and developed cult followings later. The most prominent was Liberator Simón Bolívar, who was rehabilitated by his old rival José Antonio Páez and his followers in 1842, only twelve years after his death "to bathe themselves in vicarious glory and associate themselves with [his] record. . . ."[23] In Mexico, independence leaders Miguel Hidalgo, José María Morelos, and Agustín Iturbide, all executed by the authorities, were later rehabilitated and made official heroes.[24] The list of canonical heroes is extensive, because "In Latin America, as in Europe and the United States, the names and images of dead heroes have been long-used as texts to instruct living citizens in the behaviors and values (bravery, sacrifice, and honor among others) that are useful to the nation."[25] Paraguay followed suit.

The Febreristas' most important symbolic act was to rehabilitate Francisco Solano López. The nation must honor the fallen hero.[26] One neighborhood in the capital asked to be recognized as the Barrio Mariscal López; the Febreristas happily complied. The government of 1936, allegedly based on peasants and workers, was stoutly authoritarian. Since it constituted a "national democracy," a constitutional government was not necessary,[27] nor were honest elections. No succeeding administration would take seriously any constitution not of its own making until the end of the twentieth century.

All succeeding governments honored López. In the late 1930s, the Liberal Party declined. Sometime rivals, the army and police made crucial political decisions. The dictatorship of Higinio Morínigo (1940–1948) was a prelude to the Stroessner regime. Morínigo, like López, directed the crucial defense ministry when President Estigarribia, now elevated to the highest office in the nation, died in 1940. Morínigo, a professional soldier, made himself president, outlawed the Liberal Party, and established the military control that lasted for fifty years. Authoritarianism was in. Liberalism was out. Morínigo tolerated the Colorado Party but no other.[28] His fall to a military coup in 1948 was followed by a period of confusion. This contributed to the ascendancy of the Colorado party, which would last into the twenty-first century.

Alfredo Stroessner, commander in chief of the armed forces, took power in 1954. He ruled the nation until 1989, the second longest dictatorship in all of Latin America. "His success lay in controlling two institutions, the army and the Colorado Party."[29] He disciplined the party and centralized all authority on himself, an indirect homage to Francisco López. The party penetrated Paraguayan life, including professional and business groups, those of university students, women's organizations, and neighborhood associations. Party and government were nearly interchangeable. One needed Colorado Party approval for jobs in government, education, and medicine. Liberals did poorly in business. Colorados did better. Stroessner legalized a tame Liberal faction in the 1960s for appearance's sake. Liberal politicians who played tennis normally joined the dusty, down-at-the-heels Asunción Tenis Club, where you could buy a drink and a stale sandwich surrounded by flies at the outdoor bar.[30] Colorados ate, drank, and played tennis at the sparkling Club Centenario. Colorado historians headed the national archives and library. Liberal historians never did. Stroessner oversaw economic advancement and infrastructure modernization. Much economic growth was a by-product of the new Itaipú dam on the Paraná River. It provided hydroelectric power to Brazil and cash to Paraguay.

In the early 1980s, Paraguay fell into economic recession. The aging president's popularity dwindled. In February 1989, the seventy-five-year-old Stroessner was overthrown by a subordinate, General Andrés Rodríguez, a drug lord. Elections for a new president were fairly honest. Unsurprisingly, Rodríguez won. The Colorado party remained dominant. Democracy of a sort came to Paraguay. Rodríguez stepped down at the end of his elected term, but his successors were Colorados.

LÓPEZ'S TRUE NATURE REVEALED—AND SUPPRESSED

The reputation of Francisco Solano López matched national politics. For fifty years after his death he was an outlaw and for another fifty years a hero. In the early 1870s, a few clerics who survived the war denounced him for causing useless bloodshed, sexual licentiousness, and venality.

They excoriated his using state monies for Madame Lynch's luxuries. They condemned his assumption that the wealth of the nation was family property. His sisters wished "to execrate his memory."[31] Most postwar Paraguayans knew that López was a selfish coward, not a hero. Nevertheless, beneath the widespread hostility, even anti-Lopistas believed that López stood for the nation.

A former secretary made an important assessment of López. Written between 1894 and 1904, a four-volume work by Juan Crisóstomo Centurión y Martínez painted a devastating portrait of López. Centurión's *Memorias o reminiscencias históricas sobre la guerra del Paraguay* is moving. Centurión believed that, despite all his grievous faults, López was a great man, superior to his critics. Born in 1840, Centurión studied in England on a government fellowship. Young Juan Crisóstomo returned home before Francisco attacked Brazil. During the war, he assisted the dictator, participated as an inquisitor in the purges of 1868, and was severely wounded and disfigured at Cerro Corá. After eight years as a prisoner of war and an exile in Europe, he returned to take part in politics. In 1887, he participated in the founding of the Colorado Party and opposed its anti-López faction. His connection to the dictator gives verisimilitude to the damning pictures of López that emerge from his pages.

Centurión acknowledged López's increasing cowardice.[32] He said of one battle that López's only reason for ordering an attack was to demonstrate the bravery of his soldiers, sacrificing some of his best troops. The dictator shirked responsibility when the action failed, blaming one Lt. Romero. Branding the junior officer a traitor, he forced his wife to denounce her husband in *El Semanario*.

Centurión also described how López played the race card.[33] He criticized López's tactical offensives; the marshal's purpose was merely to bring vicarious glory to their commander.[34] Centurión reported desertions to the enemy in the initial months of the war,[35] which discredits claims of Lopistas. He said that López was gleeful after the battle of Curupaity, September 22, 1866, because his army had killed so many Allied officers. López hoped that this would lead to Allied dissolution. But the sadism of Centurión's López is also clear.

The author's account exposed López's intelligence efforts as counterproductive. When the marshal sent out patrols, the men so feared his wrath that they told him only what he wanted to hear. They withheld accurate information.

Centurión judged that López's relationship with American Minister Charles Ames Washburn was a correct one until the failure of Washburn's attempt to negotiate the truce that would allow him to remain in office. The dictator again blamed the messenger, this time Washburn. Centurión said that López's failure to leave for Europe under the generous terms negotiated by British Minister Gould in August 1867, was an example of López's "caprice." His refusal to go, according to Centurión, destroyed the nation. Centurión criticized López's evacuation of Asunción in 1868, because it needlessly increased civilian suffering.[36] Centurión matter-of-factly reported López's imprisonment and execution of doña Juliana Insfran for bravely refusing to bear false witness against her hero husband, Colonel Martínez, who had surrendered his force, concluding that further resistance would be mass suicide.[37]

At the same time and arguing against the facts, other men began a campaign to glorify Francisco Solano López. In the late 1800s, they began to create the Big Lie in Paraguay. They suppressed truths and distorted facts. Two of Francisco's natural sons—Enrique Solano López, also son of Madame Lynch, and Carlos López—led the charge. The Lie's most effective publicist, however, was Juan Emiliano O'Leary. Born it 1879, his was the first generation lacking firsthand knowledge of the war. His histories are untrustworthy. Propagandist O'Leary's fables of a heroic López were so useful that a Colorado government placed a bronze bust of him in the Plaza of Heroes. In 2005, it was a sickly green.

O'Leary made a successful career by glorifying the dictator. He edited Colorado newspapers. He served a sinecure as director of the national library; he was its head in 1959 when Argentina gave Paraguay the building that is now the Biblioteca Nacional. In 1974, its disarray remained a disgrace. He also headed the national archive; his inattention to this job brought similarly calamitous results, including the destruction of valuable manuscripts. Nevertheless, O'Leary enjoyed government largess into his eighties. In 1961, he was director of protocol.[38] When the Revolution of 1936 canonized the marshal president, O'Leary heard his poetry read on national radio.[39] Nationalists cited his "histories" as proof of the marshal's greatness.[40] The López who lives gloriously, bravely, and patriotically in O'Leary's books was a fiction but a useful symbol to justify authoritarian government, political corruption, and nepotism. O'Leary's López soared from 1936 into the 1990s, his heroic image especially pushed to the front by the post-1935 governments. Most early Colorado tracts and later official pro-López propaganda were simplified versions of O'Leary's books (described later). They are uncritical. They often repeat the self-congratulatory lies that López told in *El Semanario* and *Cabichuí*. Colorados tied an honorable Marshal López to Paraguayan nationalism. The Colorado-backed campaign to rehabilitate López was for Liberals like the writer and one-time president Cecilio Baez "an effort to place a heavenly halo on the Devil himself."[41]

HIS SON'S EFFORTS

For Enrique Solano López, who collaborated with O'Leary in the rehabilitation of his father's reputation until his own death in 1917, the goal meant more than restoring the family's prestige. In 1864, he was named Enrique Mariano Lynch.[42] His father had decreed his legitimacy in 1865, and he became Enrique Mariano López. The adding of Solano to his name was apparently his own idea. The appellation Solano López, a form that Francisco did not employ, is an implicit tribute to the marshal president and distinguishes his socially prominent descendants today. Enrique's campaign subsumed his hunger for the wealth that his father and mother had stolen from the nation. He pressed Argentina and Brazil to make good his claim.[43] They refused. The claims they had denied his mother were turned over by her to Enrique. He also coveted the properties in Elisa's possession before 1870. The resurrection of his father's reputation became "the consuming passion of his life."[44] It supposedly transcended pecuniary reward, but the two were inseparable.

The only son of López and Lynch to play a role in post-war Paraguay, Enrique Solano López was born in 1858. When his father died, he was eleven and a second lieutenant in the army. Unlike many other boys of his generation, he never served militarily. He watched Brazilians kill his fleeing father. He followed his mother into exile, saw her vilified, and was in a position to know that his godfather and uncle, Venancio López, was tortured on his father's orders. Since he and his brothers accompanied their father to the end,[45] he could not have missed the open-air tortures and executions. When Brazilian forces allowed his mother to leave, Enrique followed. He enrolled briefly at St. Joseph's College in England and then at two schools in France. In 1875, he returned with Elisa to Asunción. He hastily left with her when the government ordered her departure. A crowd of women demanded that she be punished. A later story, partly concocted by Enrique, went that the Brazilians and Argentines caused the family's expulsion. Most twentieth-century accounts of the incident fail to mention that the public detested her. When he could not avoid unpleasant facts, Enrique attributed them to the Paraguayan Legion, increasingly labeled traitors, equated with Liberals.

When Enrique returned to Paraguay in 1883, his principal material asset was his genealogy; his father's rehabilitation was his primary goal. With little formal schooling, he was nevertheless briefly superintendent of public instruction, a job for which he had no training or talent. He introduced the glorification of his father into school curriculum. Until his death in 1917, he worked mostly as a journalist, serving for a time as director of the Colorado newspaper *La Patria*. Given the disputatiousness of politics at the time, it is unsurprising that he was briefly jailed in 1908 for anti-government activity, that he was exiled (also briefly), and that he returned to become a Colorado senator.[46]

Enrique, O'Leary, and others appealed to those who lacked firsthand knowledge of the suffering of the 1860s and of the marshal's true nature. In the late nineteenth and early twentieth centuries, several men began to honor López for having fought to the death. Liberals condemned López's cruelty and "the insatiable greed of his Irish mistress."[47] One part of the new López legend was to charge that incompetent subordinates like Estigarribia and Robles had betrayed their commander and to blame them for the early defeats, absolving the marshal. This ignored the fact that it was López who chose mediocre officers and was ultimately responsible. In the fable of the valiant López, his opponents were traitors who conspired with the American minister Washburn to secure defeat. The charge circulated into the 1990s and, in 2003, an intelligent but uncritical British biographer of Lynch accepted it.[48] Historical accuracy played little role in these formulations. Revisionists from O'Leary to Osvaldo Bergonzi[49] employed logic that would flunk a freshman history examination in the United States.

President Juan Bautista Egusquiza (1894–1898) was a former Legionnaire and also a Colorado, belying later Colorado smears that the two groups were separate. In the later Colorado version, the Legionnaires-turned-Liberals were traitors and Colorados were patriots. In 1898, Egusquiza opposed Lopista efforts to glorify the marshal dictator—efforts that were then gaining strength. He opposed the student notebooks that, owing to the efforts of Enrique and his allies, were for sale. These *libretas* bore an idealized likeness of the dictator and a short, eulogistic biography of López. With his glorified likeness on the cover but without the biographical sketch, they remained for sale across the street from the Paraguayan national archive in the twenty-first century.

Egusquiza's anti-Lopista stance divided the Colorado Party. Yet, "The campaign to glorify López continued to win adherents because it appealed to chauvinistic, nationalistic, and xenophobic sentiment. . . ."[50] A corollary to Lopismo was a growing hostility toward Brazil and a frustration born of the inability to act on it. Brazilian influence increased throughout the 1900s. In tandem, the campaign to exalt López gained momentum. Its liberal and Liberal opponents tried to discredit Enrique Solano's crusade by recalling his bastardy. They failed. The myth of a heroic Francisco Solano López became equated in the public mind with anti-Brazilian sentiment.

Throughout his life, Enrique Solano López pushed his financial interest, especially his claim to the millions of acres that his father had given his mother. He also demanded to have the houses and ranches obtained by her war profiteering. He never recovered any holding. Until he died, public hostility to his mother remained intense. In any event, no government, including those that wished to rehabilitate the marshal's reputation, would surrender these lands. Although Caballero once promised to help Enrique gain title to his inheritance,[51] it was an insincere gesture, not of kindness but of cruelty, encouraging a vain quest.

Enrique's ballyhoo complemented that of others. Even during the occupation, former followers cited López's memory "as a symbol around which to build a strong sense of nationalism,"[52] although the intense nationalism that men and women displayed during two terrible wars prove Paraguayans need no artificial stimuli. Most former López followers refused to admit his true nature, because to speak honestly about his character, generalship, diplomacy, and cowardice would tarnish their own reputations. Those who became Colorados used the myth of López the Honorable against Liberals. They branded opponents of López in his lifetime and accurate historical accounts of him as treason. The concept of a loyal opposition was still foreign.

PUBLIC ARENA DEBATES, PUBLISHED WORKS, AND HISTORIANS VS. PROPAGANDISTS

The propaganda war between Liberals and Colorados continued, reflecting the struggle for dominance. The parties fought over which group would govern and more fundamentally over whether the government would move toward democracy or revert to authoritarian control.

Rivarola

One of the last major attacks on Francisco Solano López was a collection of anti-López essays published in 1926 as *El Mariscal Francisco Solano López*; many of the essays previously appeared in newspapers. The book was reissued in 1996 by the Patriotic Friends of Liberty. It aimed to rebut the López legend and attack Colorados. In an editorial originally published in 1920, the director of the periodical *El Liberal*, Belisario Rivarola, said, "We swear eternal hatred of Marshal Francisco Solano López [but] we venerate the memory of his glorious soldiers." Rivarola charged that the late Enrique Solano López had defrauded the nation by trying to convince innocent youth that black was white, that López the Executioner was actually López the Hero. Rivarola thought the marshal president was morally deformed. He condemned Lopez's corruption, pointing to his alienation of the nation's patrimony, six million hectares of national territory, to please his mistress. Rivarola upbraided the creators of the abominable myth of a heroic Marshal López for tolerating his insatiable greed. Rivarola attributed much of the damage done by López to the influence of Lynch. Rivarola thought she swayed Francisco in a "magical" way, implying that she was a witch. He denounced her contribution to the nation's ruination. Rivarola insisted that López was a barbaric monster, a coward whose pride was "satanic." His "sinister personality" compounded his "military and political ineptitude." It was shocking, Rivarola said, that rehabilitators like O'Leary were then creating an image of a López who embodied civic virtue, when in fact he had been a man without virtue, the murderer of his own brothers. Charging López with needlessly prolonging an unwinnable war for selfish purposes, Rivarola nevertheless proclaimed his own patriotism by denouncing the Allies for "having despoiled an unfortunate nation."[53]

Báez

Cecilio Báez, a Liberal's liberal and an important intellectual of the first half of the twentieth century, charged that López, by prolonging the war, had hoped to destroy the Paraguayan nation. Thus, when the Allies won they would gain only desolation. As articulated by Báez, the Liberal argument was that the first three dictators had progressively declined in ability. Francia had resisted Brazil and Argentina and maintained internal peace. The elder López had fostered national development; but he then delivered the people, bound hand and foot, to his atrocious son. Francisco Solano, Báez said, ineptly plunged into conflict. With a huge army, he attacked unprepared neighbors but quixotically and without a clear military objective. Báez labeled the attacks "aggression," which they were. According to Báez, López's judgment was wretched. In the war years, *El Semanario*, truly edited by López himself, had likened the marshal president to Cincinnatus. Báez thought the comparison "disgraceful." The Roman Cincinnatus had won a quick victory and returned home, while the second López had thrown away his best and his biggest army in the first year of the war. At that point, his only alternatives were to surrender or to preside over the ruination of Paraguay.[54] He chose his own power and national ruination.

To demonstrate the depravity of Francisco Solano López and the perniciousness of his deification, Báez recounted the story of Pancha Garmendia, whose tragic fate was common knowledge. The beautiful virgin resisted the sexual predations of López. After the honorable Panchita rejected the advances of Francisco, he persecuted her brother Juan in retaliation. He terrorized potential suitors, which Washburn's *History of Paraguay* showed, and she became a recluse by necessity. For the Liberals of Baez's generation, the memory of Pancha inspired the anti-Lopistas. That she was tortured and killed on López's orders brought her martyrdom.[55]

Lopistas denied that López's judicial murder of her was personal revenge for her spurning him. Their sophism was that so many years had elapsed between her rejection of his advances and his execution of her that no one could have carried a grudge so long. Thus, they argued, there was nothing personal in López's persecution of her. She was simply part of the plot against him, although this would have been impossible in that time and place. That she had rejected his advances and that he had tortured and killed her, they generally did not bother to deny. The Liberals had founded a school named for her, the Escuela Pancha Garmendia, whose existence publicized the dictator's heinous act. It was a burr under the Lopista saddle. It is unsurprising that in 1936, as the forces of authoritarianism took power, the Escuela Pancha Garmendia ceased functioning. As the February 1936 coup created a major shift in the ideology of the government, the school lost its subsidy. A naval hospital occupied the building. The government distributed the school's furniture to other educational institutions.[56] No longer would the name remind the populace of a cruel, vindictive López. The 1926 collection ended the publication of important anti-López works. The debate was silenced. Pro-López forces dominated the public arena for the rest of the century. By the 1930s, the myth of the heroic López was the essence of Paraguayan nationalism.

The Patriotic Friends of Liberty

In 1996, in a timid effort to speak against Coloradism, the Patriotic Friends of Liberty, whose members included José Zubizarreta, Fernando Talavera, and Manuel Pesoa, protested the perverse use of the past to support the dictatorships of 1936 to 1989. Seven years after the Stroessner dictatorship had ended, they said, they hoped the republication of this tract would encourage political freedom and oppose a renewal of tyranny. They pointed out how essential the image of a brave López was to the Colorado Party. The Friends did no research themselves. They hid behind the polemicists of generations past. They denounced the dictatorships of Rafael Franco (1936–1937), Higinio Morínigo (1940–1948), and Alfredo Stroessner (1954–1989). All, they said, had waged a permanent aggression against the Paraguayan people. These critics continued to use history as a weapon, a polemical activity and not a professional pursuit.[57] Like Colorados, Liberals saw the two López presidents as precursors of authoritarian twentieth-century governments, although Colorados claimed that their actions merely favored strong government and opposed revolution and anarchy. Like the authors of the 1920s work, the late twentieth-century liberals and powerless Liberals denounced the use of the tyrant López to promote patriotism.

Had he returned from the dead, López would have approved the Colorado apologists. They employed his own justifications. He would have crowed over the lack of influence of modern opposition authors. Most Paraguayans remained unaware of the facts, Anti-Colorados said. López's political and diplomatic stupidity, like his cowardice and cruelty, must again be brought to light. Contemporaries must be made to see that López was not Paraguay's defender but a traitor who placed self-interest above country.[58] A Colorado rebuttal was that these vilifiers of López were puppets of Argentina. Their origins could be traced back to Benigno Ferreira, a veteran of the Paraguayan Legion and thus an obvious traitor.

The Lie According to O'Leary

We should return to the most influential propagandist of the López rehabilitation, Juan Emiliano O'Leary, because his tale prevailed throughout most of the twentieth century. During his long lifetime (1879/1880–1968), he created a López who symbolized heroism and inspired support for the Colorado Party. He peppered the periodical press with essays on the heroic López. In his eighties, he remained an image maker, giving public addresses about the marshal's greatness and repeating how great a debt the country owed him—and by implication owed to the dictators whom O'Leary served.

O'Leary's López was the defender of the Fatherland. One British author concluded that it was O'Leary's opportunism that made him disdain the anti-Lopista truth that he had espoused as a young man. R. B. Cunningham Graham reminded readers that O'Leary portrayed López as a "pure-minded patriot," even though the dictator had thrown O'Leary's own mother in jail for marrying the wrong man. Her second husband, the first Juan O'Leary, thought López "a jackal and the hangman of his country."[59]

His son, the propagandist O'Leary, was in fact briefly an anti-Lopista as a young man. His conversion to the cause of the fallen dictator brought him substantial material rewards, which continued all his life. He eulogized López in books like *El libro de los héroes: páginas históricas de la guerra del Paraguay* (1919), *El Mariscal Francisco Solano López* (1926 and other editions), *La alianza de 1845 con Corrientes: aparición de Solano López en el escenario del Plata* (1944), and countless articles in the popular press. He was the most effective publicist of the Colorado Party. Its ideological starting point was a "nationalist past."[60] O'Leary was so talented that he overshadowed lesser propagandists like Ignacio A. Pané and Enrique Solano López. He insisted that Colorados deserved to monopolize the nationalistic view of the past, based on the glorification of the life and career of Francisco Solano López.

O'Leary assumed direction of the Colorado periodical *La Patria* in 1902. From then until his death, he was the chief spokesman for the heroic view of the fallen marshal. O'Leary rehabilitated López. His writings answered authors in *El Cívico*, whose unflattering (and accurate) depiction of López would vie with that of O'Leary with decreasing vigor until its virtual extinction in 1936, when the Febreristas made him the major hero.

In that year, the new rulers ordered López's (or someone's) remains exhumed from Cerro Corá and placed in the Pantheon of Heroes. The rehabilitation was due substantially to the efforts of O'Leary. His impassioned, pro-López works ultimately brought him a comfortable living, national prominence, and his memorial bust. Irreverent wags in the capital came to refer to him as *El Bronce*, "The Bronzed One," ridiculing O'Leary's distortions. This joke when repeated in a tertulia, an ongoing conversation among like-minded friends, was as much dissent as was safe during the last thirty years of O'Leary's life. It was a covert expression of political dissent.

O'Leary's triumphant year was 1936, the year of the ceremonial reburial. The revolutionary government created a commission to find Marshal López. In September, a bold headline of one pro-government newspaper proclaimed "The Remains of Marshal López Were Found!"[61] According to this periodical, an unjust passion had reigned for sixty-six shameful years, when the marshal was legally a criminal. The real crime was that Marshal López's body remained buried at Cerro Corá. The Revolution of 1936 would help Paraguay retake its destiny, and Marshal López's greatness would be recognized. The "pusillanimity and treason" of the past sixty-six years, liberal falsehoods, would be corrected. The "bastard interests of the surviving Legionnaires" would be dashed.[62] The government ordered that on October 12, the anniversary celebration of the discovery of America, the remains of Francisco Solano López would be deposited in the National Pantheon, along with those of an unknown soldier of the Chaco War. A commission headed by D. Romualdo Irigoyen attested to the authenticity of López's remains.[63] The delegation's charge was to find them, and it did. Whether they were truly those of the marshal president, one cannot say. In any event, a great ceremony took place in October 1936. According to one report, "Asunción was taken over by a nationalistic fervor."[64] The celebration preceded by a decade the purported discovery in Mexico of the remains of Cuauhtémoc, the last Aztec ruler, which served similar patriotic ends.[65]

On Sunday, October 11, Francisco Solano López's corpse, or whoever's remains the commission found, entered the Bay of Asunción on the gunboat *Humaitá*. The provisional president of the republic, Colonel don Rafael Franco, government ministers, heads of all branches of the armed forces, and leaders of pro-government student organizations awaited the vessel. In an urn, the corpse was escorted by an armed guard to the National Palace. There the relic reposed in the reception hall guarded by units of the army and navy. After the doors were opened, people filed past all Sunday afternoon and evening. The armed forces passed in review. Elaborate ceremonies followed, including speeches by Dr. Juan Stefanovich on behalf of the provisional government, the mayor (intendente) of Asunción, the head of the national students' association, and the leader of the war veterans' association. A military procession came next. The troops, in uniform only two to four months, were said to have paraded impressively, all marching in step and properly dressed—which is doubtful. An "enormous crowd" was able to contain its emotion. Finally, the urns of López and the unknown soldier were taken into the National Pantheon, which was filled with floral decorations and flags.[66] Francisco Solano López had returned triumphantly to the city that he had left in 1865. O'Leary's work had succeeded. He had surmounted historical fact and vanquished the truth. The Big Lie of Paraguay was national gospel.

The propagandist O'Leary—none should dignify him with the title historian—was a skillful teller of tales. As O'Leary constructed the myth, López began his life with a "brilliant education," polishing the uneven learning schedule that in fact prepared his view of the world.[67] One of O'Leary's fables extolled the extraordinary diplomatic skill of the pre-presidential López, whose diplomatic instincts were normally wretched. That Argentines paid tribute to Justo José de Urquiza for the Pact of Union of November 10, 1859, slighted López and upset O'Leary. He denounced their ingratitude. Standing behind Francisco's diplomatic triumph, O'Leary argued, was President Carlos Antonio, a man "adored" by the Paraguayan people; contemporary accounts belie this. People respected the father without adoration. O'Leary's Francisco López, "the savior of the Argentines,"[68] was in historical reality merely his father's agent, mediating a truce that failed soon after its negotiation.

One of López's greatest weaknesses as president and commander was his inability to delegate. O'Leary reinterpreted this as a positive attribute. O'Leary's López oversaw everything because he was so superior to the bureaucrats who worked for him.[69] In fact, he *was* superior to most of them. He appointed men of lesser ability to the government and the military precisely for their mediocrity.

O'Leary, following the original López allegation, said Brazil in the early 1860s was searching for a pretext to attack. Its emperor, Pedro II, according to O'Leary, was "warlike."[70] In truth López attacked a Brazil unprepared for war. O'Leary justified the aggression by citing Brazil's violation of a treaty of 1850. However, Carlos Antonio saw no reason to consider it a provocation for violence. López's militarily imprudent attack on the Mato Grosso province of Brazil in 1864 was, according to O'Leary, neces-

Pantheon of Heroes

sary to protect the Paraguayan rear[71]—although no major Brazilian attack could have come from there, owing to the Mato Grosso's isolation. Another O'Leary story was that López ordered his armies through Argentina in 1865 to "save the government of Uruguay." In fact he supported only the Blancos, a faction out of power when López moved his forces. Repeating López's advertisements for himself, O'Leary excused the invasion of Argentina, arguing that Argentines had permitted Brazilian forces heading for Paraguay (they never got there) to sail their waters in 1855 and to camp on their soil.[72]

According to O'Leary, the impotent Congress that rubber-stamped López's orders was an authentic legislature. In the propagandist's account, it was Congress that created the position of field marshal and appointed López to the rank in 1865.[73] This fable naturally originated with López, who controlled every vote and every speech in that assembly.

When the war began, O'Leary's López was "implacable before the enemy [and] implacable in defense of the fatherland."[74] Implacable he certainly was, as long as it was other men's lives that he was risking, not his own. At the outset of the war, O'Leary says, López's plan of attack was a good one. In fact, it was dreadful. It made no military sense to divide the army or to begin an offensive without a clearly defined and attainable military objective. The failure, O'Leary said, lay in the incompetence of López's subordinates.[75] The publicist ignored the obvious fact that it was López's responsibility to appoint able commanders in the first place, not the bumblers whom he selected. O'Leary whitewashed the execution of General Robles by endorsing López's charge that Robles was a traitor,[76] although he was not. He was merely a man under stress who intemperately blurted out the truth. O'Leary attributed the failure of the Estigarribia expedition to the failure of Robles's command,[77] a curious argument that ignores López's failure to assign the Estigarribia force a military objective. He also excuses Francisco's sending his army so far away that it was isolated from its base of supply and out of touch with its commander.

One could write a volume chronicling O'Leary's distortions, but there is little point. As his career shows, much of the writing of "history" was a pre-professional endeavor, using the past as a weapon to advance a partisan cause. O'Leary made his bones in 1904, when the Liberal revolt of that year forced him to flee. He spent time in exile with General Bernardino Caballero, the "spiritual heir" of López. Until his death in 1912, Caballero was O'Leary's patron. When O'Leary returned from exile, he embarked on his "revisionist crusade." His objective was to "defend and exalt the sacred memory of Francisco Solano López,"[78] not to seek truth. He gained his objective and ignored the truth.

Chaves

One indication of how untouchable the myth of Francisco Solano López became is that none of the best historians of the second half of the twentieth century would risk his career—or possibly his life—by writing an accurate biography of the marshal president. The career of Julio César Chaves bears witness to this. Born in Asunción in 1907,[79] he attended Colegio de San José[80] and received his doctorate in law from the National University in 1929, although his thesis was on the Monroe Doctrine. He taught history in secondary schools and at the law school at the national university. He was minister to Bolivia in 1939 and ambassador to Peru in 1940. Despite his legal training, his close friend Hipólito Sánchez Quell told me, to write history was Chaves's passion, not the law. Chaves's books are essential for students of Paraguayan history. His best-known works are biographies of the first two dictators. *El Supremo Dictador*, about Francia and his regime, went through four editions. *El Presidente López: Vida y Gobierno de Don Carlos* went through two editions. Significantly Chaves never completed a natural trilogy by writing the life and times of Francisco Solano López. To do so with the care of the other two biographies would have been hazardous. It is clear from reading Chaves's study of the first President López that his treatment of the son's life would have been a far cry from O'Leary's. Thoroughly grounded in the sources of this crucial period, Chaves confined his writings about the war to such non-controversial topics as General José Díaz and the 1866 conference between López and Mitre.

In his later life, Chaves returned to Asunción from a decade in exile in Buenos Aires. He became an employee of the Colorado Party, whose director was his half-brother. Holding such non-taxing positions as director of the Francia Museum at Yaguarón, Chaves was free to write history. He published an account of the discovery and conquest of Paraguay and a life and times of the eighteenth-century Peruvian revolutionary Tupac Amaru II. But he avoided the topic of Francisco Solano López. With his children grown, Chaves and his wife lived a comfortable life at his nice but non-ostentatious house on Avenida España. He was well-off but not rich. He rented a two-room downstairs apartment to such persons as me and my family to supplement his state incomes, the royalties from his books, and fees from lecturing. Despite the importance of the second López, Chaves never wrote his biography. He could not have safely challenged the Colorado myth of the heroic Marshal López—whom Chaves knew to be a military incompetent—and have retained his privileged status. Chaves, a trustworthy craftsman, held negative opinions about Francisco Solano, which appear in his closing remarks of the biography of the elder López. He praised the father, although not uncritically, but disapproved of the son. Having already spent years in political exile, he wished to pass the rest of his days at home. His silence on the subject of Francisco Solano López is an eloquent testimonial to the suffocating pressure on society to sustain the legend of the heroic López.

THE STROESSNER CHAPTER

In 1970, Paraguay honored the hundredth anniversary of the death of Francisco Solano López. Alfredo Stroessner, the then-dictator, like López posed as a constitutional president. Stroessner, however, actually held elections and tolerated a tame opposition, which would have been anathema to López. Stroessner asked fellow Paraguayans to remember López as their "master of patriotism." By 1970, the image of the heroic López was fixed. He was the defender of a "noble and just cause." In the 1970 Stroessner version, López had neither initiated the war of the 1860s nor was he responsible for the devastation that followed. This was proved, Stroessner maintained, by the works of many historians, above all the recently departed Juan E. O'Leary. The president praised O'Leary because he trumpeted the nation's message and sang hymns to Paraguayan national glory.[81]

Stroessner said that it was his presidential duty to honor Marshal López for his skill as "diplomat, writer, strategist, and father. . . ."[82] President Stroessner told Paraguayans to remember López as a great soldier. Stroessner himself had a military record, unlike that of López, that, if not heroic, was at least honorable. He had served in the Chaco War and he wanted the Paraguayan people to remember it. Perpetuating the cult of López was one way Stroessner reinforced his power. As he praised López's punishment of the Portuguese diplomat Leite Pereira for failing to respect the president (López had executed the acting Portuguese consul), Stroessner was of course warning Paraguayans of the 1970s to respect and obey General Stroessner.

Stroessner's view of the 1860s was little more than an abstract of the arguments of President López himself funneled through O'Leary; he obtained his information from the latter's works. Stroessner, like O'Leary and López, justified the attack on Argentina by saying that that nation denied Paraguay's right of transit across its territory after having allowed Brazilian forces to do so. The López folly of attacking Brazil, however, was something that the astute Stroessner would not have done.

Stroessner stressed the importance of international law and condemned Allied violations of it. He ignored the fact that López sent a shocking number of people to their deaths after the cause was lost. Stroessner pretended that López at heart was a lover of peace, which he showed by bringing Argentines together in 1859, "an honorable triumph," a sentiment that came indirectly from the marshal by way of O'Leary. For Stroessner, López further revealed his peaceable nature in the "brilliant" note of August, 30, 1864, warning Brazil not to invade Uruguay. Stroessner's López also revealed his desire for peace in his interview with President Mitre of Argentina at Yataity-Corá in September 1866. Although López's insistence on retaining power doomed his peace effort, his desire to retain power was something that Stroessner could understand. Through López, Stroessner justified his own use of force. According to General-President Stroessner, Brazil's intervention in Uruguay gave President López the right to seize the Brazilian ship *Marquês de Olinda*. Stroessner then denied what Argentina and Brazil insisted in 1865, that the objective of the Triple Alliance was merely to remove the marshal president from office, not to end Paraguay's independence. Stroessner, whose government issued an identity card and awarded citizenship to Nazi war criminal Josef Mengele in 1959,[83] accused the Triple Alliance of a genocidal objective in the 1860s: "the extermination of the Paraguayan people."[84] Stroessner's López was not the coward of the 1860s. He was instead brave, although Stroessner found no example to support his contention. He said that López "was the incarnation of a collective sentiment inspired by justice." This was one dictator's judgment on another's claim to be the diviner of the national will. Truly competitive elections were thus unnecessary. When Stroessner said, "The people knew that to be a deserter from López's army was to desert the national cause,"[85] he was warning Paraguayans that he would tolerate no opposition that objected to the president by name. Resistance to the Paraguayan president of the 1860s, the defender of the nation's honor, seemed odious, unpatriotic, and treasonous to the nation's authoritarian ruler in 1970.

THE LEGEND IN MODERN TIMES

Schoolchildren were indoctrinated in the myth of the heroic López. At the elementary and college preparatory school Colegio de San José in 1974, the second-grade teacher told the boys, including my son, to draw pictures of the three people whom they most revered. Their first assignment was to draw a picture of their mother and to caption it "Amo a mi mamá" (I love my mother). Next, they drew their fathers, headed "Amo a mi papá" (I love my father). The final drawing was of Francisco Solano López, whose idealized likeness hung in the classroom. The teacher directed them to title this "Amo a Mariscal López" (I love Marshal López). These children, like most others young and old, lacked easy access to reliable accounts of the dictator. Most had no interest in out-of-print works by López contemporaries like Thompson or Centurión or newer books by Liberal-but-not-liberal Arturo Bray. Bray, who finished his biography of López in exile in Argentina in 1945, considered López a great man. He was honest enough, however, to show that López was a tyrant, an incompetent commander,[86] and a sadistic ruler.

In 1986, the government reissued Stroessner's 1970 eulogy. The publicist who introduced the pamphlet called López "the maximum hero of the Fatherland." He traced the line of legitimacy running from López through Bernardino Caballero[87] to the founding of the Colorado Party in 1887. That party provided the "continuity of the genuine spirit of Paraguay." The origins of the opposition Liberals, who by 1986 had been toothless for a half century, were still in Colorado propaganda to be found in the hated and reviled Legion and in the Argentine oligarchy.[88]

In 1989, democracy of a sort came to Paraguay. The military overthrew Stroessner, an old-style *golpe de estado* led by General Andrés Rodríguez, who then became president. Surprisingly, he retired at the end of his term of office. Democracy was fashionable; dictatorship was out of style. Since that time, presidents have been chosen in mostly honest elections. Nevertheless, the Colorado Party dominated the nation and praised López. Presidents Juan Carlos Wasmosy, Raúl Cubas Grau, and Luis Ángel González Macchi were all Colorados.[89] In August 2003, Paraguayans elected Nicanor Duarte Frutos president for a five-year term. Duarte took a leave of absence from his post as head of the Colorado Party. The Colorados held the largest number of seats in the Senate and the Chamber of Deputies, although not a majority in either. Their interest in maintaining the heroic image of López remained, although they seemed less than insistent about it. To deny the legend, the party would have to confess to its century-long fabrication.

In 1998, a Colorado partisan rejoined the battle over Francisco Solano López. Osvaldo Bergonzi wrote a book-length polemic that justified the indefensible killings of 1868 and 1869. Bergonzi was a Colorado legislator, a sometime university professor, and a journalist. In *El Círculo de San Fernando*, he resurrected the charge of a conspiracy against President López centered around the activities of Minister Charles Ames Washburn. He called this cabal, whose existence most historians doubt, "an act of treason."[90] Bergonzi alleged that the marshal's brothers, Venancio and Benigno, always had been envious of Francisco because he had been favored by his father. According to Bergonzi, the three brothers waged "struggle without quarter" for the presidency in 1862, and Francisco emerged victorious. The contest never occurred because Francisco controlled the army. The treason supposedly surfaced in 1868; but the usual suspects, the alleged conspirators, had no force at their command and no access to senior officers. Bergonzi sees success and genius in the murderous actions of the dictator. López's interview with President Mitre at Yataity-Corá in 1866 was, for Bergonzi's López, only a ruse to allow the marshal time to strengthen his defenses and thus win a stunning victory at Curupaity,[91] a truly Pyrrhic tactical victory that led nowhere. Despite Bergonzi's charges, the evidence, including the dictator's own statements, shows that López was then truly ready for a cessation of hostilities, providing that he could remain in power.

Bergonzi lauds the official rehabilitation of the marshal in 1936. He applauds the proclamation of then (acting) President Rafael Franco that López was "a symbol of the Fatherland."[92] Bergonzi's argument is so perversely and ineptly constructed, alleging a conspiracy so large, that his book should serve as a recommendation to parents not to allow their children to take a course from this occasional professor. The tract reveals, however, that important people in 1998 retained a stake in the myth of López's heroism; but its force was beginning to wane.

Today, the town of Piribebuy, which was López's capital[93] for several months in 1869, is about 40 miles to the east of Asunción. There, a tiny historical museum displays pictures of Francisco Solano López and Elisa Alicia Lynch. Also on display is a picture of United States Minister to Paraguay Martin McMahon, who lived down the street. Visitors hear that McMahon was Marshal López's good friend. They were not friends, though. They did not even know each other very well, although the American sympathized with the cause. Arriving in December 1868, McMahon became "one of López's major apologists."[94] The only people he knew were ardent Lopistas. Not far from the one-room Piribebuy museum is the door of the house in which McMahon lived. Only the door. In 2002, the site was occupied by an ice cream shop called El Dorado. Yet it is still referred to by locals as the place where McMahon lived. Nearby an equestrian statue of Marshal López dominates the middle of the children's park in the center of town. This tribute makes Piribebuy typical of many other Paraguayan locales.

Luque is now a busy suburb of Asunción, and buses constantly commute to the center of the capital. In 1868, it was a center of suffering and misery. The town was too small to provide services, food, or shelter for the newcomers. Despite historical reality, the public memory there is not of the suffering of the many but of the heroic marshal. In the center of Luque is a park dedicated to the memory of a valiant defender of the fatherland, not the man who caused needless suffering.

In a lovely section of Asunción about a half-hour walk from the center of the city on a street appropriately and discretely named Calle de la Residenta is the Gran Hotel del Paraguay. Part of the hotel is the original salon where Madame Lynch held court in the 1860s under the beautiful and now restored paintings on the high ceiling of the dining room. Something like her zoo is still there with reptiles, birds, and even a small deer named Bambi. The government has decreed that the hotel is a national treasure.

A few doors down the street stands the National Library of Paraguay (Biblioteca Nacional). There, a senior functionary, when asked to bring this researcher a volume titled *Papeles del tirano (Papers of the Tyrant)*, reacted with shock. "He was not a tyrant!" she exclaimed. "He was a hero!"[95] In her reaction we can see how even educated Paraguayans with access to primary sources accept the marshal's heroic status. The rightwing, revisionist effort of the past ninety years has succeeded in glorifying an evil and disgusting man. His nature reveals itself most clearly by his torture and execution of his unthreatening brothers and brothers-in-law, by his torture and imprisonment of his sisters, by his ordering the sinister Aveiro to beat his own mother—but, most importantly, by his needless sacrifice of three-fifths of all Paraguayan men, women, and children on the altar of his ego.

Iconic images of López abound. One of the most prominent malls in Paraguay is Marshal López Shopping. A British author says this "is rather like going to Berlin and finding the Adolf Hitler shopping mall."[96] Under one prominent bust of the marshal are the words "Never will fall from my hands this sacred standard of my country," attributed to the fallen hero. It even correctly identifies the year of his birth as 1826, unlike the deceptive memorial in the heart of the capital.

In the 1990s, uncertainty attended the arrival of democracy. Considerable press freedom exists in twenty-first-century Paraguay. But the Colorado Party is the government's institutional voice, and Francisco Solano López remains its most treasured hero. Professional historians and a significant number of able men and women know the truth. They fear giving the public an honest appraisal of López. Ambivalence characterizes the twenty-first-century view of him. Privately, competent historians have taken the measure of the cowardly López. They gleefully tell visitors that none of Lynch's claims about her birth are true. They like her lover even less, they say quietly.

At Cerro Corá, where López died, the republic maintains a large park, some 5,583 hectares. Animals, birds, and reptiles native to the region roam the preserve. What was once intended as the showplace of the park is a great cross and a monument to Marshal López *and his army*, thus distributing the tribute more broadly and removing a few chinks from the honor armor of the former dictator. Indicating a small but perceptible twenty-first-century hint of unconcern for López, a reporter for one Asunción newspaper in 2002 wrote, "One finds the park in a lamentable state of abandonment. The historic places, like the monuments and busts of the

Bust of López with the inscription "Never will fall from my hands this sacred standard of my country."

heroes of the Great War, can scarcely be seen," overgrown by vegetation. The park's functionaries and guards receive little financial support beyond their salaries. In early 2002, the tractor used to cut the grass was broken, and the employees had little hope of a new machine. Traditionally on the first of March, national dignitaries visit the monument to praise the "maximum hero of our country." The rest of the year, though, they forget the park and him. They have allowed the large, impressive, modernist sculpture, the "Monument to Marshal López and his army" to crumble from the humidity and neglect.[97]

On February 25, 2002, the newspaper *Ultima Hora* issued a color magazine for children to prepare them for the anniversary of the hero-marshal's death. It contained a tribute to the beardless boys whom López recruited to fight in one of the last battles of the war. The biography of López himself actually occupied little space in the magazine. Other heroes whose lives the children were told to emulate included an unnamed Guarani shaman, Domingo Martínez de Irala, José Gaspar de Francia (not identified by his title, Supreme Dictator), and José Feliz Estigarribia. This *Magazine for Children* (*Revista de los Chicos*) buried the one-page biographical sketch of Francisco Solano López on page 17, as if he were a national embarrassment. It correctly lists the year of his birth as 1826 and names his mother, father, and siblings. The anonymous author says that López joined the army while young and rose rapidly, and that "at nineteen, he was already a colonel," neglecting to mention that his appointment came from his father. The author mentions Francisco's trip to Europe and says that he performed other diplomatic missions for Carlos Antonio. The magazine points out that Francisco succeeded his father but lauds the long peace before 1864, contrasting Paraguayan amity with the strife in neighboring countries, meaning especially Argentina. The article notes Francisco's contribution to national progress and the modernization of the nation, mentioning the Oratory (Pantheon of Heroes), the Municipal Theater, and the fellowships that sent young Paraguayans to Europe. The author places the Triple Alliance treaty before López's attack on Brazil, implying a cause and effect that reverses historical fact. He makes no mention of the dictator president's aggression or his seizure of the *Marqués de Olinda* or that his invasion of the Mato Grosso occurred before the Brazilian government knew that it was at war. This now traditional version says that López's armies won major victories over the Triple Alliance. The author fails to mention that most victories occurred against largely phantom opponents. About the war itself, the author says only that as the fighting went on and that after many years and battles, the Paraguayan position deteriorated. He says that López had now been promoted to field marshal without mentioning that he had promoted himself. Blandly, the author says that many (unidentified) observers then saw the marshal's death as the solution to the war, without explaining why. Other people, the author continues, including his family, followed him faithfully to the end. His torture and execution of some of his family are missing from the account. The author says that in death López fulfilled his promise not to surrender. Thus, the story that is fed to schoolchildren is as important for what it leaves out—virtually López's whole presidency and his military ineptitude—as for what it includes. It suggests a new ambivalence about the national hero.

In 2002, the annual tribute commemorating López's death, the Day of Heroes, de-emphasized the dictator's importance by a process of stealth. No public official called the López legend a sham. That would reveal that the Colorado party had promoted a lie. But changes have occurred. On July 24, 1961, the Stroessner government celebrated Francisco Solano López's birthday with a gala. Its highlights were the return of the remains of Elisa Lynch to Paraguay, a military parade, and a speech by the aged Juan Emiliano O'Leary. On López's birthday in 2005, however, in the central plazas of Asunción, there was no celebration. No ceremony honored López's natal day. Perhaps the acceptance of historical accuracy is building momentum.

In 2002, an American with decades of experience in Paraguay, with close family ties there, and with great affection for the country, posed the crucial question: "Why," he asked, "do they celebrate this man on the day of his death? He ruined the country! They don't have just one national holiday to honor him; they have two."[98] In 2005, at least, the people in downtown Asunción ignored the anniversary of his birth.

NOTES

1. Thomas Whigham and Barbara Pothast-Jukeit, "The Paraguayan Rosetta Stone," *LARR* 34, no. 1 (1999): 174–86.

2. Vera Blinn Reber, "The Demographics of Paraguay," *HAHR* 68, no. 2 (May 1988): 289–319.

3. R. B. Cunningham Graham, *Portrait of a Dictator: Francisco Solano López* (London: William Heinemann, 1933), xiii.

4. Cunningham Graham, *Portrait of a Dictator*, 265.

5. Cunningham Graham, *Portrait of a Dictator*, 76.

6. Elisa Alicia Lynch, *Exposición y protesta que hace Elisa Alicia Lynch* (Buenos Aires: M. Biedma, 1875), 15.

7. Harris Gaylord Warren, *Paraguay and the Triple Alliance: The Post-War Decade, 1869–1878* (Austin: Institute of Latin American Studies, University of Texas, 1978), 20, 331, n. 66. A peso was roughly equal to a dollar.

8. Warren, *Paraguay and the Triple Alliance*, 234.

9. Cunningham Graham, *Portrait of a Dictator*, 270–71.

10. Cunningham Graham, *Portrait of a Dictator*, 272.

11. Cunningham Graham, *Portrait of a Dictator*, 272–73.

12. Lynch, *Exposición y protesta*, 9.

13. Lynch, *Exposición y protesta*, 58–63.

14. Cunningham Graham, *Portrait of a Dictator*, 274.

15. Siân Rees, *The Shadows of Elisa Lynch: How a Nineteenth-Century Courtesan Became the Most Powerful Woman in Paraguay* (London: REVIEW, an imprint of Headline Book Publishing, 2003), 311, 312.

16. This summary follows Paul H. Lewis, "Paraguay from the War of the Triple Alliance to the Chaco War," *The Cambridge History of Latin America; Vol. V: c. 1870–1930* (Cambridge, UK: Cambridge University Press, 1986), 475–96; and Lewis, "Paraguay since 1930," *Cambridge History of Latin America; Vol. VIII: Latin America since 1930: Spanish South America* (Cambridge, UK: Cambridge University Press, 1991), 233–66.

17. Harris Gaylord Warren and Katherine F. Warren, *Rebirth of the Paraguayan Republic: The First Colorado Era, 1878–1904* (Pittsburgh: University of Pittsburgh Press, 1985), 5.

18. Warren and Warren, *Rebirth*, 39.

19. The faction took its name from Cándido Bareiro, the nation's president from 1878–1880. He had been López's minister to the United Kingdom and France during the war. He was an outspoken Lopista in the 1870s. On his death in 1880, Bernardino Caballero took office. The Bareiro Faction was the precursor to the Colorado Party.

20. Lewis, "Paraguay . . . to the Chaco War," 492.

21. Paul H. Lewis, *Political Parties and Generations in Paraguay's Liberal Era, 1869–1940* (Chapel Hill: University of North Carolina Press, 1993), 33.

22. The Chaco Central was lost after 1870.

23. John Lynch, *Simón Bolívar: A Life* (New Haven, CT: Yale University Press, 2006), 300.

24. Christon I. Archer, "Death's Patriots–Celebration, Denunciation, and Memories of Mexico's Independence Heroes: Miguel Hidalgo, José María Morelos, and Agustín Iturbide," in *Death, Dismemberment, and Memory in Latin America: Body Politics*, ed. Lyman L. Johnson (Albuquerque: University of New Mexico Press, 2004), 63–104.

25. Lyman L. Johnson, "Why Dead Bodies Talk: An Introduction," in *Death, Dismemberment, and Memory in Latin America*, ed. Johnson, 1–26.

26. *El Diario*, issues of March 3–4 and July 4, 1936.

27. *El Diario*, March 13, 1936.

28. The Liberal Party enjoyed legal status in 1946, as did the Febreristas.

29. Lewis, "Paraguay since 1930," *Cambridge History of Latin America, VIII*, 252.

30. By 2005, the Asunción Tenis Club had been considerably spruced up.

31. Lewis, "Paraguay since 1930," 254.

32. Centurión, *Memorias*, I, 332, II, 8–16.

33. Centurión, *Memorias*, II, 34.

34. Centurión, *Memorias*, II, 100–101.

35. Centurión, *Memorias*, II, 8; III, 255.

36. Centurión, *Memorias*, II, 282–87, 337, 346–47, 350.

37. Centurión, *Memorias*, III, 116–17, 175–79.

38. *La Tribuna*, March 11, 1961.

39. *La Lucha: Diario de la Tarde*, May 19, 1936.

40. *El Diario*, July 11, 1936.

41. Warren and Warren, *Rebirth*, 102.

42. Testamento de FSL, Asunción, June 4, 1865, *Proclamas y cartas del Mariscal López* (Buenos Aires: Editorial Asunción), 1957.

43. D. Enrique S. López, *Documentos referentes a la venía solicitada ante el honorable Congreso* [de Argentina], Buenos Aires, 1884.

44. Warren and Warren, *Rebirth*, 111.

45. It is a measure of Francisco's feeling for his children with Lynch that he kept them with him. They were his possessions. Had he truly been concerned with their welfare, he would have sent them to safety. He did not. McMahon could have escorted them from the country in 1869.

46. See Victor Simón, *Enrique Solano López: El Periodista* (Asunción: Partido Colorado, 1972).

47. Warren and Warren, *Rebirth*, 111.

48. Rees, *Shadows of Elisa Lynch*, 216, 226–27.

49. *El Círculo de San Fernando* (Asunción: Industrial Gráfica Comuneros, 1998).

50. Warren and Warren, *Rebirth*, 112–14.

51. Warren and Warren, *Rebirth*, 174–76.

52. Warren, *Paraguay and the Triple Alliance*, 27.

53. Belisario Rivarola Rivarola, "Cincuentenaria de Cerro Corá: Muerte del Tirano," in *El Mariscal Francisco Solano López* (Asunción: Junta Patriótica, 1926), 71, 69, 66. This piece originally appeared in *El Liberal* on March 1, 1920.

54. Cecilio Baez, "Guerra del Paraguay," in *El Mariscal Francisco Solano López* (Asunción: Junta Patriótica, 1926), 50–52, 43.

55. Cecilio Baez, "La heroina de su honor: Pancha Garmendia," in *El Mariscal Francisco Solano López* (Asunción: Junta Patriótica, 1926), 187–99 [originally published May 14, 1892, in *El Combate*].

56. *El Liberal*, February 6, 1936.

57. Patriotas Amigos de la Libertad, "Al Lector," *El Mariscal Francisco Solano López*, 3. In all eras, some historians valued historical accuracy, but they made smaller impact than polemicists like O'Leary.

58. Junta Patriótica, "Razón de esta obra," *El Mariscal Francisco Solano López* (introduction to 1996 reprint), 5–9.

59. Cunningham Graham, *Portrait of a Dictator*, 82–84.

60. Victor N. Vasconcellos, *Juan E. O'Leary: el reivindicador* (Asunción: Partido Colorado, 1972), 7.

61. *La Hora: Organo de la Asociación Nacional de ex-Combatientes*, September 5, 1936.

62. *La Hora*, September 5, 1936.

63. The commission also found the remains, the members said, of Panchito López. They honored him in all seriousness as "Colonel of the Nation."

64. *La Hora*, October 14, 1936.

65. Lyman L. Johnson, "Digging up Cuauhtémoc," in *Death, Dismemberment, and Memory in Latin America: Body Politics*, ed. Johnson, 207–44.

66. *La Hora*, October 14, 1936.

67. Juan E. O'Leary, *El Mariscal Francisco Solano López*, 3rd ed. (Asunción: Casa America-Moreno Hnos., 1970). This edition appeared after O'Leary's death.

68. O'Leary, *El Mariscal . . . López*, 93, 103, 153.

69. O'Leary, *El Mariscal . . . López*, 117.

70. O'Leary, *El Mariscal . . . López*, 117, 121–26.

71. O'Leary, *El Mariscal . . . López*, 153.

72. O'Leary, *El Mariscal . . . López*, 156.

73. O'Leary, *El Mariscal . . . López*, 163.

74. O'Leary, *El Mariscal . . . López*, 164.

75. O'Leary, *El Mariscal . . . López*, 177.

76. O'Leary, *El Mariscal . . . López*, 178.

77. O'Leary, *El Mariscal . . . López*, 178.

78. Vasconcellos, *O'Leary*, 11, 13.

79. Carlos R. Centurión, *Historia de la cultura paraguaya*, 2 vols. (Asunción: Biblioteca Ortiz Guerrero, 1961), I, 239.

80. Chaves used his prestige and influence to get the author's sons admitted to Colegio de San José.

81. Alfredo Stroessner, *En Cerro Corá no se rindió la dignidad nacional*, 2nd ed. (Asunción: Cuadernos Republicanos, 1986 [1970]), 20.

82. Stroessner, *En Cerro Corá*, 23.

83. Stroessner revoked Mengele's Paraguayan citizenship in 1979 under strong international pressure.

84. Stroessner, *En Cerro Corá*, 43–44.

85. Stroessner, *En Cerro Corá*, 67.

86. A combat veteran, Bray explains López's military incompetence by saying that there are only two ways to become an able commander: by formal education in a military school or in combat itself—and López was not privileged to experience either.

87. Leandro Prieto Yegros, "Presentación," [introduction to] Alfredo Stroessner *En Cerro Corá no se rindió la dignidad nacional* (Asunción: Partido Colorado, 1986 [1970]), 11–12.

88. Prieto Yegros, "Presentación," 15. Some Liberals were truly former Legionnaires, but that many Legionnaires helped found the Colorado Party was ignored.

89. Liberals one time managed to elect a vice president.

90. Osvaldo Bergonzi, *El Círculo de San Fernando* (Asunción: Industrial Gráfico Comuneros, 1998), 6.

91. Bergonzi, *El Círculo*, 85–100.

92. Bergonzi, *El Círculo*, 364.

93. There were two capitals of Paraguay in 1869. One was wherever López was and the other was the provisional government in Asunción.

94. Chris Leuchars, *To the Bitter End: Paraguay and the War of the Triple Alliance* (Westport, CT: Greenwood Press, 2002), 209–10.

95. Personal communication, Asunción, February 8, 2002.

96. Nigel Cawthorne, *The Empress of South America* (London: William Heinemann, 2003), 296.

97. *ABC Color*, February 16, 2002.

98. Personal communication, Asunción, March 1, 2002.

Bibliography

ARCHIVES AND ABBREVIATIONS

The Americas: A Quarterly Review of Inter-American Cultural History (TAM)
Archivo Nacional de Asunción (ANA)
Cambridge History of Native Peoples of the Americas (CHNPA)
Carlos Antonio López (CAL)
Colección Rio Branco (CRB)
Eliza (Elisa) Alicia Lynch (EAL)
Francisco Solano López (FSL)
Hispanic American Historical Review (HAHR)
Latin American Research Review (LARR)
Sección Historia (SH)
Sección Nueva Encuadernación (NE)

ASUNCIÓN NEWSPAPERS: WAR YEARS

Cabichuí
El Centinela
El Semanario de Avisos y Conocimientos Útiles

ASUNCIÓN NEWSPAPERS: TWENTIETH CENTURY

ABC Color
El Diario
El Liberal

La Hora: Organo de la Asociación de Ex-Combatientes
La Lucha
La Tribuna
Ultima Hora

BOOKS, ARTICLES, AND DISSERTATIONS

Abente, Diego. "The War of the Triple Alliance: Three Explanatory Models," *LARR* 22, no. 2 (1987): 47–69.

Andrews, George Reid. *Afro-Latin America, 1800–2000*. Oxford: Oxford University Press, 2004.

Archer, Christon I. "Death's Patriots—Celebration, Denunciation, and Memories of Mexico's Independence Heroes: Miguel Hidalgo, José María Morelos, and Agustín Iturbide." Pp. 63–104 in *Death, Dismemberment and Memory*, edited by Lyman L. Johnson. Albuquerque: University of New Mexico Press, 2004.

Archivo del General Mitre: Guerra del Paraguay. Vols. II, IV. Buenos Aires: Imprenta de la Casa Editorial Sopena, 1911.

Baez, Cecilio. "Guerra del Paraguay." Pp. 39–53 in *El Mariscal Francisco Solano López*. Asunción: 1996 [1926].

———. "La heroina de su honor: Pancha Garmendia." Pp. 187–99 in *El Mariscal Francisco Solano López*, Asunción: Junta Partriótica, 1926.

———. "La tiranía de Solano López: su aspecto comercial." Pp. 127–35 in *El Mariscal Francisco Solano López*. Asunción: 1996 [1926].

Barman, Roderick J. *Citizen Emperor: Pedro II and the Making of Brazil, 1825–1891*. Stanford, CA: Stanford University Press, 1999.

Barrett, William E. *Woman on Horseback: the Biography of Francisco López and Eliza Lynch*. New York: Fredrick A. Stokes Company, 1938.

Beattie, Peter M. *Tribute of Blood: Army, Honor, Race and Nation in Brazil, 1864–1945*. Durham, NC: Duke University Press, 2001.

Beezley, William H. "Caudillismo: An Interpretive Note." *Journal of Inter-American Studies* 11 (1969): 345–52.

Benítez, Luis G. *Historia diplomática del Paraguay*. Asunción: Fondo de Carátula, 1972.

———. *Breve historia de grandes hombres*. Asunción: Industrial Gráfica Comuneros, 1986.

———. *Cancilleres y otros defensores de la república*. 2 vols. Asunción: Talleres Reprográficos Vercam S.R.L., 1994.

———. *Manual de Historia del Paraguay*. Asunción: n.p., 2002.

Bergonzi, Osvaldo. *El círculo de San Fernando*. Asunción: Industrial Gráfica Comuneros, 1998.

Beverina, Juan. *La Guerra del Paraguay: las operaciones de la guerra en el territorio argentino y brasileño*. Tomo 3. Buenos Aires: Establecimiento Gráfico Ferrari Hnos., 1921.

Box, Pelham Horton. *The Origins of the Paraguayan War*. Urbana, IL: University Studies in the Social Sciences, 1930, repr. New York: Russsell and Russell, 1967.

Bray, Arturo. *Solano López: soldado de la gloria y del infortunio.* Asunción: Editorial Lector, 1996 (orig. publ. Buenos Aires, 1945).

Burkholder, Mark A. "Honor and Honors in Colonial Latin America." Pp. 18–44 in *The Faces of Honor,* edited by Lyman L. Johnson and Sonya Lipsett-Rivera. Albuquerque: University of New Mexico Press, 1998.

Burns, E. Bradford. *A History of Brazil.* 3rd ed. New York: Columbia University Press, 1993.

Cardozo, Efraím. *Hace cien años: crónicas de la guerra de 1864–1870 publicadas en "La Tribuna" de Asunción en el centenario de la epopeya nacional.* 13 vols. Asunción: Ediciones EMASA, 1967–1982.

Cawthorne, Nigel. *The Empress of South America.* London: William Heinemann, 2003.

Centurión, Carlos R. *Historia de la Cultura Paraguaya.* 2 vols. Asunción: Biblioteca Ortiz Guerrero, 1961.

Centurión, Juan Crisóstomo. *Memorias o reminiscencias históricas sobre la guerra del Paraguay.* 4 vols. Buenos Aires and Asunción: Imprenta de Obras de J. A. Berra / Imprenta Militar, 1894–1901.

Chaves, Julio César. *El Supremo Dictador,* 4th ed. Madrid: Atlas, 1964.

———. *El Presidente López: Vida y gobierno de Don Carlos.* 2nd ed. Buenos Aires: Ediciones Depalma, 1968.

Chaves, María Concepción L. de. *Madame Lynch y Solano López.* Buenos Aires: Artes Gráficas Negri, 1976.

Cooney, Jerry W. "Economy and Manpower: Paraguay at War, 1864–1869." Pp. 23–43 in *I Die with My Country,* edited by Hendrik Kraay and Thomas L. Whigham. Lincoln and London: University of Nebraska Press, 2004.

Cunningham Graham, R. B. *Portrait of a Dictator: Francisco Solano López.* London: William Heinemann, 1933.

Davis, Arthur H. *Martin T. McMahon: Diplomático en el estridor de armas.* Asunción: Arthur H. Davis, 1985.

Decoud, Hector Francisco. *Los emigrados paraguayos en la guerra de la Triple Alianza.* Prólogo por José Juan Biedma. Buenos Aires: L. J. Rosso, 1930.

Diagnostic and Statistical Manual of Mental Disorders. Washington, DC: American Psychiatric Association, 1996.

Dictamenes jurídicos sobre propiedades en el Paraguay pertenecientes a Don Enrique Solano López y otros. Buenos Aires: Imprenta de Stiller y Lass, 1887.

Durán Estrago, Magarita. *Presencia franciscana en el Paraguay (1538–1824).* Asunción: Biblioteca de Estudios Paraguayos, Universidad Católica, 1987.

El Mariscal Francisco Solano López. Asunción: Junta Patriótica, 1926 (repr. 1996, Patriotas Amigos de la Libertad).

Escobar, Ticio y Osvaldo Salerno. "Introducción" Pp. 1–4 in *Cabichuí: periódico de la Guerra de la Triple Alianza,* edited by Ticio Esobar and Osvaldo Salerno. Asunción: Museo del Barro, 1984.

———, eds. *Cabuchuí: periódico de la Guerra de la Triple Alianza.* Asunción: Museo del Barro, 1984.

Feros, Antonio. "'Spain and America: All is One': Historiography of the Conquest and Colonization of the Americas and National Mythology in Spain c. 1892–1992." Pp. 109–34 in *Interpreting Spanish Colonialism,* edited by Christopher

Schmidt-Nowara and John M. Nieto Phillips. Albuquerque: University of New Mexico Press, 2005.

Fuente, Ariel de la. "Federalism and Opposition to the Paraguayan War in the Argentine Interior." Pp. 140–53 in *I Die with My Country*, edited by Hendrick Kraay and Thomas L. Whigham. Lincoln and London: University of Nebraska Press, 2004.

Ganson, Barbara J. "Following their Children into Battle: Women at War in Paraguay." *TAM* 46, no. 3 (January 1990): 335–71.

García, Frederico. "La prisión y vejámenes de doña Juana Carrilla de López." Pp. 77–97 in *El Mariscal Francisco Solano López*. Asunción: Junta Patriótica, 1926.

Gaydol, Sandra. "*Honor moderno*: The Significance of Honor in Fin-de-Siecle Argentina." *HAHR* 84, no. 3 (August 2004): 475–501.

Gelly, Juan Andrés. *El Paraguay: lo que fue, lo que es y lo que será*. Prólogo de J. Natalicio González. Asunción: Editorial El Lector, 1996 (orig. publ. 1849).

Gibson, Charles. *Spain in America*. New York: Harper and Row, 1966.

Gimlette, John. *At the Tomb of the Inflatable Pig: Travels through Paraguay*. London: Hutchinson, 2003.

Godoi, Juan Silvano. *Documentos históricos: El fusilimiento del Obispo Palacios y los tribunales de sangre de San Fernando*. Asunción: Imprenta Cromos, 1996 (orig. publ., 1916).

Goetz, Robert. *1805: Austerlitz: Napoleon and the Destruction of the Third Coalition*. London: Greenhill Books and Mechanicsburg, PA: Stackpole Books, 2005.

Grant, Ulysses S. *Personal Memoirs*. New York: New American Library, 1999 (orig. publ. 1885).

Gutiérrez, Ramón. *When Jesus Came, the Corn Mothers Went Away: Marriage, Sexuality, and Power in New Mexico, 1500–1846*. Stanford, CA: Stanford University Press, 1991.

Hopkins, Edward A., Raymond E. Crist, and William P. Snow. *Paraguay, 1852 and 1968*. New York: American Geographical Society, 1968.

Hutchinson, Thomas J. *The Paraná; with Incidents of the Paraguayan War and South American Recollections from 1861 to 1868*. London: Edward Stanford, 1868.

Jeffrey, William H. *Mitre and Argentina*. New York: Library Publishers, 1952.

Johnson, Lyman L. and Sonya Lipsett-Rivera, eds. *The Faces of Honor: Sex, Shame, and Violence in Colonial Latin America*. Albuquerque: University of New Mexico Press, 1998.

———. "Introduction." Pp. 1–17 in *The Faces of Honor: Sex, Shame and Violence in Colonial Latin America*, ed. by Lyman L. Johnson and Sonya Lipsett-Rivera. Albuquerque: University of New Mexico Press, 1998.

Johnson, Lyman L., ed. *Death, Dismemberment, and Memory in Latin America: Body Politics*. Albuquerque: University of New Mexico Press, 2004.

———. "Why Dead Bodies Talk: An Introduction." Pp. 1–26 in *Death, Dismemberment, and Memory: Body Politics*, edited by Lyman L. Johnson. Albuquerque: University of New Mexico Press, 2004.

———. "Digging up Cuauhtémoc." Pp. 207–44 in *Death, Dismemberment, and Memory: Body Politics*, edited by Lyman L. Johnson. Albuquerque: University of New Mexico Press, 2004.

Jones, Kristine L. "Warfare, Reorganization, and Readaptation at the Margins of Spanish Rule: The Southern Margin (1573–1882)." Pp. 138–87 in *CHNPA, Vol. III*,

Pt. 2: South America, edited by Frank Salomon and Stuart Schwartz. Cambridge, UK: Cambridge University Press, 1999.

Keegan, John. *The Face of Battle: A Study of Agincourt, Waterloo, and the Somme.* Harmondsworth, UK: Penguin Books, 1976.

Kolinski, Charles S. *Independence or Death! The Story of the Paraguayan War.* Gainesville: University of Florida Press, 1965.

Kostianovsky, Olinda Masare de. *José Berges: malogrado estadista y diplomático.* Asunción, n.p., n.d. [1969].

———. *La mujer paraguaya: su participación en la Guerra Grande.* Prólogo del R. Antonio Ramos. Asunción: Talleres Gráficos Escuela Silesiana, 1971.

Kraay, Hendrik, and Thomas L. Whigham, eds. *I Die with My Country: Perspectives on the Paraguayan War, 1864–1870.* Lincoln: University of Nebraska Press, 2004.

Leuchars, Chris. *To the Bitter End: Paraguay and the War of the Triple Alliance.* Westport, CT: Greenwood Press, 2002.

Lewis, Paul H. "Paraguay from the War of the Triple Alliance to the Chaco War." Pp. 475–96 in *The Cambridge History of Latin America, Vol. V: c. 1870 to 1930*, edited by Leslie Bethell. Cambridge, UK: Cambridge University Press, 1986.

———. "Paraguay since 1930." Pp. 233–66 in *The Cambridge History of Latin America, Vol. VIII, Latin America since 1930: Spanish South America.* New York: Cambridge University Press, 1991.

———. *Political Parties and Generations in Paraguay's Liberal Era, 1869–1940.* Chapel Hill and London: University of North Carolina Press, 1993.

Livieres Argaña, Juan A., ed. *Con la rúbrica del Mariscal: Documentos de Francisco Solano López.* 5 vols. Asunción: Escuela Silesiana, 1970.

López, Enrique Solano. *Documentos referentes a la venia solicitada ante el honorable Congreso por D. Enrique Solano López en representación de la señora Doña E. A. Lynch.* Buenos Aires: Imprenta Martínez, 1884.

———. *Revalidación de títulos de terrenos al sud del Pilcomayo.* Buenos Aires: n.p., 1884.

López, Francisco Solano. *Proclamas y cartas del Mariscal López.* Buenos Aires: Editorial Asunción, 1957.

Lynch, Elisa Alicia. *Exposición y protesta que hace Elisa A. Lynch.* Buenos Aires: Imprenta de M. Biedma, 1875.

Lynch, John. *Caudillos in Spanish America, 1800–1850.* Oxford, UK: Oxford University Press, 1992.

———. *Simón Bolívar: A Life.* New Haven, CT: Yale University Press, 2006.

Maíz, Fidel. *Etapas de mi vida: contestación a las imposturas de Juan Silvano Godoy.* Asunción: Imprenta La Mundial, 1919.

———. "Una carta famosa al señor Pérez Martínez." Pp. 336–44 in *El Mariscal Francisco Solano López.* Asunción: Junta Patriótica, 1926 (repr., 1996).

Masterman, George. *Seven Eventful Years in Paraguay: A Narrative of Personal Experience Amongst the Paraguayans*, 2nd ed. London: Samson Low, Son, and Marston, 1870.

McPherson, James M. *Crossroads of Freedom: Antietam, the Battle that Changed the Course of the Civil War.* Oxford, UK: Oxford University Press, 2002.

Millett, Allan R. *The General: Robert L. Bullard and Officership in the United States Army, 1881–1925.* Westport, CT: Greenwood Press, 1975.

Mitre, Bartolomé. *Memoria militar: Sobre el estado de la guerra con el Paraguay . . . demostrando la probablilidad de forzar el Paso de Humaitá (con los documentos comprobantes)*. Buenos Aires: Imprenta de *La Nación*, 1903.

Necker, Louis. *Indios Guaraníes y chamanes franciscanos: las primeras reducciones del Paraguay, 1580–1800*. Asunción: Centro de Estudios Antropológicos, Universidad Católica, 1990.

Nickson, R. Andrew. *Historical Dictionary of Paraguay*, 2nd ed. rev. Metuchen, NJ: Scarecrow Press, 1993.

O'Leary, Juan E. *El Mariscal Solano López*. 3rd ed. Asunción: Casa America-Moreno Hnos, 1970.

———. *Nuestra Epopeya (1.a. parte)*. Asunción: Ediciones Mediterraneas, 1985 (orig. publ. 1919).

Papeles del tirano: tomados por los aliados en el asalto de 27 de diciembre de 1868. Buenos Aires: Imprenta Buenos Aires, 1869.

Pastore, Carlos. *La lucha por la tierra en el Paraguay*. Montevideo: Editorial Antequera, 1972.

Patterson, Loren S. "The War of the Triple Alliance: Paraguayan Offensive Phase—A Military History," Unpublished Ph.D. diss., Georgetown University, 1975.

Pereyra, Carlos. *Francisco Solano López y la guerra del Paraguay*. Madrid: Editorial America, 1919.

Pitaud, Henri. *Madama Lynch*. 4th ed. Asunción: Talleres "El Gráfico," 1978.

Plá, Josefina. *Hermano negro: la esclavitud en el Paraguay*. Madrid: Paraninfo, 1972.

———. *Los Británicos en el Paraguay, 1850–1870*. Asunción: Arte Nuevo, 1984.

Potthast-Jukeit, Bárbara. *"Paraíso de Mahoma" o "País de las Mujeres"?: El rol de la familia en la sociedad paraguaya del Siglo XIX*. Asunción: Instituto Cultural Paraguayo-Alemán, 1996.

———. "Protagonists, Victims and Heroes: Paraguayan Women during the 'Great War.'" Pp. 44–60 in *I Die with My Country*, edited by Hendrik Kraay and Thomas L. Whigham. Lincoln and London: University of Nebraska Press, 2004.

Quevedo, Roberto. *Antequera: Historia de un Silencio*. Asunción: Editorial La Voz, 1970.

Ramos, R. Antonio. *Juan Andres Gelly*. Buenos Aires: Asunción, 1972.

Reber, Vera Blinn. "The Demographics of Paraguay: A Reinterpretation of the Great War, 1864–1870." *HAHR* 68, no. 1 (May 1988): 289–319.

Rees, Siân. *The Shadows of Elisa Lynch: How a Nineteenth-Century Courtesan Became the Most Powerful Woman in Paraguay*. London: REVIEW, an imprint of Headline Book Publishing, 2003.

Resquín, Francisco Isidoro. *La guerra del Paraguay contra la Triple Alianza*. Asunción: Editorial El Lector, 1996 (orig. publ. 1895).

Rigual, Miguel. *Lo mejor de la Historia Paraguaya*. Asunción: Editorial Gráfica Mercurio, S.A., 2002.

Rivarola, Belisario. "Cincuentenaria de Cerro Corá: Muerte del Tirano." Pp. 64–71 in *El Mariscal Francisco Solano López*. Asunción: Junta Patriótica, 1926.

Rock, David. *Argentina, 1516–1987: From Spanish Colonialism to Alfonsín*. Berkeley and Los Angeles: University of California Press, 1987.

Saeger, James Schofield. "Survival and Abolition: The Eighteenth Century Paraguayan Encomienda." *TAM* 38, no. 1 (July 1981): 59–85.

——. "Warfare, Reorganization, and Readaptation at the Margins of Spanish Rule—The Chaco and Paraguay (1573–1882)." Pp. 257–86 in *CHNPA, Vol. III, Pt. 2: South America*, edited by Frank Salomon and Stuart B. Schwartz. Cambridge, UK: Cambridge University Press, 1999.

——. *The Chaco Mission Frontier: The Guaycuruan Experience*. Tucson: University of Arizona Press, 2000.

Salomon, Frank and Stuart B. Schwartz, eds. *The Cambridge History of Native Peoples of the Americas, Vol. III, Pt. 2: South America*. Cambridge, UK: Cambridge University Press, 1999.

Sarmiento, Domingo F. *Life in the Argentine Republic in the Days of the Tyrants, or Civilization and Barbarism*, trans. Mary Mann. New York: Hafner, 1960.

Scheina, Robert L. *Latin America's Wars: the Age of the Caudillo*, Vol. I. Washington, DC: Brassey's, Inc., 2003.

Schmidt-Nowara, Christopher and John M. Nieto-Phillips, eds. *Interpreting Spanish Colonialism: Empires, Nations, and Legends*. Albuquerque: University of New Mexico Press, 2005.

Shumway, Jeffrey M. "'Sometimes Knowing How to Forget Is Also Having Memory': The Repatriation of Juan Manuel de Rosas and the Healing of Argentina." Pp. 105–40 in *Death, Dismemberment, and Memory*, edited by Lyman L. Johnson. Albuquerque: University of New Mexico Press, 2004.

Simón, Victor. *Enrique Solano López: el periodista*. Asunción: Partido Colorado, 1972.

Skidmore, Thomas. *Brazil: Five Centuries of Change*. New York: Oxford University Press, 1999.

Stroessner, Alfredo. *En Cerro Corá no se rindió la dignidad nacional*, 2nd ed. Asunción: Cuadernos Republicanos, 1986 (1a. ed., 1970).

Tasso Fragoso, Augusto. *Historia da Guerra entre a Tríplice Aliança e o Paraguai*, 5 vols. Rio de Janeiro: Imprenta do Exerxito, 1934 (2nd ed. 1956–1960).

Thompson, George, C.E. *The War in Paraguay with a Historical Sketch of the Country, Its People, and Notes upon the Military Engineering of the War*. London: Longman, Green, and Co., 1869.

Twinam, Ann. *Public Lives, Private Secrets: Gender, Honor, Sexuality and Illegitimacy in Colonial Spanish America*. Stanford, CA: Stanford University Press, 1999.

Vargas Peña, Benjamín. *Espías del dictador Francia (los Pyragüés)*. Asunción: n. p., 1982.

Vasconcellos, Victor N. *Juan E. O'Leary: el reivindicador*. Asunción: Partido Colorado, 1972.

Vera, Mirian Isabel and Féliz de Guarania. *Guía para el estudio de la Historia del Paraguay*. Asunción: Instituto Profesional de Artes y Ciencias de la Comunicación, 2003.

Walzer, Michael. *Just and Unjust Wars: A Moral Argument with Historical Illustrations*. New York: Basic Books, 1977.

Warren, Harris Gaylord. *Paraguay: An Informal History*. Norman: University of Oklahoma Press, 1949.

——. "The Paraguayan Image in the War of the Triple Alliance." *TAM* 19, no. 1 (July 1962): 3–20.

——. *Paraguay and the Triple Alliance: The Post-War Decade, 1869–1878*. Austin, TX: Institute of Latin American Studies, University of Texas, 1978.

Warren, Harris Gaylord and Katherine F. Warren. *Rebirth of the Paraguayan Republic: The First Colorado Era, 1878–1904*. Pittsburgh: University of Pittsburgh Press, 1985.

Washburn, Charles A. *The History of Paraguay, with Notes of Personal Observations and Reminiscences of Diplomacy under Difficulties*. 2 vols. Boston: Lee and Shepard, 1871.

Weigley, Russell. *The American Way of War*. New York: Macmillan, 1973.

———. *A Great Civil War: A Military and Political History, 1861–1864*. Bloomington: Indiana University Press, 2000.

Whigham, Thomas L. "The Iron Works of Ybicuí: Paraguayan Industrial Development in the Mid-Nineteenth Century." *TAM* 35, no. 2 (October 1978): 201–18.

———. *The Politics of River Trade: Tradition and Development in the Upper Plata, 1780–1870*. Albuquerque: University of New Mexico Press, 1991.

———. *The Paraguayan War, Volume I: Causes and Early Conduct*. Lincoln: University of Nebraska Press, 2002.

———. "The Paraguayan War: A Catalyst for Nationalism in South America." Pp. 179–98 in *I Die with My Country*, edited by Hendrik Kraay and Thomas L. Whigham. Lincoln: University of Nebraska Press, 2004.

Whigham, Thomas L. and Hendrik Kraay. "Introduction: War Politics, and Society in South America, 1820s–60s." Pp. 1–22 in *I Die with My Country*, edited by Hendrik Kraay and Thomas L. Whigham. Lincoln: University of Nebraska Press, 2004.

Whigham, Thomas L. and Barbara Potthast. "Some Strong Reservations: A Critique of Vera Blinn Reeber's 'The Demographics of Paraguay.'" *HAHR* 70, no. 2 (November 1990): 665–75.

———. "The Paraguayan Rosetta Stone: New Insights into the Demographics of the Paraguayan War." *LARR* 34, no. 1 (1999): 174–86.

White, Richard Alan. *Paraguay's Autonomous Revolution, 1810–1840*. Albuquerque: University of New Mexico Press, 1978.

Williams, John Hoyt. "Paraguayan Isolation under Dr. Francia: A Reevaluation." *HAHR* 52, no. 4 (February 1972): 102–22.

———. "Observations on the Paraguayan Census of 1846." *HAHR* 56, no. 3 (August 1976): 424–37.

———. *The Rise and Fall of the Paraguayan Republic, 1800–1870*. Austin: Institute of Latin American Studies, University of Texas, 1979.

Yegros, Leandro Prieto. "Presentación." [introduction to] Alfredo Stroessner. *En Cerro Corá no se rindió la dignidad nacional*. Asunción: Cuadernos Republicanos, 1986.

Zubizarreta, Carlos. *Cien vidas paraguayas*. Asunción: Ediciones Nizza, 1961.

Index

About the Author

James Schofield Saeger is professor of history at Lehigh University. He has published articles on rebellion, bureaucratic politics, church-state conflict, labor relations, and film in Latin America. His previous book was *The Chaco Mission Frontier: The Guaycuruan Experience*. He is currently working on a book about the invasion of Puerto Rico by the United States.